THE CASE STUDY GUIDE TO COGNITIVE BEHAVIOUR THERAPY OF PSYCHOSIS

The Wiley Series in

CLINICAL PSYCHOLOGY

Titles published under the series editorship of:

J. Mark G. Williams   *School of Psychology, University of Wales, Bangor, UK*

A list of earlier titles in the series follows the index.

THE CASE STUDY GUIDE TO COGNITIVE BEHAVIOUR THERAPY OF PSYCHOSIS

Edited by
David Kingdon
*University of Southampton,
Royal South Hants Hospital,
Southampton, UK*

and

Douglas Turkington
*Department of Psychiatry, Royal Victoria Infirmary,
Newcastle Upon Tyne, UK*

JOHN WILEY & SONS, LTD

Copyright © 2002   John Wiley & Sons Ltd, The Atrium, Southern Gate, Chichester,
West Sussex PO19 8SQ, England

Telephone   (+44) 1243 779777

Email (for orders and customer service enquiries): cs-books@wiley.co.uk
Visit our Home Page on www.wileyeurope.com or www.wiley.com

This publication is designed to provide accurate and authoritative information in regard to the
subject matter covered. It is sold on the understanding that the Publisher is not engaged in
rendering professional services. If professional advice or other expert assistance is required, the
services of a competent professional should be sought.

Other Wiley Editorial Offices

John Wiley & Sons Inc., 111 River Street, Hoboken, NJ 07030, USA

Jossey-Bass, 989 Market Street, San Francisco, CA 94103-1741, USA

Wiley-VCH Verlag GmbH, Boschstr. 12, D-69469 Weinheim, Germany

John Wiley & Sons Australia Ltd, 33 Park Road, Milton, Queensland 4064, Australia

John Wiley & Sons (Asia) Pte Ltd, 2 Clementi Loop #02-01, Jin Xing Distripark, Singapore 129809

John Wiley & Sons Canada Ltd, 22 Worcester Road, Etobicoke, Ontario, Canada M9W 1L1

Library of Congress Cataloging-in-Publication Data

The case study guide to cognitive behaviour therapy of psychosis / edited by
David Kingdon and Douglas Turkington.
      p.   cm.—(The Wiley series in clinical psychology)
      Includes bibliographical references (p.) and indexes.
      ISBN 0-471-49860-2 (cased)—ISBN 0-471-49861-0 (pbk.)
      1. Psychoses—Treatment—Case studies.   2. Cognitive therapy—Case studies.
    I. Kingdon, David G.   II. Turkington, Douglas.   III. Series.

   RC512.C36   2002
   616.89′142—dc21   2002071301

British Library Cataloguing in Publication Data

A catalogue record for this book is available from the British Library

ISBN 0-471-49860-2 (cased)
ISBN 0-471-49861-0 (paper)

Typeset in 10/12pt Palatino by TechBooks, New Delhi, India
Printed and bound by CPI Antony Rowe, Eastbourne

CONTENTS

Part II: Training, Supervision and Implementation

ABOUT THE EDITORS

David Kingdon is a Professor of Mental Health Care Delivery and a consultant psychiatrist with a mental health team in Southampton. He is co-author, with Douglas Turkington, of *Cognitive-Behavioural Therapy of Schizophrenia* (New York: Guilford Press, 1994) and has produced many papers and chapters on CBT in severe mental illness over past decade. He has worked as a senior medical officer with the Department of Health, is a member of many project groups, including the National Service Framework for Mental Health external reference group, and is chair of a Council of Europe expert working party on "Psychiatry and Human Rights".

Dr Douglas Turkington is a senior lecturer and consultant psychiatrist based at the Department of Psychiatry in the University of Newcastle-upon-Tyne. Having trained in Glasgow he moved to Sheffield where he received basic cognitive therapy training and achieved the advanced certificate in rational emotive therapy. He has worked with CBT for psychotic patients for the last 15 years and has co-authored one of the first books on the subject. He has lectured and run workshops throughout Europe and North America, and has published widely on the process of therapy and on the evidence base for CBT in schizophrenia and other psychoses. Currently he is attempting to prove that the good outcomes found in randomised controlled trials can be replicated using mental health team workers in community settings.

LIST OF CONTRIBUTORS

Andy Benn: *Principal Clinical Psychologist, Department of Psychology, Rampton Hospital, Woodbeck, Rampton, Nottinghamshire DN22 0PD.*

Alison Brabban: *Consultant Clinical Psychologist, Maiden Law Hospital, Lanchester, County Durham DH7 0NQ.*

Pauline Callcott: *Clinical Nurse Specialist, Newcastle Cognitive and Behavioural Therapies Centre, Plummer Court, Carliol Square, Newcastle-upon-Tyne, Tyne and Wear NE1 6UR.*

Isabel Clarke: *Senior Clinical Psychologist, Department of Psychiatry, Royal South Hants Hospital, Southampton SO14 0YG.*

Lars Hansen: *Research Fellow, Department of Psychiatry, Royal South Hants Hospital, Southampton SO14 0YG.*

David Kingdon: *Professor of Mental Health Care Delivery, Department of Psychiatry, Royal South Hants Hospital, Southampton SO14 0YG.*

Laura McGraw: *Psychosocial Interventions Team, University of Sunderland, Industry Centre, Enterprise Park West, Wessington Way, Sunderland SR3 3XB.*

Nick Maguire: *Chartered Clinical Psychologist, Community Mental Health Team, Bay Tree House, Graham Road, Southampton SO14 0YG.*

Paul Murray: *Insight into Schizophrenia Nurse, Innovex (UK) Ltd., Innovex House, Marlow Park, Marlow, Bucks. SL7 1TB.*

Madeline O'Carroll: *Nurse Tutor, School of Nursing, Royal London Hospital, Philpot Street, Whitechapel, Hackney, London E1 1BB.*

Jeremy Pelton: *Field Manager, Insight into Schizophrenia Programme, Innovex NHS Solutions, Innovex (UK) Ltd., Innovex House, Marlow Park, Marlow, Bucks. SL7 1TB.*

Ron Siddle: *Consultant Cognitive Behaviour Therapist, Manchester Mental Health Partnership, Department of Clinical Psychology, North Manchester General Hospital, Delaunays Road, Manchester M8 5RL.*

Douglas Turkington: *Senior Lecturer in Psychiatry, Department of Psychiatry, Leazes Wing, Royal Victoria Infirmary, Queen Victoria Road, Newcastle NE1 4LP.*

PREFACE

Within the past year, research has confirmed that non-expert community psychiatric nurses can safely and effectively deliver cognitive behaviour therapy (CBT) to patients with schizophrenia and their carers (Turkington et al., 2002). It is reasonable to expect that other disciplines within mental health would achieve similarly encouraging results (Turkington & Kingdon, 2000). Such interventions are greatly appreciated by patients and carers, improve job satisfaction for the practitioner and lead to improved insight and coping. It is now contended that case management should be supplemented by such viable, high-quality psychosocial interventions if improved outcomes are to be achieved for patients with schizophrenia (Thornicroft & Susser, 2001). It certainly seems that low case loads alone do not produce such outcomes, as the UK 700 study (Burns et al., 1999) has demonstrated: how the increased time available is spent would appear to be fundamentally, and not unexpectedly, important.

This pathway towards the application of CBT principles to their psychotic patients has been trod by increasing numbers of community mental health team professionals over the last ten years in the United Kingdom, Australia, Canada and certain European countries. The dissemination of these techniques in other areas has depended upon local initiatives and has often lacked published case material to support enthusiastic practitioners; thus the pressing need for this casebook. CBT is a collaboration between patient and therapist, so to illustrate the variation that can occur, each chapter begins with a description of a mental health professional's own personal development and training in CBT for psychosis. The contributors then describe a case to illustrate certain key principles, which are explained in varying depths. The cases have been carefully chosen to give the early practitioner a good feel for the process of therapy in a variety of different psychotic presentations. A brief introduction to the general techniques is given at the beginning of the book, and it ends with a discussion on training, supervision and implementation issues.

The first case describes the key principles of working with a patient who has a systematised, grandiose delusion which is antipsychotic-resistant. Douglas Turkington, a psychiatrist, stresses the importance of maintaining collaboration, working up a formulation and generating interesting home-work exercises. Laura McGraw, a community nurse (with the assistance of Alison Brabban), describes her experience of introducing CBT to a pa-tient whom she has known for many years. She describes the complexi-ties for the patient and the therapist of making sense of their experiences and of working towards a shared explanation on which reality testing and activity scheduling can begin. Lars Hansen, a senior trainee psychia-trist, shows how to work with hallucinatory experiences, some of which are seen as pleasant and supportive by the patient. Isabel Clarke illus-trates her model of therapy with a patient with long-standing problems whom she met through her work as a senior clinical psychologist in a rehabilitation service. David Kingdon, together with Nicky, shows how practising consultant psychiatrists can integrate CBT into their workload to produce improved quality of management—in this particular case by understanding the link between Nicky's underlying guilt and psychotic symptoms. With Damien, a process of therapy is clearly described for those very difficult patients who abuse hallucinogenic drugs thereby exacerbat-ing psychotic symptoms. Ron Siddle, a nurse therapist, shows us how to work with those voices that command actions and are linked to depres-sion. Such patients, unless effectively treated, are of course at high risk of eventual suicide. Paul Murray provides a detailed description of a patient who received a brief intervention as part of the Insight into Schizophrenia study (Turkington et al., 2002), but nevertheless seemed to gain signifi-cant benefits from it. Nick Maguire, a clinical psychologist, describes two patients with paranoid delusions, and shows clearly not only how to help the patients to recognise that their delusions are beliefs and not facts but, in a guided discovery manner, to help the patients to test them gradually in a real situation. His model for doing so is clearly explained. Pauline Callcott, a nurse therapist, describes work with a very traumatised and fearful woman using CBT for psychosis, combined with some of the treat-ment methods used in post-traumatic stress disorder. This had mixed results—symptoms improved but admission was necessary and remains quite a controversial way of working with psychotic patients. Jeremy Pel-ton, a nurse therapist with the Insight project, describes how to engage the family as co-therapists and shows how beneficial that can be in im-proving joint understanding and coping, which can be of real and last-ing benefit to psychotic patients who, it would seem, can be helped to move into 'the real world'. The casebook should provide great encour-agement to those mental health professionals who have always intuitively believed that such interventions could be appropriate for the many pa-tients experiencing severe mental health problems. We hope that by clear case illustrations, and by describing the research evidence available, we

may also help those who are more sceptical to understand why we believe these developments to be so important in the management of such
disorders.

Douglas Turkington
David Kingdon
18 December 2001

INTRODUCTION

"We can talk", a major American journal announced in 1997: "Schizophrenia is no longer a disorder in which psychological approaches have no place" (Fenton & McGlashan, 1997). Many people, including users of services, their carers and staff, are now trying to understand why people who are going through a troubled period in their life, feel or behave the way they do, and think about frightening, confusing, depressing or distressing matters. Irrespective of whether they are users or patients, carers, friends, nurses, social workers, doctors or psychologists, it is important that they have the capacity to control their emotions effectively. Some people seem able to do this intuitively, but most of us need help. We hope this book can provide some of that help by giving examples of how a variety of people from different backgrounds have spent time trying to understand and offer assistance in these circumstances.

People who have participated in the use of CBT—of one form or another—will be described. This will include not only users or patients who have experienced psychotic symptoms, but also those who have worked with them as carers or therapists. Both groups vary considerably in their experiences of symptoms and of using CBT with these symptoms. Participation and collaboration in therapy has been an essential basis for any progress that is seen. In their guided discovery of the experiences that have led to their meeting for therapeutic purposes, the patient and therapist will both have taken a lead.

Over the years, we have also been closely involved in training and supervising mental health workers and describe some of the positive and negative experiences involved. Similarly, the implementation of CBT in mental health services has progressed and is gradually becoming embedded in clinical services—but not uneventfully. Again this will be discussed and evidence for the effectiveness of CBT in psychosis will be reviewed briefly.

Finally, we would recommend that you read one or more of the available texts on CBT in psychosis, as they differ and complement each other in a

A Case Study Guide to Cognitive Behaviour Therapy of Psychosis. Edited by
David Kingdon and Douglas Turkington. © 2002 John Wiley & Sons, Ltd.

variety of ways. Hazel Nelson's book (1997) is thorough and detailed in its description of therapy. David Fowler and colleagues (1995) have produced a book which is enlivened by case studies and broad clinical experience, while the text by Paul Chadwick and colleagues (1996) provides a very clear exposition of the use of the ABC framework in CBT. Our own text (Kingdon & Turkington, 1994) provides a theoretical basis for normalising symptoms and working systematically with them. However, in case such books are not readily available, we will present below a brief description of the key issues.

TECHNIQUES USED

Basis in cognitive behaviour therapy

The use of CBT in schizophrenia has been drawn from Beck's theory of emotional disorders (Beck, 1976). It has been founded on a tradition of evaluation, using experimental and research studies of defined therapeutic techniques. These techniques are problem-oriented and are aimed at changing errors or biases in cognitions (usually thoughts or images) involving the appraisal of situations and modifying assumptions (beliefs) about the self, the world and the future. The Cognitive Therapy Scale (Young & Beck, 1980) is used in research studies to ensure fidelity to the treatment model described by Beck and colleagues, but it is also a valuable tool in training. There have been adaptations to this for general use (e.g. Milne et al., 2001) and also for use in psychosis (Haddock et al., 2001). It describes the general therapeutic skills used in psychological treatment and the more specific conceptualisation, strategy and techniques used in cognitive therapy. The use of CBT in schizophrenia builds on these skills and techniques, although there are some differences in emphasis.

General skills

The general therapeutic skills described are those that are applicable to any psychological approach. They are aimed at enhancing what have been described as "non-specific factors" (Truax & Carkhoff, 1967)—the development of accurate empathy, non-possessive warmth, unconditional positive regard and non-judgementalism.

These skills also include agenda setting, which needs to be performed quite sensitively with patients with schizophrenia. Developing and agreeing an agenda may not be easy for them because of thought disorder, negativity or preoccupation with delusions and hallucinations, and this may involve more prompting and suggesting, while retaining collaboration and elicit-ing feedback, than would occur when setting agendas for patients with different disorders. The agenda may even be implicit rather than explicit; for example, an initial session usually concentrates on engagement and as-sessment, so the agenda may simply be "to find out what problems you're having at the moment and begin to understand how they came about". Developing such understanding, displaying interpersonal effectiveness, and collaboration are further general skills. Pacing and the efficient use of time are important in engaging and retaining the patient in therapy. As si-lences can be anxiety-provoking and increase symptoms they are generally to be avoided but, on the other hand, patients need time to respond when their concentration is impaired and the pace of sessions needs to be judged carefully. The length of sessions may also need to be responsive to the men-tal states of patients. If they are becoming tired or particularly distressed, sessions may be wound down early. Occasionally if a complex delusional system or a particularly sensitive area is being explored, more time can be taken (within the constraints of the therapist's working schedule).

Cognitive therapy differs from other therapeutic interventions in its man-ner of conceptualisation and strategy, and the specific techniques, used. The concept of guided discovery is very important when working with patients with schizophrenia. Therapy is a journey of exploration into pa-tients' beliefs, understanding them and finding out more about them, as far as possible, without preconceptions. That does not mean, of course, that the therapist will agree with the conclusions that the patients have reached, but he or she will understand how the conclusions developed, which will be explained further in discussion of the management of delusions and hal-lucinations. There is a focus on key cognitions; that is, "voices", delusional beliefs and behaviours—e.g. ways of coping with "voices" or avoidant behaviour in response to delusions of reference. The use of an ABC formu-lation can be valuable in clarifying the association between Antecedents, Beliefs and Consequences and assist patients to review their voices and beliefs constructively (see Chadwick, Birchwood & Trower, 1996).

A broad strategy for change is developed collaboratively with the patient from a formulation. The formulation will include discussion of predis-posing factors (e.g. early childhood experiences), precipitating factors (life stresses, e.g. leaving home, adverse illicit drug experience) and perpetuat-ing factors (e.g. continued unrealistic expectations and criticisms, or social circumstances). The development of key symptoms and beliefs will form part of this formulation.

The application of specific cognitive behaviour. techniques will be de-scribed. Patients with schizophrenia may find difficulty in collaborating with homework assignments and we tend to avoid the term. Instead we discuss "finding out" about something (e.g. satellite broadcasts: if the patients believe that these are influencing their thoughts). Where patients find difficulty with diaries, detailed recall of specific days can be used, e.g. "Do you remember what you did yesterday?", "What time did you get up?", "What time did the voices start?", "Where were you and what were you doing?", "What were they saying?".

Engagement

Developing a working alliance with patients with schizophrenia can be difficult where they have paranoid symptoms or have had difficulties with services in the past. They may not feel listened to and may expect you to dismiss their beliefs as 'mad'. However, when they find that the therapist is interested in their symptoms, their content, what they mean to them and how they have developed, engagement can be effectively secured. Studies in this area consistently find that, once they agree to participate in a study, less than 15% drop out. Engaging them in such studies or therapy can be difficult but the opportunity to state their case about their beliefs is frequently taken up with alacrity. This can be further improved by allowing them to lead a discussion, where they are able to do so, taking their concerns as primary—but prompting with known information when silence occurs—with the ultimate aim of having sessions that are relatively relaxing and comfortable. When it becomes hard work or distressing, it is generally better to pull back and use relaxation methods or casual conversation to conclude the session. Sometimes the patients will want to work through painful issues, but this needs to be carefully paced.

Tracing antecedents of symptoms

Understanding the circumstances in which delusional ideas or hallucinations began, even when they may be 30 years previously, can be invaluable in finding out why particular beliefs have arisen. For example, paranoid delusions and hallucinations may have occurred for the first time during a drug-induced psychosis ("bad trip") and need to be relabelled as originating with, although not currently caused by, that experience. Also, voices may relate to a specific traumatic event that is often accompanied by a depressive episode. A good conventional psychiatric assessment of the personal history can allow the pathological process to be charted using "guided discovery". This is particularly important for patients who have been ill for a number of years, as the mists of time have often obscured the original precipitants. A direct approach—"When did you first think that...." or "When were you last well or OK?"—may elicit the information needed, but may sometimes be less successful where distressing events are involved. Developing the story through personal history—beginning with birth and progressing to childhood, adolescence and the period preceding illness—may, by association, draw out the relevant precipitants where they exist. Accounts from relatives, clinical records or family doctor notes may be useful to prompt the patient. There remain a small number of patients who are unable to locate specific precipitants but can be overcome by the minor stresses of life.

Understanding patients' explanations

Patients use a variety of explanations for their symptoms, and these are elicited. Romme and Escher (1989) found that people who experienced auditory hallucinations described them as being caused by "trauma repressed", "impulses from unconscious speaking", "part of mind expansion", "a special gift or sensitivity", "expanded consciousness", "aliens", "astrological phenomena" and, more rarely, "a chemical imbalance or schizophrenia". To this can be added spiritual beliefs ("God or the Devil speaking") and technological explanations (satellites or radar, etc.).

To understand patients' explanations it may first be necessary to allow them to lead and explore the models of their mental health problems. It is often helpful to normalise, but this is not to minimise or be dismissive of their symptoms. A vulnerability/stress model is useful in explaining the illness, and is credible scientifically. Some patients have vulnerabilities that may have been inherited or caused by some physical effects on the brain, and the presence of stressful events (which might include chemical interaction, e.g. illicit drugs or viral illness) which may have precipitated the illness. For some people their vulnerability is very low, but the stress they have experienced has been high and overwhelming. Others seem very vulnerable to stress, and illness precipitates readily.

Alternative explanations for specific symptoms may be developed through discussion. Prompting the patients may be necessary, but the more the patients are able to provide their own alternative explanations the more likely they are to accept them. Anxiety symptoms are frequently misunderstood; e.g. the thought that 'my boss is controlling my mind' can arise from the giddiness associated with hyperventilation, or "I'm being shocked" from paraesthiae.

Delusions

Two factors appear important in delusion formation (Hemsley & Garety, 1986): prior expectation, i.e. "what you expect affects what you believe"; and the current relevant information provided by the environment, i.e. "the events occurring at the time and circumstances you find yourself in". Working with delusions involves establishing engagement, tracing the origins of the delusion, building a picture of the prodromal period, identifying *significant* life events and circumstances, identifying relevant perceptions (e.g. tingling, muzziness) and thoughts (e.g. suicidal, violent), and reviewing these negative thoughts and any dysfunctional assumptions. Patients are particularly prone to taking things personally, getting things out of context and jumping to conclusions.

The content of the delusion needs to be explored: the nature of the evidence that the patient has assembled *for* the delusion; and the evidence he or she can produce that seems to argue against the delusion. Alternatives are developed: "Are there any other possible explanations?"; "If someone said that to you, how would you respond?". The process continues by gentle prompting: "What about...?", "Do you think just possibly...?" Where delusions are resistant or if the discussion appears to be going round in circles, a technique described as inference chaining may be valuable. However, *if the patient is becoming agitated, distressed or hostile, discontinue* the session. Discussion with a cognitive therapist who is experienced in this area, if available, may allow the recommencement of therapy. Inference chaining can proceed through the factual implications of a belief, e.g. "If you have a transformer in your brain, doesn't it need electricity to work?" or emotional consequences, "OK, I do have some problems with this belief that you have... but if other people accept what you are saying, what difference would that make to you." This can then be followed through to specific concern, e.g. "I'd be respected", "By whom in particular?", "My family". These issues can then be worked with: "Although I may not be able to accept your belief" (e.g. that you are the Jesus Christ), "I may be able to help you to look at how you can gain the respect of your parents."

Hallucinations

Working with hallucinations involves initial assessment of the relevant dimensions, i.e. conviction, preoccupation, distress, content, frequency and pattern of occurrence. Any "voices" are discussed and differentiated from illusions and delusions of reference. Agreement will usually be reached that they resemble "someone speaking to you as I am doing now" (or perhaps shouting or mumbling). The individuality of the perception is established: "Can anybody else hear what is said?...not parents, friends, etc.?" This is agreed although it may involve the person checking with others about whether they can be heard. Beliefs about the origin of voices are explored: "Why do you think they can't hear them?" Often the patient is unsure of his or her origin or produces delusional beliefs. Techniques for delusions (see above) can be used if appropriate. Possible explanations will then be explored: e.g. "it may be schizophrenia". Stressful situations in which voices can arise may usefully be described as they can help to normalise the experience, i.e. many people under certain forms of stress can hallucinate. This can be induced through sleep deprivation (Oswald, 1984), sensory deprivation states (Slade, 1984) and other stressful circumstances, such as bereavement, hostage situations (Grassian, 1983), PTSD and severe infections. In other words, 'voices can be stress related—because you hear them does not mean that you are a different sort of person from everybody else. When people are put under certain types of stress, e.g. sleep deprivation, they may also hallucinate.'

The aim is to raise the possibility that voices are internal—the person's own thoughts. The analogy with dreams and nightmares may help with this: 'a living nightmare'. Medication and coping strategies, e.g. listening to music, a warm bath, attending 'Hearing voices' groups (of other patients who suffer similarly), then become more relevant. Also, exploration of the content of voices can occur. Where this is abusive, violent or obscene, perhaps making commands, the voices are often related to previous traumatic events or depressive episodes, and specific work can then be efficacious. Voices may seem omnipotent (Chadwick & Birchwood, 1994) but: 'Just because a voice says something, however loudly and forcefully, does not mean it is true...or that you have to act upon it.'

Thought disorder

Disorder of the form of thought, however caused, interferes with communication, and techniques have been developed for clarifying verbal communication in these circumstances (Turkington & Kingdon, 1991). They involve allowing patients' speech to flow, then gently prompting them to focus down on specific themes as they emerge. Usually the themes selected are those which, on the surface, sound distressing—e.g. distressing events that may be mentioned. Neologisms and metaphorical speech are clarified by gentle questioning, and once a theme is selected the patients are drawn back to it each time they stray. The process is one that enables communication. It can be improved by audiotaping sessions and then reviewing them, as pertinent themes may emerge from such reviews for discussion at the next session.

Negative symptoms

There is evidence that CBT improves negative symptoms (Sensky et al., 2000). Techniques involve eliciting specific positive symptoms, especially ideas of reference, thought broadcasting and hallucinations, which may emerge under stress. Patients may become essentially agoraphobic or socially phobic because of a fear of reactivating distressing positive or panic symptoms. They may also require a convalescence period after an acute episode, and a reduction in pressure and the postponement of some immediate expectations may be indicated. The protective function of stress avoidance, e.g. sleeping during the day and getting up in the quiet of the night, needs to be considered. Avoidance of stimulation may be a reasonable coping strategy while work with positive symptoms and stress management is pursued. Retaining hope is essential, so the development of realistic five-year plans may reduce the immediate pressures to "get better and get back to work/college". The aims may be the same, but the time scale is more realistic.

Clinical subgroups

Although a symptomatic approach is valuable in working with patients with psychoses, there are limitations to it in that, for example, hallucinations may present quite differently and cause different levels of distress in a person presenting with a range of psychotic symptoms than in someone for whom this is the predominant symptom relating to previous life events. This has increasingly led us to consider whether psychoses, including the schizophrenias, can be subgrouped (see Kingdon & Turkington, 1998). If valid and reliable groups can be developed, this could help with their management in determining responses to medication, psychological treatment, family work and rehabilitation measures. Such groups would also be expected to give indications of prognosis and assist substantially in research and training. Differentiation into bipolar disorder and schizophrenia has, arguably defined a spectrum rather than discrete entities. Previous descriptions of "the group of schizophrenias", as it was originally described (Bleuler, 1950), have included those appearing in International Classifications of Diseases, such as *simple, hebephrenia, catatonia, paranoid* or *schizoaffective*, and symptomatic classifications (e.g. Liddle et al., 1994), such as *positive, negative* or *disorganised*. These classifications have not proved useful in clinical practice, yet there seems to be very general agreement that substantial differences between groups of patients exist. We have described four such groups (Kingdon & Turkington, 1998) that have proved helpful in planning treatment strategies, based on individual formulations. For convenience, these have been provisionally described as:

Gradual onset

- "sensitivity psychosis": individuals who develop psychosis gradually in adolescence with predominant negative symptoms;
- "trauma-related psychosis": individuals with traumatised backgrounds (usually from sexual abuse) with abusive hallucinations as predominant and most distressing symptoms.

Acute onset

- "anxiety psychosis": individuals who initially develop anxiety and depressive symptoms in response to a life event, are often socially isolated, who suddenly 'know' the reason for their distress and generally develop a single 'core' delusion elaborated into a delusional system with or without hallucinations;
- "drug-related psychosis": individuals whose initial presentation is with drug-precipitated psychosis followed by persisting psychotic symptoms, of the same nature and content, as the initial episode.

Management is focused on these specific symptoms, but the "core" delusion in "anxiety psychosis", for example, rarely responds to direct reasoning approaches although these help to establish a relationship with the patient, and often prompts investigation into underlying issues, e.g. isolation or poor self-esteem.

Medication issues

All the studies into CBT in schizophrenia have stressed the importance of medication. It is sometimes necessary to wait for medication to reduce acute psychotic symptoms before using CBT, especially with thought disorder, although the use of a CBT approach often allows negotiation on the use of medication or hospitalisation to occur. 'Compliance therapy', a brief form of CBT, has been specifically aimed at this. Where patients begin to understand that their voices are internal phenomena and that their beliefs just *might* be self-induced, they are more likely to take medication to alleviate these problems. Conversely, if medication has a positive effect, this reinforces work on helping them to accept voices as their own thoughts.

CONCLUSION

Cognitive behaviour therapy is a major advance in treating schizophrenia. In combination with medication, it offers effective interventions for a range of positive and negative symptoms and is very acceptable to most patients and carers. The techniques involved build on basic training for cognitive therapists and psychologists, and also case managers, nurses and psychiatrists, who are experienced in working with patients with schizophrenia. Manuals are available to assist with the development of skills. In some areas, training courses for mental health workers have been developed but there are currently far too few trained personnel; however, this situation may change with the emerging evidence of effectiveness and increased training opportunities (see later chapters).

CASES: SUBGROUPS AND PROMINENT SYMPTOMS

Cases	Subgroups				Prominent symptoms									
	PTSP[1]	Drug-related	Anxiety psychosis	Sensitivity psychosis	Hallucinations —abusive	Hallucinations —other	Paranoia	Thought disorder	Other delusions	Negative symptoms	Depression	Anger	Anxiety	Suicidality
1 John			*		*		**		*			*		
2 Janet				*	*		*		*	*	*	*	*	
3 Pat	*				**	*	*			*	*			
4 Helena	*				**					*	**		*	*
5 Kathy				*		** visions	*	*		*	*			
6 Nicky	*				**		*			*	**			*
7 Damien		*					*	**	*	*	*	*		
8 Sarah	*				**		*				*		*	*
9 Carole	*				**				*		*			*
10 Mary			*				**					*	*	
11 Karen			*				**		*				*	
12 Jane				*	*		**			**	*		*	
13 Malcolm				*		*	**		*		*			*
14 Colin			*				**				*		*	

*   Present

**   Prominent symptom

---
[1] 'Post-traumatic stress psychosis'

PART I

CASE STUDIES

Chapter 1

"THE ADMIRAL OF THE FLEET"

Case 1 (John): *Douglas Turkington*

There are a number of patients with antipsychotic-resistant schizophrenia who derive minimal benefit even with Clozapine (Kane et al., 1988). These patients often suffer from delusions which are systematised and entrenched. Such delusions are usually not only impervious to treatment with antipsychotic medication, but they are also very difficult to treat psychologically. The problem in relation to these cases is that the delusion is often systematised with a grandiose or paranoid theme and insight is usually virtually completely lacking. The delusion is often held with a very marked conviction and the patient sometimes acts in a dangerous way upon the content of the delusion. The questions then arise as to whether patients with such systematised grandiose or persecutory delusions can be understood within a cognitive therapy framework and whether the application of the principles of cognitive therapy (Fowler, Garety & Kuipers, 1995) can produce benefit. One of the key issues that has always prevented the development of a viable rational intervention with grandiose or paranoid systematised delusions has been the apparent incomprehensibility of the content. There is, however, evidence that such delusions are based on pre-existing beliefs and attitudes within the patient's life history (Harrow, Rattenburg & Stoll, 1988). Some of the key principles in working with the chronically grandiose or paranoid patient with schizophrenia are therefore to understand the case by means of a jointly generated case formulation, to introduce doubt into the delusional system and to allow chinks of insight to develop gradually. There is also the question: What is the most efficient way to work with such patients? The description of techniques and the process of application as described in the case of "The Admiral of the Fleet" should give guidance to therapists who are dealing with such patients, who often end up chronically institutionalised in long-stay wards and within rehabilitation settings, or struggle in the community and are episodically admitted into acute wards, often for prolonged periods, after they have acted on their delusions. This group of patients with schizophrenia who have grandiose

A Case Study Guide to Cognitive Behaviour Therapy of Psychosis. Edited by
David Kingdon and Douglas Turkington. © 2002 John Wiley & Sons, Ltd.

or paranoid systematised delusions are best described within the therapeutic framework as being anxiety psychoses (Kingdon & Turkington, 1998)—that is, they often have some degree of vulnerability to develop schizophrenia but it is actually an accumulation of highly significant life events, salient to schema vulnerability, that tip them over into the development of a particular protective delusion that acts to protect self-esteem (Lyon, Kaney & Bentall, 1994).

Prior to describing the process of cognitive therapy with this case, I should describe something of my own background. I trained as a general psychiatrist in Glasgow, primarily in biological treatments but also in the importance of psychodynamic psychotherapy. My experience of working with schizophrenic patients in Glasgow showed me that the content of their psychotic symptoms was often more understandable than I had been led to believe in relation to their life history and the life events they had experienced. However, I could not see a way forward in treating them with psychodynamic psychotherapy as it appeared that they were too psychologically fragile to cope with a regressive psychotherapy modality. Indeed, this was confirmed by Stanton and colleagues (1984) where psychodynamic psychotherapy with schizophrenia led to a symptomatic deterioration, but supportive psychotherapy showed some degree of benefit. Thereafter I was trained in cognitive therapy, having become very interested in the cognitive model as described in depressed persons by Beck (1967). A very clearly described process of therapy was available in manualised form for the treatment of patients with clinical depression (Beck et al., 1979). This seemed to show that there was a clear way forward and a clear direction of therapy with such patients, which gave the therapist hope of a possible therapeutic process that might benefit such patients systematically. Remaining fascinated in psychotic patients from my time in Glasgow, I moved to Sheffield and was trained in the cognitive therapy of depression, as described by Beck. This training involved working systematically through Beck's cognitive therapy of depression and having audiotaped supervision of therapy sessions. I was then instructed in the rational emotive therapy of Ellis, and achieved the advanced certificate in this therapy modality. Being well trained in the techniques of Beck and Ellis, I was then able to apply the principles of therapy from both approaches. It was, however, the Beckian approach that seemed most appropriate for patients with schizophrenia. Beck's approach was much more gradual and collaborative and was much less active/directive; it was dependent upon a case formulation and a variety of techniques used at different levels. The techniques of Ellis (1962) remained useful for working with the above beliefs, which often underpinned and maintained psychotic symptoms.

While working with Professor Kingdon at Bassetlaw Hospital, and noting his application of cognitive therapy techniques to his entire schizophrenic population, I began to understand how the principles of Beckian cognitive therapy could be applied to patients with schizophrenia. Certain principles from rational emotive therapy, however, remained highly useful in the treatment of this patient group, particularly in certain subgroups of schizophrenia. The case that follows shows a typical example of my work with a patient with a grandiose systematised delusion. It stresses the importance of maintaining collaboration and gradually working with techniques from superficial to deep, and at the same time maintaining rapport and working together to produce acceptable homework experiments.

JOHN

"The Admiral of the Fleet" (John) was admitted under Section 3 of the Mental Health Act as he was considered to be a danger to the community. He had been making positive actions on his belief that he was highly involved in world politics and was, indeed, at the centre of all military actions on behalf of the Western nations. At the time of admission his self-care had deteriorated and he had begun to become threatening towards his landlord, who had been very tolerant of his behaviour for a prolonged period. He had also been sending voluminous numbers of letters to leading politicians and military personnel. On admission he made it very clear to staff that he viewed the admission as a form of military detention against his wishes, and that it was unacceptable for the allied commander-in-chief to be detained in a psychiatric unit in this way. He indicated that he had been in charge of the NATO fleet and the entire allied operation during Desert Storm. He believed that he had been involved in all recent military campaigns including Chechnya, Bosnia, Lebanon, Iraq and Zaire and had delusions that references were made to him in the book by Norman Schwarzkopf and, on a daily basis, on cable network news. The Schwarzkopf book was kept on his bedside table and he spent most of the day watching cable network news. He believed that certain facial expressions and gestures by leading political and military figures were related directly to his involvement in these activities. He went on to tell staff that he was a candidate in the 1992 US presidential election and that George Bush had stolen a number of his key strategies and policies. He was abusive towards staff on the ward, threatening to have them struck off through a High Court action.

John was a middle-aged man at the time of admission but he had first been admitted to a psychiatric ward in October 1995. At that time the psychiatric

Registrar had indicated that John was grossly deluded, claiming that he was not only involved in global politics and military action, but that Bill Clinton was taking the credit for his activities. He also indicated that the Queen of the United Kingdom was not doing her job properly. His medical notes stated that he had been given full doses of Olanzapine, Risperidone, Clopixol Depot and Droperidol, all to very little effect, and that he had developed severe side effects. He was discharged at that time on no medication, and was just as deluded as previously. John's landlord tolerated his deluded mental state for a two-year period, during which he was not acting as obviously on his delusions until the time of his most recent admission under the Mental Health Act. He had no pertinent previous medical problems of any kind. His parents, however, had separated in his childhood and he had not seen his father for many years. He had by and large lost contact with his mother through the years of his psychosis. His sister had a very successful job; however his brother had a history of chronic schizophrenia. John, who described himself as being "the black sheep of the family", had a normal birth and development in childhood and was brought up in the south of England. He described having a poor upbringing due to tensions in the family, which ended in the parental divorce. He was to a degree resentful that his brother had taken the main role in helping his mother. He went through a normal schooling, reporting no behavioural difficulties, and achieved two "O" levels at the age of 16. At that time he left school and joined the Royal Air Force. He spent two years in training and qualified as an electronic engineer, and was then involved in aircraft inspection and radar maintenance throughout Europe. He was promoted to Corporal and at the age of 28 reached the rank of Sergeant in the Royal Air Force. At 33 years of age he was involved in a dispute over the cause of a helicopter crash, and ended up resigning from the forces over this issue. He had married in 1972, but the couple had separated shortly after the dispute about the helicopter crash. He had lost contact with his two children. He had been teetotal throughout his life and had never used any illegal substances. His premorbid personality was described as independent, assertive and sociable. He was a stable extrovert with no particular religious orientation but had always been interested in military history and politics.

Mental state examination at the time of his admission revealed that his self-care was poor, his hair was unkempt and he was unshaven. There was a degree of emotional blunting with occasional knowing smiles. There was no evidence of any disorder of affect such as incongruity, depression or elation and hallucinations or thought disorder were not in evidence. There was, however, evidence of a systematised grandiose delusion linked to delusions of reference from television, radio and newspapers.

His behaviour on the ward continued to oscillate between positive actions on his delusions—i.e. watching cable network news and reading the newspapers and writing to politicians—and resting on his bed thinking. Testing of organic function revealed no abnormality; his intelligence quotient was certainly in the above-average bracket. Discussion with John's mother prior to his first session confirmed that he had developed his delusion after becoming mentally ill at the time of the public enquiry over the helicopter crash and his resignation from the forces. His mother confirmed that for the following two years he had been mentally ill and unemployed, living away from his family in the community. He then left the United Kingdom and worked in Ireland for a period before again acting on his delusions. He moved to the United States and started to sleep 'rough' outside the White House in Washington. After a period of 18 months, he was deported from the United States and lived "rough" for a period prior to his first admission in the north-east of England.

Over the period of his admission prior to being referred for cognitive therapy, he was given 6 months of the maximum tolerable dose of Clozapine which was causing him side effects of excess salivation and hypotension. He was deemed totally neuroleptic resistant but it was clear that there had been some minimal benefits from the use of Clozapine. After a word round, he was referred for cognitive therapy "more in hope than in expectation" prior to being moved to a long-stay bed in a mental hospital. He had been refused admission into any hostel accommodation in the community as he was considered to be too dangerously deluded. At his assessment session for cognitive therapy he was assessed in terms of the Comprehensive Psychopathological Rating Scale (Asberg, Montgomery & Perris, 1978) with a score of 27, indicating a moderate degree of disability. His symptoms mostly comprised delusions of grandeur, emotional blunting, hostility, lassitude, fatigability and autonomic disturbance. His Global Score was 6, indicating a maximal degree of psychotic disability. His assessment on the Maudsley Assessment of Delusion Schedule (Taylor et al., 1993) and the Global Scale for Delusional Severity (Turkington et al., 1996) revealed that he had almost a maximal positive score of 18/19. His score on the Dysfunctional Attitude Scale (DAS; Weissman & Beck, 1978) revealed that he had a normal profile except for a strong vulnerability on entitlement. Entitlement vulnerability is defined on the DAS as 'a belief in entitlement to things including success, money, love and happiness'. It is quoted as indicating that the person with entitlement vulnerability expects and demands his or her wants to be met by other people because of his or her inherent goodness or hard work. When this does not happen, as is often the case, the person with this vulnerability feels either depressed or inadequate or can become very angry. Such people complain loudly and often, but do little to solve their problems. As a result of their bitter demanding attitudes they invariably get far less of what they want from life.

During the first session on the ward John was hostile and defensive, and would only talk about his delusions. Owing to the fact that this was the only material that was possible for the agenda, and the only way that collaboration could be maintained, it was decided to chart the chronological development of his delusions, i.e. an examination of the antecedents.

Focusing the discussion on the antecedents of the emergence of the delusions led to a very productive session. John became interested in talking about the problems which predated his "new role". He told me that, in the late 1980s, five aircrew were killed in a helicopter crash; he also said that he had inspected the wreckage and, in his view, compensation should have been paid to the families of the men who died as he believed that the crash had been the result of instrument failure. It is also clear that John probably carried a genetic vulnerability to the development of schizophrenia as there was one close family member who was chronically ill with the disorder. He reported becoming increasingly angry and anxious between March and April of that year, and by the time he presented his report to a public enquiry, he was having paranoid ideas that threats were being made against him and his family. He believed that his house had been burgled in an attempt to remove key information, and indicated that his wife was becoming extremely distressed by the situation. His major affect through this time was of anger and frustration. He stood alone against the investigating team and the evidence of superior officers, and resigned shortly after the public enquiry. In the following month he described a period of having a very unusual change of mood. He said that it felt "as if something was about to happen", and it seemed to be linked to increasing anxiety and depersonalisation. Initially he developed delusions of reference and significance from the literature and music from that time, and his interlinked grandiose delusions emerged shortly thereafter with the key roles of his grandiosity being of avenger, controller and peace-maker. It was clear that the affective investment of this grandiose delusional system was of anger, and the behaviour linked to it was of episodic violence and a positive information search. This combination of parameters made his likelihood of admission under a section of the Mental Health Act very high and made him a potential danger to others in the community. During this first session, despite initially being very distressed and remaining deluded throughout, he was able to remain in touch with the therapy and was able to discuss the chronology of the antecedents for approximately one hour.

Cognitive therapy Session 2 revealed that he was still very angry that he received no credit for his stance against the lack of compensation for the families of the aircrew. He was given homework to find the news clippings from that time, if he still had them in his possession (his bedside cabinet was full of documents and papers), and, if possible, to find his report for the public enquiry. We agreed that we would both read extracts from the Schwarzkopf book which, John claimed, made direct references to him and we would discuss these in the following session. Throughout this session the main target was to gain more information and begin to understand what might have triggered the psychosis. The plan was to use guided discovery to lead towards an improvement in insight, and gentle peripheral questioning was used around the grandiose delusions. Any sign of increasing agitation was dealt with by tactical withdrawal and by refocusing the discussion on a more neutral area.

In cognitive therapy Session 3 it was clear that we were making some progress towards our joint understanding of the development of his "new role". Work on his delusions was largely unproductive, and the sessions were most usefully spent working on the antecedents and his own anger that he had lost his RAF career. He went on to tell me that it was very unfair that he had lost "uniform, salary and pension". Again he was given homework to itemise clearly the issues over the helicopter crash and the item of equipment failure that he believed was responsible.

By the time we reached cognitive therapy Session 4 it was clear that the work done in previous sessions had, to some degree, made the grandiose delusional system even more impenetrable. More detailed questioning during this session led to an expansion of the delusion, which included his involvement in the crash of the Bank of Credit and Commerce International, the Watergate Incident and the bombing of the World Trade Centre. An attempt was made to use Socratic questioning over his claims to have such a colossal degree of influence and political power. This Socratic questioning was also unhelpful and led John to indicate that he might be the Messiah, and remembered that children on the streets of Washington were calling him Jesus. This apparent increase in delusional severity and arousal seemed to be linked to the excessive amount of material being covered in the sessions, and it was decided that the next sessions should be paced more slowly and we should attempt to organise some regular time each day to allow him to relax using a relaxation tape. At this time, unfortunately, the Kosovo crisis was deepening and it was clear that he was becoming increasingly concerned about this.

In cognitive therapy Session 5, which was taken very slowly, he told me that the Queen as Head of Forces was symbolically responsible for his bad treatment, and he indicated a strong identification with Princess Diana in relation to the way the Royal Family had treated her. He seemed more relaxed now, and in Session 6 there was more discussion about how authority figures could, and often did, abuse their power and how people could best deal with this. His own beliefs about entitlement in relation to his current role with his consultant psychiatrist were explored, together with issues in relation to his own resignation from the RAF.

Cognitive therapy Session 7 showed the first signs of less direct involvement in current world affairs. He told me that he did *not* order the strike on Saddam Hussein. The focus through much of this session was at the schema level, i.e. on people's powerlessness to change some world situations, and in this he was able to agree that certain economic and natural disasters were actually not within his power to avert. The session proceeded with peripheral questioning and the generation of alternative hypotheses along with gentle schema level work on his entitlement demands.

In Session 8 it was decided to set up an experiment. By this time we had re-established a good therapeutic alliance, although there was no sign of any change in his insight. He indicated that his orders were being sent out of the psychiatric unit and being put into action by various military forces across the globe, so we decided to explore the mechanism by which these orders might be sent out. He indicated that he wrote instructions on a board in the day room and that staff and patients took the orders out. An experiment was set up, which in retrospect was probably too demanding, in which John was to have Tony Blair removed from office as Prime Minister within the next two weeks by issuing a direct order on the day hospital board.

In Session 9 it was agreed that Tony Blair was still in power and John had to agree that other people might be involved in the chain of command, which would slow down the implementation of his orders. In this session we returned to his case formulation and set up an inductive formulation by breaking his life down into five-year periods from birth until the onset of his psychotic symptoms. Through this process of inductive formulation we were both able to write up on the white board the various key influences on his life, and he was able to identify some of his own core beliefs. We came to some agreement on a mini-formulation that he had come to view himself as "the black sheep of the family". He indicated this most clearly in a belief about himself, i.e. "I am a rebel". This would appear to be a core belief that came from early childhood when his father died, and his brother had assumed the main paternal role. At this time he viewed himself as markedly rebellious against his brother's domination. He developed a compensatory schema that authority figures must be just and fair at all times, and it was this combination of core schema and compensatory schema that was massively activated by the injustice which, he believed, occurred at the time of the helicopter crash and led to the emergence of delusions directly linked to his compensatory schemas. During this session he seemed, remarkably, to have no delusions and was able to concentrate well on the underlying themes on his psychosis. It is commonly seen that when the focus is on the linked underlying schemas the delusion itself intrudes less into the session. As homework, he was asked to develop further some of the key areas surrounding the themes—i.e. other situations in which he may have behaved in a manner driven by these beliefs—and these were discussed at the start of Session 10. He placed his next order on the board in the day room: he ordered Japanese troops to be sent to Bosnia to support the deepening crisis in Albania. Three weeks later he showed me a paper clipping reporting that Japanese troops had been sent to Honduras. We found this a very interesting experiment as he accepted that his orders were being interfered with and that he couldn't have total control of everything. He did, however, indicate that it must have been a more junior officer who made this mistake with his orders and their implementation. It was therefore agreed that we would proceed with these experiments to understand his actual role more fully. At this point his CPRS score was checked and was found to be 25, indicating that there had only been minimal changes in his symptoms; his GSDS score was also checked and found to be 16, and therefore had only minimally changed. He was, however, becoming actively involved in his cognitive therapy and was doing reality-testing experiments which might in due course allow him to become less deluded. He was apparently less hostile and more sociable on the ward and was writing less voluminous letters to politicians.

By the end of Session 12, having performed a further experiment in which his order was not carried out to his satisfaction, John admitted that "the joint Chiefs of Staff do have a fair bit of power". We were then able to enter the debate that an alternative explanation for his partial success in predicting the outcome of various political and military scenarios was due to a high level of informed and intelligent speculation. This alternative explanation was to be tested against John's own explanation, i.e. "command and control". The homework was set up and he agreed at this point, surprisingly, to apply for his RAF pension and on the application form he signed his name with the rank of sergeant. At this time he also began to talk about his family and was seen to have become low in mood and near to tears for a period at the end of the session.

In cognitive therapy Session 13 the therapist and John both decided to make predictions about what would happen in the situation of the escalating

Kosovo crisis. I, as therapist, predicted:

1. The Serbs will show brinkmanship but will back down.
2. No military involvement from NATO will be needed.
3. No missiles will be fired against Belgrade.

John's predictions were:

1. War would break out in Kosovo.
2. There would be massacres of the local population.
3. NATO will go in and enter the arena of armed conflict.
4. There will be a Serb–NATO conflict.
5. Tomahawk cruise missiles will be fired against Belgrade and that he would give the command for the missiles to be fired.

In Session 14 he indicated that when the missiles were to be fired he would issue a strike command and would expect this to happen within 48 hours. By this point it was clear that John's predictions about what would happen in Kosovo were becoming very near to the truth and my predictions, as therapist, were being seen as completely false. This scientific testing of John's predictions, however, did not lead to an entrenchment of his delusional state. On the other hand, he actually became more involved in the scientific process of setting up experiments to test them and was very kind to the therapist in relation to his erroneous predictions. John indicated that it didn't matter that I had been wrong as I had much less in the way of background military knowledge. He also indicated that if he did receive a lump sum payment from the RAF, that he would pay off some of his wife's mortgage.

In Session 15 he informed my secretary that a strike had been ordered. The strike did not happen, but he was now highly involved in the scientific process of looking at the available information rather than positively looking for confirmatory information that would support his delusion. The nursing report was that John was much more appropriate and sociable on the ward and was doing more normal activities.

In Session 16 which was now back up to 45 minutes in length, he indicated that he was watching and following what was happening in the military and political arena rather than issuing commands. He was offered a lump sum pension and contacted his wife for the first time in many years.

In Session 17 of the cognitive therapy course he indicated that he was now scientifically testing out the situation himself. He said that he did not put his last order on the board, and only told me about it. He said that, as I was not allowed to tell anybody because of my position of trust with him, the last order must have been a prediction rather than a command. He also showed some improvement in relation to his own entrenched attitudes towards his own consultant and the taking of Clozapine.

By Session 18 he indicated that his last three orders were not carried out and he accepted that he was just watching and following world affairs. His entitlement demands seemed to be less powerful and he was more accepting of a need for medication and a need to work with his consultant on his rehabilitation. By this time in therapy he had agreed this case formulation and understood that a very large change had occurred in his life which had ended up with his admission to hospital. He had agreed the main schemas and beliefs that lay at the heart of his psychosis and he had begun hypothesis testing. By this time both positive and negative symptoms were improved: his CPRS had fallen to 11 and his GSDS had halved to a score of 8. The Dysfunctional Attitude Scale now revealed a normal profile.

This description of cognitive therapy for an inpatient with a grandiose systematised delusion indicates a number of key principles.

1. The generation of a collaborative, therapeutic alliance is crucial to any further progress, and this may mean that the therapist has to spend a lot of time talking about the impact of the delusions upon the patient's life.
2. Techniques that are applied too rapidly or in too probing a manner are liable to lead to increased arousal and increased systematisation of the delusion. It is therefore appropriate to work at a slow and steady pace and to work with homework that the patient is ready for.
3. Progress in this case only came when the antecedents of the psychotic period were explored and a mini-formulation and a full formulation generated as to why this change might have occurred in John's life. A focus on the pre-psychotic period would seem to be very important to enable patients to put their life history into perspective and understand some of the key triggers that have led to changes in their beliefs about themselves and their world.
4. Reality testing with appropriate homework exercises can be creative and interesting. They do not tend to make patients more deluded; on the contrary, it introduces them to an objective scientific method that can lead them to reduce their conviction in their delusion.
5. It would seem very important to understand the underlying schemas in this case of rebellion/entitlement and on understanding these key dysfunctional personal beliefs to work at this level beneath the grandiose system, thus allowing the system to settle gradually.
6. At all times it would seem crucial to pace the sessions reasonably slowly and, as far as possible, to retain rapport by using word perfect accuracy and avoid being drawn into confrontation or collusion.

7. The information given by the patient, although apparently incomprehensible, should always be taken seriously with the expectation that the pieces of the jigsaw will gradually fall into place as the sessions proceed.

This case gives very real hope to those patients with antipsychotic-resistant delusional systems. Cognitive therapy can show a different way of making the psychotic material much more comprehensible to both the treating clinical team and the patient, and can engage the patient as an agent in allowing the delusions to become the subject of testing within a collaborative, trusting and supportive therapeutic alliance.

Chapter 2

FROM A POSITION OF KNOWING: THE JOURNEY INTO UNCERTAINTY

Case 2 (Janet): *Laura McGraw and Alison Brabban*

The main purpose of this chapter is to provide some insight into the impact that developing new ways of understanding and new skills has on the therapist and their clinical practice. This in itself may not seem particularly revolutionary, however, the transition from believing you know most things to realising you know very little can be both demanding and emotionally challenging (Salzberger-Wittenberg, Henry & Osborne, 1990). I will use a case study to illustrate this experience.

In 15 years as a community mental health professional there have been very few moments when I have wanted to leave my job. However, in the early 1990s I found myself working as a lecturer and a community psychiatric nurse and becoming increasingly exposed to an array of literature commenting on the practice of Psychiatric Nursing. The reports touched on all aspects of service delivery and found that practice did not match expectations, despite policy recommendations. Community psychiatric nurses' caseloads had a low proportion of people with long-term mental illness on them; multidisciplinary team reviews rarely happened; the Care Programme Approach was not fully implemented; users and carers seemed poorly served; clients' physical health education was unsatisfactory; monitoring of medication was unsystematic; and the training of staff in appropriate interventions for schizophrenia was minimal (Gournay, 1996). The overall conclusion appeared to be that community psychiatric nurse (CPN) caseloads were made up of low proportions of severely mentally ill people and concerns were raised around current knowledge, skills and attitudes in such teams (McFadyen & Vincent, 1998).

This disarray of mental health services and low staff morale within overshadowed all the progress that had been made and sent signals to the public that community care was out of control (Muijen, 1996). Although it

A Case Study Guide to Cognitive Behaviour Therapy of Psychosis. Edited by
David Kingdon and Douglas Turkington. © 2002 John Wiley & Sons, Ltd.

seemed that CPNs had been moved away from working intensively with people suffering severe mental health problems and encouraged merely to administer depot injections and deliver anxiety management groups, I still attempted to do something meaningful with clients with psychosis. However, I experienced an increasing frustration with my clinical practice. Those people diagnosed as suffering from schizophrenia were the individuals with whom I enjoyed working. However, in my nurse training I had been taught that: *"Delusions are false beliefs. It is best not delve into them or you will become part of the delusional system."* Or, if someone talked to you about hearing voices or seeing things, it was best to: *"Ignore the content and concentrate on how they feel, get them involved in some activity, like making tea."*

A typical visit for me would consist of administering a depot injection, asking about side effects and spending approximately 10–20 minutes with the person. If he or she touched on personal experiences I employed core-counselling principles. I was empathic and understanding and I conveyed warmth and fostered trust. I had worked with many clients for six to seven years and had developed an alliance and a "comfortable relationship" (Barker, 1999). I was aware of certain aspects of their lives and knew my clients' presentations well, but was unable to underpin my "knowing" with any evidence. For example, I knew that a particular lady was becoming unwell if she painted her nails bright red, when to be alarmed if I didn't get an answer at the door and when it was okay. However, when clients wanted to talk about their hallucinatory or delusional experiences I became increasingly uneasy with my responses. I was acutely aware that after experiencing such extraordinary and often terrifying phenomena they wanted to talk about them. I was also aware that this in itself could be cathartic. What I did not know was how to respond other than a sympathetic nod or a desultory discussion about medication.

I perceived the "Medical Model" as something I was not party to, however, on reflection I see that I was only too happy to suggest either a change or increase in medication or possibly an appointment with the psychiatrist as the solution to any uncertainty. At least I believed that if anything were to happen I had followed "the correct procedure". I became increasingly aware that the content of my conversation stayed on safe subjects such as football or the day centre.

When people experience something as strange as hearing voices it can lead to a range of reactions from confusion and fear to depression. It is not just the experience itself that can be distressing, but the potential consequences can haunt the individual: "I'm mad", "they're going to lock me up", and "I'm going to have my children taken away". We all try to make sense of our experiences and this does not change even when the experiences are of an extraordinary nature (Chadwick, 1997). I was aware that my clients were trying to make sense of their "symptoms" and yet all I was offering was "maintenance medication" and "stability".

I had known many of these clients for a long time. They had shared aspects of my life with them, as I had been party to facets of theirs. My inability to reduce the distress they felt as a result of their psychosis was alarming to me, to say the least. Peter Wilkins (2001) expressed my feelings eloquently:

> Moments of madness are unpredictable—cliff edges with no railings; sheer drops that cause the mind to accelerate and the soul to brake hard. The psychiatric nurse stands, aroused by her own fears of madness and taunted by her inadequacies. She is naked under her own gaze—as much the watched as the watcher.

The conclusion: something had to be done. I needed to understand more and build on what I perceived was my "solid" knowledge base.

It took a determined two years to secure a place to train in Cognitive Behaviour Therapy for psychosis. My interview date actually coincided with the solar eclipse though I was so preoccupied by my determination to pursue the training that the astronomical events of the day escaped me. After I had been offered a place I left to go to the station. As the sky became a jaundiced hue, I pondered whether the strain had been so immense that I was shifting into a different reality . . . and indeed I was. However, embarking on such training did not simply involve "learning some new stuff". The path to knowledge turned out to be treacherous and full of potholes.

The first morning of the course I sat in a room full of what appeared to be very young people and listened to a debate about "What is schizophrenia?" Afterwards we were recommended to read *Recovery from Schizophrenia: Psychiatry and Political Economy* (Warner, 1985). I had memories of books with such seemingly obscure titles from my sociology degree a hundred years and two children ago. For me the surprise with this title was the term *"Recovery"*. Being the vigilant (and panic-stricken) student that I was, I purchased the book immediately.

In my experience, professionals use language and narrative based on the notion of the "chronic schizophrenic", talking of remission and maintenance. In a meta-analysis by Hogarty (1993), 40.2% of people recovered from a first episode of psychosis—a significant proportion of people have a fair to good outcome. However, that impression of hope is not what carers take away from their contact with mental health services. There is a fog of pessimism that seeps into our clinical practice so that we often omit hope and recovery from our care plans. Manfred Bleuler described this pessimism:

> The patient and those who are healthy had ceased to understand one another. The patient gives up in abject resignation, any effort to make himself understood. In doing so the naive observer declares that the patient has lost his reasoning powers. (Barham, 1995, p. 417)

A critique of CBT and PSI has stated that these approaches are technical cookbook affairs with little compassion and notion of the individual. The concept of recovery, and by that I mean the individual's concept of recovery (Reeves, 2000), is, however, the essence of these approaches.

JANET

The course demanded that I identified a number of clients with a diagnosis of psychosis or schizophrenia for me to work with within a CBT framework. One of the clients I decided to work with was a lady I had visited fortnightly for six years whom I felt I knew well. Much was made on the course of engagement and assessment of individuals. I wanted to give myself a break and chose her, as I knew I could skip the first part and move on to the therapy with ease. There would be no difficulties there. I visited the client and she was keen to work with me. I reassured her that it would be no different from previous sessions, just a little longer and probably more detailed. I also had to explain that the sessions would be taped. This was alarming for me, but not for her, as I had never used a tape recorder in sessions before. (For anyone embarking on this activity I suggest two things: firstly, chose a machine with a red light that flickers when you are recording or you will spend the whole session frantic that you have pressed the wrong button; and, secondly, set the machine to record in your home and get used to hearing your own voice before you have to present it in your supervision sessions.)

Reason for referral

Janet lived at home with her mother. She was diagnosed as having paranoid schizophrenia in the 1970s when she had a brief stay in an acute mental health ward. I met Janet in 1993 as her CPN when I was asked to "maintain her mental state and ensure medication compliance". Since that time, I had been unable to offer her much in the way of therapeutic opportunities. Day services were unsuitable and visits were focused on coping strategy enhancement. When I offered a new therapeutic approach Janet was interested.

Engagement

The shift in the therapeutic relationship with Janet was more difficult than I had ever anticipated. I had believed that because I had already established a positive relationship with Janet the process of engagement would be smooth. I found that establishing a structured approach to the sessions was more problematic than I had imagined: I found it difficult to set the agenda, limit the time and set homework (Kingdon and Turkington, 1994). I became anxious and worried that I would look foolish in her eyes. I had always been the professional and now I was reduced to a confused mess, fumbling to get a tape into the machine in the right way.

Janet was fascinated by the intellectual ideas of CBT and enjoyed the visits which, at first, were lasting an hour and a half. This may seem beyond the capacity of most CPNs—caseloads are high and the pressure is on to keep visits short. I confess that this considerable time was largely due to my inexperience, but I do ask the question: Why do we always feel visits should be as short as possible? While we are racing around completing risk assessments, unable to find time to write our notes or attend meetings, what do we achieve? If we are merely trying to see as many clients as possible, how useful is this to the person receiving the rationed visit and how rewarding is this for us as professionals?

We discussed the "awkwardness" we both felt. She was used to me chatting about my life, my children, the holiday, and I was used to giving her an injection and having occasional discussions about "getting out more" or "doing more in the house". We had once spent 6 months trying to help her to use the washing machine effectively, without success. This felt more formal, and like a true novice I was clumsy and inept at my delivery. I discussed with her that it was important to have an agenda and a structure and why homework was crucial to the therapy (having barely understood the reasons myself). Working within a structured framework feels daunting and renders the experienced clinician ill at ease. It became apparent, however, that without these props the session can become meandering and diverse. The agenda reassures the client that there is a purpose to the meeting and maintains the focus of the therapist. I now explain to clients that doing homework means that I would not have to move in with them to get all the information I need. Clients feel that you are genuine, and that it matters to you what they are experiencing when you are not there.

Again, it is interesting to note how many times we actually explain to people why we want them to do tasks between sessions. Those who, like myself, have executed a million anxiety management groups will recall with clarity how difficult it is to persuade people to do homework tasks, and then how to tell them sympathetically that it didn't matter anyway. Put yourself in the position of the person: If you were unclear about the purpose of what appeared to be both a difficult (try doing a thought diary for a week) and meaningless (think about courses you have been on when you had to do formative assignments) task, what conviction would you apply in trying to achieve it? It is important to give a clear rationale and explanation for the purpose of your interventions and, indeed, your presence in their home.

It was important to explain to Janet the purpose of CBT and the aims of therapy. This was discussed using Kingdon and Turkington's (1994) framework where therapy is seen as an opportunity for Janet to describe her experiences and generate discussion about them. There was to be a focus on areas of her life that she found distressing, ensuring that any co-existing depression or anxiety was treated. Finally, underlying core beliefs or schema would be identified and worked with.

"Schema" is a term meaning core beliefs—those beliefs we hold as true from our childhood experiences about the world, ourselves and those in it. So, for example, someone who has a childhood characterised by physical abuse may grow to be an adult who believes that the world is a dangerous place to be in. These beliefs are not necessarily pathological: most individuals do not believe that people as a whole are dangerous or trustworthy, or that they themselves are worthless.

The notion of concentrating on the "areas of her life that *she* found distressing" (as opposed to those that we as practitioners find upsetting) is hardly revolutionary, but is still something with which some clinicians have difficulty. It transpired that Janet did not view all of her "psychotic" experiences as negative or distressing. As the sessions developed an ebb and flow of their own, the anxiety reduced for both of us. Janet tended not to talk about her feelings at first and would state that "voices, pictures and mood swings" had troubled her. It seemed that Janet needed to be confident that I would not leave her feeling exposed and vulnerable after she had discussed her experiences. I find it astounding that people who have had negative experiences within mental health services are still bold enough to embark on new encounters, to tell their usually painful story again and again. I would like to think that Janet believed I was trying to help her reframe her experiences. I think, however, that she actually believed that she was doing *me* a favour.

Assessment

The assessment process was essential to help me to gain insight into Janet's current problems. I needed to develop an understanding of her personal history, i.e. the events leading up to her first psychotic episode, as well as to comprehend what had maintained her problems since the first episode of psychosis. I had never used many of the assessment tools I administered, and was anxious to ensure that Janet did not feel overwhelmed. During the assessment stage Janet talked at length about her experiences and I found it difficult to focus on gathering information without getting dragged into the therapy. I was not used to structuring my work, and when Janet described her delusions I was intrigued and found it difficult not to be pulled down a narrow path before I had a wider picture.

As time went by and I explored Janet's experiences, she became angry. After 25 years in mental health services she could not understand why other professionals had never wanted to know about such things. This was devastating for me; after all, that was *me* she was referring to. She wasn't describing a different service in a strange location or an unfortunate incident with a colleague. I have always been one who struggles with the notion "don't take things personally". Surely I had asked her details about her experiences before, and indeed I must have done. I knew about them, so I must have asked. It was extremely difficult to stop myself from seeking reassurance from her, getting her to say that I had not been totally ineffective for the last seven years, making her believe that she needed to add on "present company excepted". Instead it was important to acknowledge her frustrations with the services and with her life. Janet needed to feel that she could talk openly about her experiences without fear of upsetting me. I needed to listen to what she was saying and to take her seriously. It seems harder to appreciate someone's point of view when it touches on you and your view of yourself.

Presenting problem

Janet believed that she had an implant in her brain. She did not know who put it there or how it was done, though she had ideas that it could have been done through telekinesis. She believed it had probably been implanted at birth, or possibly beforehand, as she had no knowledge of having any major operation and "it couldn't have got in without surgery". She believed the implant functioned using electricity and was 100,000 times more powerful than the brain. There were seven strands to the implant, each one carrying out a function within the body:

- STRAND 1: Sensory function
- STRAND 2: Emotions/feelings/mood psychic ability
- STRAND 3: Limb movement
- STRAND 4: Intellect/cognition

- STRAND 5: In her right eye—a fibre optic camera shows pictures
- STRANDS 6 and 7: Both of these go to her ears which is why she hears voices

Janet believed that there were others with similar implants and that the implants could sometimes be facilitating. Those with a functioning Strand 3 succeed at sport; those with Strand 4 using "random excess memory" are mathematicians, and so on. For her the difficulty was that Strand 2 was damaged and this caused her mood changes and paranoia. Janet was ambivalent about the implant. She was pleased that it allowed her to engage in space flight but was angry that it interfered with her ability to concentrate and succeed. Additionally, Janet saw "pictures" of war, space, other planets and nuclear destruction. When asked about this she had a complex explanation. The tale went back 10,000 years to the planet Orio. The emperor of Orio had heard a message saying "Esso has stolen a particle" and since then there had been mass destruction and the inhabitants of this world and Orio had connected "Janet Mary Smith" (Janet) with "Esso".

Janet spent her days "listening to stories and going to other galaxies". She said she literally saw the "remains of war, starvation and torture" and struggled with feelings of paranoia, as she believed she had been blamed for this destruction.

Developmental and social history

Janet was 51 years old when I started this work. She had one older sister and a younger brother who now had successful careers and lived away from home. Her father had been a solicitor (though he was now dead) and her mother had worked as a teacher. The family had lived in a large detached house in a small economically deprived village. Janet had never associated with anyone from the village and described them as "different from her". She received her primary education as a day pupil at a private school in a nearby town and afterwards she had attended boarding school. She had liked the boarding school regime and endorsed the school motto "Work hard, pray hard, play hard". Janet left school at 18 with ten "O" levels and four "A" levels and studied economics at university.

Her first year had been uneventful. She had boarded with a couple known to her family, but as she had felt "left out" of student life she later moved into a student house accompanied by her boyfriend. At the same time she became involved with a drama group. Two members of the group had moved into the house, but this had not proved successful. Her fellow housemates had been a distraction and her work suffered as a result. Her boyfriend later ended their relationship, stating that Janet was "odd", and subsequently began a relationship with one of the other women in the house.

Looking back, Janet described how she had experienced "intellectual paranoia" during this time. Her fellow residents had been "violent and hypnotic" and her boyfriend had been "using" her. Janet started to experience difficulties at this time: she was becoming more disorganised and her concentration was suffering. As a consequence she failed her end of term exams. It was at this time that she experienced her first hallucination. It had been an "orange planet, accompanied by pictures of soldiers underground causing mass destruction and torture". She had returned home at this point, whereupon she was diagnosed with "paranoid schizophrenia" (though she was unaware of this until 1985). Her treatment was an antipsychotic depot injection and an oral major tranquilliser and she was still on this treatment regime when I started the therapy.

Janet viewed her upbringing as positive, but was angry about the restrictions her illness had placed upon her life. She talked at length about her academic achievements prior to university and the subsequent "paralysis" she believed the implant had caused. She believed it had robbed her of her destiny and her ability to express her feelings. It was difficult to put together a picture of what had happened since then. Time was a difficult concept for Janet: her clothes and surroundings remained unchanged since the 1970s and her statements regarding dates and times were often vague—"I was upset in 1982". After coming home it seemed that Janet had tried to find employment doing office work but had been unsuccessful in her quest. Although she had had two brief admissions to hospital, little appeared to have changed. She continued to live at home with her mother, who seemed to be her only social contact. She rarely left the house and had no friends.

Standardised assessments

The *KGV psychiatric assessment scale* (Krawiecka, Goldberg & Vaughan, 1977), although designed for a more chronic population, has also been found to be a quick and reliable measure for assessing hallucinations, delusions and thought disorder in those with less chronic conditions (Manchanda, Saupe & Hirsch, 1986). Two years of regular use later, I would agree wholeheartedly with this. However, as a student using it for the first time, it is an alarming document, both in size (meaning that it is long) and content (meaning that it asks questions that you may have never asked before). The assessment, according to guidelines, takes 30–60 minutes:

I finally completed it after two 90-minute sessions. I felt clumsy and inept; my questioning was stilted and laboured. The amount of information that Janet gave me was overwhelming in both amount and content. I found it difficult to limit myself to asking questions as the responses promised such complex detail that I wanted to know more. I presented an assessment tape to my clinical supervisor, who, as tactfully as possible, enquired if I had in fact been administering the KGV or carrying out the therapy, as she had been unable to determine this from my tape. The KGV identified that Janet was feeling depressed: she complained of lack of concentration and inability to "shake it [the low feeling] off"; and she talked about guilty ideas of reference and blame. She had experienced hallucinations every day in the past month, and was also experiencing delusions, indicating that her belief was held, with full conviction, every day. Having believed that delusions were unshakeable, I also assumed that people held them with 100% conviction, hence the "fact" that they were fixed.

Although I had spent a number of years "monitoring" Janet's medication, this had consisted of asking her if she had any side effects and breathing a sigh of relief when she said she had none. The *LUNSERS* (Liverpool University Neuroleptic Side Effect Rating Scale; Day et al., 1995) helps us to identify groups of side effects and has since proved to be excellent ammunition when battling to have a person's medication altered. Janet's score was not high but nonetheless it was apparent that she was unhappy with her medication. She hated the injection and believed the tablets "numbed" her mind.

Reflections on the assessment process

The assessment process prompted a catastrophic response, not from the client but within me. I was astounded that I knew so little about a person whom I had professed to know for so long. It seemed unthinkable that I had not known the details of her experiences and had not asked these questions in the time I had known her. It seemed that I had let her down and done her a great disservice. I had never categorised myself as the best clinician in the world but I believed that I was a reasonable one. This now felt shaky to say the least. At this point I felt I had two options, I could either give up the job and open the fantasy coffee shop that we talk about in our dark days or decide that this training was not for me after all—what's wrong with just giving depots anyway? I chose neither, but it was a difficult time requiring massive tolerance and patience from my colleagues, clinical supervisor and family.

Initial case formulation

A very basic cognitive formulation links a person's mood and behaviour to the way that he or she interprets or thinks about an event. Using this simple model we can understand that a person who believes that hearing voices is a sign of madness and impending incarceration is likely to feel anxious, and may hide away as a result. This would contrast with a person believing the experience of hearing voices means that he has special powers who may feel quite elated and may want to spread the word of his newly found gift.

Formulating can be done at different levels of complexity. A more detailed cognitive formulation examines *why* the person is interpreting events in a particular way. Following a cognitive model it is proposed that early experiences determine the manner in which the person sees himself in the world. These core beliefs then colour the person's view of events from there on, and such interpretations will influence the person's moods and behaviour.

Previously I had trained using Schneider's first rank symptoms of schizophrenia to "help me", and had spent my early years in nursing trying to reason why all the people I ever met who had been given a diagnosis of schizophrenia seemed to have so little in common. Formulation, as opposed to diagnosis, seemed just as baffling at first but did seem to offer more to my clients and to me. The experience of psychosis is overwhelming to both the client (Romme & Escher, 2000) and the therapist. The formulation provides an opportunity to understand and normalise psychotic experiences. I shared a client's formulation with her recently and she announced at the end of the session: "It's no wonder I'm like this".

> Without a formulation the therapist can be likened to a General engaged in battle without planned tactics to guide him in the deployment of his troops and in the timing of his offensive. (Blackburn & Davidson, 1990).

This therapist had seemingly never timed "her offensive" before—hours were spent pouring over the inference of words. Was it that Janet believed she was special or was it that she believed she had not succeeded? As a true novice I was unable to generalise the approach I had been taught. That the formulation is actually a hypothesis did not reduce my desire to "get it right first time". I saw it as a static conclusive statement rather than a flexible starting point and was determined to gain an understanding of Janet's viewpoint and develop the formulation. This was not only to help me to make sense of her problems and guide my intervention but also to protect me from being overwhelmed by the labyrinthine constructs of her experiences.

Janet's childhood had been characterised by being "set apart". Her social position in the village was elevated by her parents' jobs. Her detached house overlooking the village was unique and her attendance at boarding school appeared to contribute to the development of two beliefs: that she was different and that academic achievement was important.

Janet was brought up in a family that placed great emphasis on academic and financial success. She enjoyed the school regime and had faith in the school motto "Work hard, pray hard, play hard". Her university years were characterised by a shifting of boundaries. She was living with other students without any routine and had struggled with an emotional relationship, feeling that it was "distracting her from her work". She was involved with an art group and involved in drama, living with artists in the early 1970s but then started to have difficulties with her studies, was unable to concentrate and was gripped with "intellectual paranoia". She must have felt confused and bemused as this was not her perceived destiny. Her family had "mapped out" that she should finish university and go into business with her sister. It was all planned. What was happening?

It appears that the stress surrounding these critical incidents may have contributed to her first episode, although Janet did not recognize how stressed she was. As a result of her emerging psychosis she was removed from university and returned home. Following her return she discovered that her family reacted differently to her. They appeared awkward in her presence and the comfortable, close relationship she had with her siblings now felt strained. Janet retreated to her bedroom on the very few occasions that they visited.

I wondered whether Janet's belief that she had an implant served two functions. It could be seen that by externalising blame for her perceived failures (i.e. it is the fault of the implant) Janet feels less personally responsible for her perceived inadequacy. How could she possibly have succeeded with an implant in her head? Secondly, her delusional beliefs appear congruent with her beliefs about the world and about herself, that she is different and special.

Her auditory hallucinations echoed her schema in that the voices she heard told her she was worthless. Sharing the entire formulation with Janet did not seem appropriate as it was at odds with her own explanation, and to have divulged this viewpoint might have jeopardised our relationship.

Formulation of Janet's problems

- *Early experiences*
  Elevated social position in home village
  Emphasis on academic success from parents

- *Dysfunctional beliefs and assumptions*
  I am different/special
  Emotions detract from achievement
  Success is about academic and professional accomplishment
  Unless I am a complete success I am a failure

- *Critical incidents*
  Perceived rejection by peers at university
  Struggling to keep up with work
  Distracted from academic work
  Fails exams

- *Negative automatic thoughts*
  There is something wrong with me
  I have an implant controlling me
  "You are a waste of space" *(voice)*
  "You know nothing" *(voice)*

- *Maintaining factors*
  Isolation
  Defensive function of delusion
  Continued emphasis on academic achievement

- *Behaviour*—Avoidance/withdrawal
- *Feelings*—Depression/anger/paranoia
- *Physiological*—Poor sleep/anxiety/unable to concentrate.

Course of therapy

I had had the notion that when I carried out cognitive behaviour therapy it would be in a serene environment; a quiet pale-green room with a carefully placed pot plant and coffee percolator bubbling in the background. I would be calm and knowledgeable and the client would be attentive and willing. This couldn't have been further from reality.

Medication management

After years of visiting Janet it was important to me that the benefits of this new style of intervention were evident to her. I wanted to provide her with some hope that things could be better and to show her that I was taking her concerns seriously.

She had let me know she was unhappy with her medication and this seemed to be a straightforward and achievable first step for my intervention. Having assured the team that I would monitor any new medication and that compliance would not be an issue as her mother administered oral medication, she was given an atypical neuroleptic. Janet was delighted about this and reported feeling "less subdued". I felt relieved: hopefully I was making a difference.

Normalising

For many people the experience of psychosis is worsened by the fear that they see themselves as "mad, a lunatic, a nutter". They are subject to the media portrayal of mental illness and fear the arrival of the "knife wielding maniac" that lies dormant within them. Many people diagnosed as having "schizophrenia" have little idea of what this actually means, clutching onto beliefs that it has something to do with "a split personality or two minds". Along with that belief is the fear of the implications of madness. What is going to happen to them; when will the alter ego emerge; will they be carted off to the mental hospital; and will the key be thrown away?

The cognitive model would predict that such an interpretation of events would be related to feelings of anxiety and general stress. Needless to say, the stress-vulnerability model (Zubin & Spring, 1977) links stress to relapse and further symptoms of psychosis. This adds to the importance of reducing the fear that is linked to the interpretation of psychotic symptoms. The aim of a "normalising rationale" (talking about those people who, when they are subjected to stressful situations, experience a different reality) is to lessen the fear surrounding a person's experience by linking those experiences to common/expected phenomena (Nelson, 1997).

To facilitate the normalising process Janet and I looked at the cultural context of her "psychotic" experiences (Kingdon & Turkington, 1994). As part of this we discussed how, in other cultures, the experience of hearing voices was not always perceived as a sign of "mental illness" and could be seen as having a spiritual link. This evidently had some impact on Janet as at the end of the session she announced, "Just think, if I lived in India, I'd be a priestess". The impact of the cultural interpretation of symptoms on social status had been felt.

The cognitive model views delusions as being at the end of the spectrum of a normal misinterpretation. After learning about this framework it was interesting to find that, once understood, the basic principles of CBT permeated into the whole of my life. I became overaware of the cognitive distortions I made, the negative thoughts that leapt into my mind, and the selective attention I had to certain facets of my experiences. How many times have I spoken to a less than happy friend and suddenly thought "What's wrong with her, she must be annoyed with me", or sat anxiously in a meeting, certain that everyone thought I was stupid. At night in the dark I often get scared, convinced I am being followed, and often have a need to check the empty back seat of the car. It is often helpful to share some of these everyday experiences with a client. The rationale is that by normalising thinking errors, such as the process of jumping to conclusions, the person feels less weird. Although I feel it is important to normalise the client's experiences, this must not be done at the expense of detracting from their experience. The distress related to a delusional belief cannot be compared with that related to the misinterpretation of the actions of a friend.

Stress-vulnerability model

As therapy proceeded we moved on to the stress-vulnerability model and the antecedents to her first episode. The stress-vulnerability model is an effective way to reach a shared understanding of what may have contributed to a person's experience. Janet appreciated the attempts to make sense of her situation. She found that by exploring events surrounding her first episode she was able to see the stress she had experienced prior to her "breakdown." This personalised view was important in helping Janet to become actively involved in a collaborative therapeutic approach.

Treating coexisting depression

Janet had scored highly on the Beck Depression Inventory (Beck & Greer, 1987) suggesting her depression was of a moderate to severe level. One feature of her depression was sleep disturbance. Janet was going to bed at 8 p.m. and rising at 3 a.m. Interestingly, her paranoia was worse at 6 a.m.

It was difficult for Janet to identify the way in which she could make her life worth while. To her, happiness equated to success and she believed many "non-academic" activities to be pointless. She perceived her previous employment as an insurance salesperson as a demeaning activity. In contrast, she would tell me on a regular basis that she had achieved ten "O" levels (basic school examinations) and four "A" levels (advanced examinations).

At this point I felt it was important to reframe Janet's sense of worthlessness. I tried to encourage her to keep a diary of her activities throughout the day, dividing them into things she enjoyed doing and those that gave her some sense of achievement. This was a difficult task for Janet (and me) because whenever she enjoyed doing something she minimised its worth. She constantly compared what she was achieving with what she believed she should be achieving at this stage in her life. She enjoyed reading, but she was only able to read for short periods of time owing to problems with concentration. Any pleasure that could have been gained was negated by her belief that she should be able to do more.

In an attempt to normalise Janet's dismissive thoughts about her achievements I used the analogy that study skills are talents that need constant practice. Many people find it difficult to return to successful study after taking time out: I was a perfect example of that! Telling Janet of my fear of taking exams after a 15-year gap seemed to give her hope. She seemed to realise that her lack of concentration did not indicate that she was generally inept and therefore a complete failure.

To improve her concentration and subsequent pleasure from reading, we gradually introduced articles of increasing length for her to read. Janet chose articles of interest and read them one section at a time. Although she tackled this, she was still concerned that she was not able to remember everything. I thought it was important to normalise this: most people do not remember all they have read. I discussed my methodology of underlining important sentences and writing copious notes as a memory aide. This worked. Her anxieties about her concentration went down and she started to read again.

Janet needed other interests apart from reading to fill her days. In the past she had enjoyed painting and visiting art galleries and yet these were no longer part of her life. This was a difficult issue to tackle since there were no cultural opportunities of this kind nearby. In a desperate attempt to expose Janet to the outside world and increase her pleasurable activities, we arranged to go further afield and found a number of art galleries in neighbouring towns. At the same time she thought it might be interesting to see if there were any television programmes about art, so we scoured the television guides for programmes about art and literature. As a result, Janet started to watch the TV with her mother until 9.30 p.m. Because she was going to bed later she started sleeping till 4 or 5 a.m. which reduced the length of time she spent alone in her bedroom in the morning.

Janet and I visited local museums and art galleries; it had the effect (for me) of stepping into her shoes and falling into her world . . . headfirst. She had been apart from this world for so long that all our activities were tinged with comments such as:

"So, this is how they park cars now", "People seem very strange to me", " I stayed in the 70s", "It is all very foreign to me". Although Janet experienced some increase in activity and pleasure as a result of this approach, she often stated that she could not carry out the tasks she wanted to because of her implant. She believed that her implant was 100,000 times stronger than her brain and overpowered her own wishes. To me it seemed that Janet used the power of the implant as a reason for not trying anything new and as a rationale for inactivity. Did this mean that I should be challenging her belief in the implant? I was worried about what would happen if she no longer had an external reason for her problems. Janet, however, stated that she would like to be "free again". It was at this point of the therapy that I developed a similar desire as Janet's to be "free again": not from the implant, but from this intervention. The familiar appeared useless to me and I did not feel confident or competent with cognitive behaviour therapy. I felt I would never be able to talk to a client in a meaningful way again. I was terrified of working with entrenched beliefs and read and re-read the literature, reassuring myself that I was following a recognised procedure. When the pressure is increased, reverting to the familiar becomes an easier option.

Delusional beliefs

One particular aspect of cognitive therapy that I found intriguing was asking the client to rate conviction in his or her delusional beliefs. I had always assumed that those with delusions were absolutely 100% convinced of their beliefs and it never occurred to me otherwise. Using this approach I found that Janet had some doubt about her implant, though she was 90% sure it existed and was controlling her.

The next stage of my intervention was to explore the evidence that Janet was using to support the existence of her implant. Janet must have some evidence, but surely there was more evidence that no such implant existed. We started to collect data for and against her explanation of the implant. On further exploration I discovered that Janet believed that the implant had been put into her head by "telekinesis". This was an interesting explanation but when I asked about how this worked, it was apparent that Janet did not have all the answers. It was obvious to me that neither Janet nor I would be able to explore the evidence for the implant being inserted by telekinesis if we had limited knowledge of the subject. I therefore set a task for both of us to find out more, and we spent the next few weeks studying the paranormal (Carroll, 1994). It is interesting to note that as we started to delve into worlds with which we were unfamiliar, a strange phenomenon occurred: our own certainty of "truths" started to crumble. Prior to my reading, I had a vague notion of what telekinesis was; and Janet had thought she had some idea of what it involved. However, in all of our research we could find nothing on the use of telekinesis as a method of implanting material into the human body.

CBT uses Socratic questioning as a means of exploring a person's interpretations and conclusions about events, but there appears to be very little literature on how this translates into practice, although there are references indicating that it should be 'Colombo style' (reflecting the naïve style of questioning used by the TV cop in the dirty raincoat) as opposed to Sherlock Holmes's interrogatory approach. I was soon to discover the difference. Janet and I had a discussion about the implant:

ME: How do you think the implant was put in your head?
JANET: I don't know.
ME: Have you ever had any operations on your head?
JANET: No.
ME: Have you any scars on your head?
JANET: No.
ME: Do you have *any* evidence to prove it is in there?
JANET: I thought I did.
ME: (*becoming more excited and pressured in my speech*): So, you have no evidence?
JANET: (*pausing longer and becoming more timid*): I don't appear to, no.

I later discovered that this was not a good example of Socratic questioning. I submitted this tape to my supervisor, feeling I had done rather well. I knew the response was not as I expected when she struggled to think of a positive comment at the start of the next session. As she tried to put it tactfully, the principle of this style of questioning is not to beat the client into submission, admitting she is wrong, but to explore the explanations that may be available and debate the likelihood of each. The therapist should have a genuine interest in trying to understand how the person has reached his or her conclusion. Unlike my initial attempt, the tone should be inquisitive and questioning. We decided to run the session again under the guise that it would be good to have a résumé. The session started with Janet asking, "So, are we going to argue about the implant again?". It seemed she hadn't felt that we were exploring her belief at all—more that I was trying to impose my own conclusions.

The re-run of the session was significantly different. The main evidence Janet had for the existence of the implant was a 20-year-old X-ray that "showed it was there". Not only that, but Janet had actually kept the original X-ray. What an opportunity to explore the evidence! As Janet produced this precious photograph, I felt my stomach turn. There in front of me, quite plain to see, was something in her skull that did have the appearance of an object with wires coming from it. Perhaps she was right all along and did have something implanted in her skull. I could definitely see how she had made the assumption. What should I do now? I couldn't possibly tell her I agreed with her, could I? I kept quiet hoping she wouldn't ask my opinion. "Do you think it looks like an implant?", she asked.

Agreeing that this object did in fact look like an implant was probably one of the most significant moments in the therapy. Janet felt understood and validated and this no doubt helped the therapeutic relationship enormously. Of course it dawned on me that there must have been some evidence that Janet had developed a belief in the implant, and it was naïve of me to think that we would find nothing. I had to help Janet to explore whether or not she may have jumped to a conclusion (a typical cognitive error). Just because there was something on the X-ray that *looked* like an implant, did not mean that it necessarily *was* an implant.

When we looked for further explanations of what the object may be, we found that Janet had originally been told that the X-ray showed 'a pineal body'. Neither of us knew exactly what a pineal body was or how likely it was that it would be evident on an X-ray. Once again I set the task to find out more. We searched through medical texts and talked to medical colleagues and found out a considerable amount about this harmless gland. It was indeed an alternative explanation for the object on the X-ray. As we found out more it was evident that Janet's belief in the implant was starting to shift. I thought it would be wise to take a similar approach to the brain implant theory as I had with the theory of the pineal gland. If brain implants did exist then they should be mentioned in scientific texts. After an extensive search Janet was surprised that she could find no mention of them at all.

One of the fears I had about working with people in this way was that it would unearth painful thoughts and feelings for them and I would be unable to help them to deal with these. It was my formulation that Janet's core belief of being special was maintained by her view that she had the gift of space flight. Without this I worried that she may have to confront her ordinariness. Whether Janet was 'subconsciously' aware of this I will never know, but her decision to change the focus of the sessions could be viewed as having a self-protective function. Janet decided she no longer wanted to explore her beliefs about the implant and her special powers and instead asked if we could concentrate on her voices.

Working with voices

Before delving into any therapeutic intervention with Janet's voices I felt it was important to find out more. Did she recognise the voices? What were they saying to her? Could their occurrence be predicted? After completing a 'voice diary', I realised that Janet heard one male voice that was worse in the morning when she was alone in her bedroom. The voice, identified as her sister, was generally offensive, saying she "was a waste of time" and "knew nothing". Her usual response was to get angry and shout back at her. She was keen to point out that her sister was wrong and was lying. I wondered what it would mean to Janet if the voice was correct. The answer was final: she believed she would be better off dead than be a waste of time and know nothing.

Various cognitive-behavioural approaches to dealing with auditory hallucinations are described in the literature: modifying the voices themselves (Haddock, Bentall & Slade, 1996; Tarrier, 1992), exploring the content of voices in relation to their personal experiences and core beliefs or schema (Fowler, Garety & Kuipers, 1995; Brabban & Turkington, 2001) and exploring the attributions the person makes about his or her symptoms (Chadwick & Birchwood, 1994; Morrison, 2001). In the modification of positive symptoms (Tarrier, 1992) the existing coping strategies of clients are examined and developed to help them to cope with their hallucinations (this is referred to as Coping Strategy Enhancement). Fowler, Garety and Kuipers (1995) believed that it is important to tackle the voices as though they are types of automatic thoughts, examining evidence for and against what they are saying. Finally, Chadwick and Birchwood (1994) and Morrison (2001) emphasised the importance of looking at the individuals' attributions about their voices as they believed it was what individuals made of their symptoms that determined whether they became distressed or not.

As a starting point with Janet I spent time exploring her beliefs about the origins of her voices, where they came from and what this meant. Janet believed that her sister was communicating via telepathy but did not understand why she would be doing so. While exploring this further, I presented a number of possible alternative reasons to explain why she may hear voices. She was interested to look at the literature describing experiences of people who heard voices but who did not have a diagnosis of mental illness (Romme & Escher, 2000). We also re-examined the stress-vulnerability model (Zubin & Spring, 1977) and looked at the possibility of her voices being a reaction to stress. Although Janet was not swayed by this bio-psychosocial explanation, she recognised that her voices seemed to arise in times of stress but not when she was relaxed.

To pursue the origin of Janet's voices further, we tried "Coping Strategy Enhancement", which I saw as having two functions. Firstly, if Janet could control her voices to some extent, then she should feel less distressed. Secondly, if she found she had some control over her symptoms, then that would be further evidence that the voices were not externally generated. Janet used re-attributional statements such as "I'm not a waster" when the voices started. We had identified that her hallucinations tended to occur in the early hours of the morning when she sat alone in her bedroom listening to her radio. To avoid this trigger Janet started to switch off her radio, come out of her room and make tea for her and her mother. It seemed that her mother was usually awake at this time, so we agreed that they should talk together thereby avoiding any inner focus. This proved to be a very effective strategy: not only did Janet's voices diminish, but her mother was delighted to have the cup of tea.

Janet was still insistent that it was her sister who was talking to her. Rather than spend more time on this attribution I changed my focus to explore the content of the voices. I asked Janet to rate how much she believed what the voice (her sister) was saying. I was surprised to hear that she did not believe that she was a waste of time at all. She did think, however, that her sister believed this. Her evidence was that on her sister's rare visits, Janet perceived a "psychological barrier" between them. She found her sister polite but unsympathetic. Although I accepted that Janet's sister could present in this way, I questioned whether this was actual proof that she believed Janet to be worthless. Perhaps she was unsure how to converse with Janet, or was worried about upsetting her by saying the wrong thing. We also explored how Jane's own behaviour could impact on others' reaction to her. Janet took these alternatives on board and agreed to see whether her sister's reaction would be different if she initiated a conversation. She concluded that she might have mis-attributed her sister's behaviour as evidence that she disliked her.

By the end of therapy it was evident that Janet understood the stress-vulnerability model, and although she could see how this linked to her first episode she was not quite so convinced of any ongoing relevance. Moreover, there were definite improvements in her quality of life; her sleep pattern was more regular and during her waking hours she seemed to be getting more enjoyment from her activities. She was now visiting galleries and museums and, when she was at home, had started to pursue a former interest in painting. As for her symptoms, the KGV showed that the severity of her hallucinations and delusions had reduced significantly, and her score on the Beck Depression Inventory reflected that her symptoms had reduced and were now more indicative of a mild depression.

At the end of my therapeutic pursuits I approached Janet to see whether she would be happy for me to publish her case. Part of the deal was obviously that she would be able to read my description of her case, and I must admit that this caused a few anxieties, particularly as I knew I would be mentioning that some of her symptoms might be acting as defences against feelings of worthlessness. I avoided the subject of what I would be saying until Janet allayed my misery: "Lets face it, I enjoy the space flight, what else have I got to do all day? If I didn't have that to look forward to, I think my life would be very miserable indeed."

SOME AFTERTHOUGHTS

Although it appeared that Janet had changed within the course of therapy the most significant impact had been on myself. Although I had believed I was to learn a new set of skills when I started my course, I quickly realised that it was a lot more than that. To work in this way required a complete change in attitudes and values to "severe mental illness" and these took much longer to accommodate than practical skills. I felt as though my entire working practice was deconstructed during this process and it took me some time to return order to the chaos of my life. Possibly as an attempt to find some certainty I adopted the psychological framework with evangelical zeal. I was sure that this approach was the 'Holy Grail' yet at this point in my training I had neither the understanding nor the experience to back this up. This is a lonely position to be in—and an annoying one for colleagues to experience. I was able to see the limitations of the approaches they were using but could not avoid highlighting their inadequacies. In retrospect I realise they were being quite tolerant of my preaching, but from my perspective I was feeling dislocated and removed from the safety of the familiar. On reflection this is probably what Janet was experiencing at some level as I challenged her state of knowing and asked her to enter an arena of uncertainty.

As time went by my confidence grew and I felt more secure with my new set of beliefs and skills; however, I quickly learned that this was only the start. I realise that what I have learned is merely one perspective explaining psychosis. Although I now have a psychological understanding of mental illness I appreciate that there are many models that can be used to formulate this experience. I no longer see uncertainty as an unhealthy state of mind, but see it as a requirement for further development. The journey continues.

Chapter 3

MANAGING VOICES

Case 3 (Pat): *Lars Hansen*

From an early age I have been fascinated by human behaviour and always harboured a strong desire to understand more about the underlying reasons for normal and abnormal responses. As a young medical student I naively believed that psychiatry *was* psychotherapy—the reason why I chose to study medicine. I was soon to learn otherwise! But after recovering from the initial disappointment, over the next few years I began to believe that my newly acquired biological knowledge could serve my quest for a fuller understanding of the human soul. In the mid-1990s as I ventured out into the junior psychiatric posts, I realised to my horror that the trench warfare between the biological and the psychological fraction of psychiatry was still flourishing, with neither camp being any less dogmatic than the other. Every opportunity was exploited to ridicule and belittle the "enemy's" attempts to explain its comprehension of the world ... with the utterly predictable result that no winner, but two losers, appeared: the psychiatrists and, more importantly, the patients' well-being that was supposed to be our main objective.

In this climate an inexperienced clinician was not sure where to turn for assistance. It was therefore thoroughly refreshing to discover that a new, rapidly developing branch of psychology provided a more integrated perspective of how the mind functions, and indeed dysfunctions. Cognitive Behaviour Therapy (CBT) shed new light on everyday life experiences in the ward-round and in the outpatient clinic that simply made straightforward sense to both myself and the patients. And "oh, relief", without disregarding that other measures could have an additive or even synergistic effect. It was possible in a non-dismissive and respectful way to organise the patients thoughts into more understandable structures—a process which sometimes in itself seems therapeutic; "by switching the light in a dark room ... the beast is still there, but at least you know who you are fighting" as one patient said following an outline of the formulation.

A Case Study Guide to Cognitive Behaviour Therapy of Psychosis. Edited by
David Kingdon and Douglas Turkington. © 2002 John Wiley & Sons, Ltd.

As CBT in its nature is collaborative it also challenges the therapist and improves interpersonal skills immensely. The guided discovery and normalisation approach sometimes make it appropriate to tell the patient some well-chosen personal experiences. Never are timing and human intuition more of the essence than in these situations. The demands on the therapist are huge, but so are the rewards, and it is difficult to imagine encounters being more giving than when new insight is gained for both parties. That applies maybe even more so to therapy for psychotic patients—an area that psychotherapists have been fighting shy of for decades. Evidence is emerging that psychotic patients can benefit significantly from discussing their experiences with others. Many of these particularly vulnerable patients have spent years holding back their innermost thoughts and interpretations of their experiences out of fear of upsetting their relatives . . . and out of fear that the doctor automatically will increase their medication. Many patients find it, not surprisingly, greatly relieving finally to have somebody to talk to about their experiences—experiences that tend to get more and more distorted the longer they are not bounced off someone else. We are still not clear about the exact mechanisms that are working in the therapy and as long as that is the case, and probably even after that, it is advisable for the therapist to be guided by the proverbial Rogerian triad of Warmth–Empathy–Genuineness.

THE ROLE OF SUPERVISION AND TEACHING

After years of self-study and supervision from more or less well-qualified supervisors I was fortunate enough to be accepted at the newly established Diploma Course in CBT at Southampton University year 2000–01. The course consisted of three teaching modules: axis I disorders, personality disorders and finally psychotic disorders. I was at this stage doing my specialist registrar training in general adult psychiatry in the area and was therefore able to be granted one day's study leave each week for the 30 weeks of the course.

To my surprise the knowledge that I had from psychodynamic experience stood me in good stead, especially with regards to therapeutic relationship, engagement and containment. On the other hand, it took my supervisor lots of energy to convince me that it was all right to loosen up, use examples from your personal life (without flooding the therapeutic alliance) and not shy away from normalising seemingly extreme experiences. Thus, it was not without trepidation that I commenced therapy with my first psychotic patient after the first of three terms of the course. In spite of having spent significant amounts of time with psychotic patients in my training in the hospital, this was a qualitatively different experience. Somewhere in the back of my mind was a feeling that this was dangerous for the patient. Was there any truth in the old dictums about psychotherapy not being suitable for these vulnerable people? This latent fear certainly did flare up when a young, male patient that I had known as an outpatient for more than a year prior to his CBT started to cut himself and not turn up for appointments. This seemed to coincide with the keen therapist collecting painful childhood material to complete the formulation. The supervision was very helpful by advising me to make a "tactical withdrawal" and simply befriend him for a while to keep the relationship going. There is little doubt that if things had carried on the way they did the patient would either have disappeared or harmed himself seriously. He showed me that I had overstepped his safety distance and that he could not cope with it.

As mentioned, the course was divided into three modules and those of us who had chosen to specialise in psychosis had to wait until the last module to get the teaching course. This meant that we theoretically had a relatively poor base to start off with, which obviously put extra pressure on the supervisor over the first months. During this period the supervisor and the other trainee in the group were especially indispensable. As soon as the teaching got underway pieces in the jig-saw would little by little fall into place, while understanding on a grander scale had to wait until the final written assignment was completed at the end of the course.

Minor adjustments on this new course are understandably needed but this course and similar settings are clearly the way forward to create more therapists in a service that is crying out for more, relatively short-term therapy availability provided in an evidence-based manner.

PAT

Pat was referred from the community mental health team for treatment-resistant auditory hallucinations. The hallucinations were assessed by her psychiatrist to have a serious effect on the patient's quality of life.

Personal history

Pat was a 62-year-old white woman. She had never been married, did not have children. and lived with her younger brother. She had no formal qualification and was semi-retired from a job as a cook in a rest home. She described herself as a non-practising Christian.

She was born in Southampton with no known complications at delivery. She developed well as a small child, but was extremely scared of the dark and refused to sleep on her own until the age of 9 or 10. She described herself as "generally, a very nervous child". She grew up in the same house as her mother's sister and her family, and therefore had a very close relationship with her two cousins, Moira and Shelley. She hated school and felt that teachers thought: "She is daft." She said, "I felt everything I did was wrong." She left school at 15 with no formal qualifications. Soon after leaving school she started working in a laundry, and worked there for 25 years only interrupted by two years of sickness around the time of her first breakdown in 1958. Looking for new challenges and better pay, she found a job as a cook in a mental health day centre in 1981. She worked there for ten years before she moved to her present job as a cook/care assistant in a rest home. After a period of poor physical and mental health in the winter prior to starting therapy, she decided with the agreement of the rest home management to semi-retire and only work when required. When she started the therapy she was unable to work as "the voices stress me out". She enjoyed her work and the contact with carers and clients and was therefore very unhappy about this. Through her working life she has had long spells of unemployment due to poor psychiatric health, e.g. eight years during the 1970s.

Psychosexual development

She had only had one long relationship, lasting 20 years. He died 15 years ago. She had not had a relationship since and stated that she did not miss the company of men but emphasised with laughter that she was not afraid of them.

Family history

She was eldest of four siblings; she had three younger brothers. A female cousin spent several years in Knowle Hospital in the 1960s (reason unknown) and her father suffered from alcoholism. He died in 1984 aged 66 from stomach cancer, but the patient claimed "I took no notice". He worked as a driver until retirement at 60. The patient did not feel close to her father even though she "did not mind him". She later disclosed that he was drinking day and night, but denied that he was violent or had similar problems to her own.

Her mother died in 1996 aged 81 from cancer of the uterus. Pat was devastated and felt that she herself may have been partly responsible because she felt that she should have alerted the doctor at an earlier stage. Pat was very close to her mother and has often dreamt about her after her death.

The mother was described as caring and loving... "We could talk about everything... I would never leave our mum for any man in the world." She worked intermittently as a canteen assistant but took time off regularly to look after Pat.

Her three brothers were, respectively 54, 53 and 43 years old. She had regular contact with all three but they did not talk about "emotional things". The older two brothers were in their 50s and were both married with children while the younger brother lived with her in their childhood home. About the two older brothers: "They come every Sunday, leave some money and then they are off." The youngest brother was working full time but was known to have an alcohol problem. She had daily contact with the two cousins she grew up with, Moira and Shelley. They lived nearby and provide good support for one another.

Past psychiatric history

1958   First episode of schizophrenia, hospitalised for one year.
1969   Schizophrenia, local Mental Hospital, self-discharged after a few hours.
1976   Schizophrenia, Psychiatric Unit, self-discharged after 10 days.
1997   Schizophrenia, Psychiatric Unit, self-discharged after a week. Admission precipitated by mother's death and severe skin infection of the arm (leading to high temperature).

Past medical history

She had been remarkably well until December of the year prior to therapy when she developed a pulmonary embolus. She was fully recovered. She also had some chronic back pain.

Medication

She took Olanzapine (antipsychotic) 10 mg daily since September 2000 and had a number of other antipsychotics in the past. Her adherence to medication was good.

Social history

She lived with a brother in rented accommodation, the same two-bedroomed house in which they were born. She received weekly benefits and her rent was paid. Until recently she also received a considerable amount of money from her work at the rest home. She had no debts. She smoked ten cigarettes daily and said she used to drink too much alcohol when she was in her twenties ("It calmed me down") but drank very little now.

Premorbid personality

She describes herself as always having been anxious. She had a keen interest in other people and especially loved the company of her family. She enjoyed bingo and gossiping with neighbours and cousins.

Forensic history

None.

Mental state presentation

She came across as a lively, friendly, English lady who was slightly short of breath, but well kept. Her speech was unremarkable but she was very talkative. Her mood was assessed initially to be low and anxious. Subjectively she claimed to be feeling "fine, but anxious". She was considered to be at low risk of self-harm or harm to others. Her thoughts were normal in form but focused on understanding the origin of the voices. She believed that the voices were started by the "Robsons" who had been living next door for two generations. She also maintained that the doctors were withholding the truth from her. In the past she had had visual hallucinations in the form of seeing ghosts around the house, but this had not happened over the last years.

The auditory hallucinations consisted for the time being of three female voices: those of Moira and Shelley were well known to her as they were the voices of her cousins; the third was the voice of Jenny, who claimed to be a psychiatrist. The voices talked to her (second person) and about her (third person). Usually the content was friendly and gave her advice on different issues; e.g. "go and play bingo... it is time for Pat to do the vacuum-cleaning". She was convinced that the voices had an external source. The abusive voices from the past had not been heard for years. She believed that the voices were omniscient but not omnipotent.

- *Cognitive State:* She was assessed to be of normal intelligence with no evidence of dementia.

- *Insight:* She was compliant with medication and believed she had a mental illness, but did not accept that the voices could be emanating from her own mind.

Initial assessment

She presented with the following complaint: "Voices are driving me mad . . . the Robsons have gone, now it is just Moira, Shelley and Jenny's voice. They are all friendly, but I would like to get rid of them . . . do you think I ever will? After all these years of searching will I ever find the truth? Will I ever be normal?" There were some minor discrepancies between her explanation and the information gathered from case notes and other health professionals, e.g. in her work history she did not talk about the periods of unemployment; and the family doctor that she believed had been her doctor since childhood was younger than she was. An attempt to write her experiences down in diary form failed as "the voices went dead quiet every time I tried to write anything down" (paradoxical intention).

Rating scales were discussed in supervision and the following three were decided upon: the Health of the Nation Outcome Scale (HoNOS; Wing, Curtiss & Beevor, 1996), the Psychosis Rating Scale (Haddock et al., 1999)—auditory hallucinations (AHRS); and delusion rating scales (DRS). The ratings were carried out in session III:

- HoNOS: overall score, 12 points, mainly on depressed mood, physical health, and problems with hallucinations and activities.
- AHRS: 24 points, mainly on frequency, duration, beliefs about origin, distress, disruption and lack of control.
- DRS: 5 points, scored on conviction and duration.

Formulation

- *Formative experiences:* Nervous child, scared of the dark. Felt ostracised by other children. Father an alcoholic. Felt an academic failure. Felt close to the rest of family. Experienced first breakdown at 19.
- *Core beliefs:* "Nothing will ever change . . . I'll never find the truth."
  Self–self: "I'm stupid and mad . . . I'll never be normal."
  Self–others: "Most people are helpful and stronger and brighter than me."
  Others–self: "People that do not know me think I'm weird . . . my family likes me."
- *Rules for living:* Others cannot be fully trusted. Avoidance. People will not help me find the truth.

- *Onset:* Poor physical health. Sleep deprivation. Stress. Brother drinking. Increased isolation.
- *Maintaining cycle*

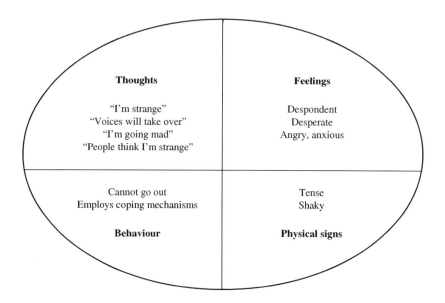

To ensure that the formulation that was performed in collaboration with the patient was not seen as solely focusing on negative aspects, we decided to add another category to the three traditional "P's" of "Predisposing," "Precipitating" and "Perpetuating" (Table 3.1). We called this category "Strengths Factors"—i.e. coping strategies that she recognised could decrease the voices in intensity and frequency.

- Talking to her cousins.
- Seeing the doctor (including the GP, psychiatrist and therapist).
- Living an active life style (going to work, playing bingo, inviting people for tea and visiting family).
- Taking the tablets.
- Helping other people.
- Thinking about other things.
- Going to sleep.
- Talking on the phone.
- Write down what the voices are saying.

The ABC model (Ellis, 1962) was introduced later (see Chadwick, Birchwood & Trower, 1996). The voices (A) were viewed as activating

Table 3.1 The three P's

	Biological	Psychological	Social
Predisposing factors	Intermittent alcohol abuse; possible genetic predisposition	Anxious, father alcoholic; scared of darkness; felt ridiculed at school	Poor academic achievements; "teachers thought I was stupid"; fearful of strangers
Precipitating factors	Alcohol, physical illness, sleep deprivation.	Depression, family members on holiday; death of mother; stress.	Social isolation; inactive lifestyle; fears about losing job
Perpetuating factors	Physical illness; chronic pain.	Brother drinking; anxious personality	Not going out; not seeing other people

events; B was the belief or personal interpretation; and C was the behavioural or emotional consequence of the belief (Table 3.2).

Treatment plan

The treatment plan was developed in collaboration with the patient and discussed at length in supervision. The following stages were chosen.

Engagement stage

Initially the therapist would state clearly what the therapy was about (safe, collaborative method of looking at the causes of distress) and what

Table 3.2 The ABC model

A	B	C
Second and third person voices. (See Mental State)	"Voices are driving me mad." "I'll never find the truth." "The doctors will not tell me the truth." "I'll never be normal." "Voices are in control of my life."	"Sad, depressed. Makes me feel the odd one out." Desperate, "they will never shut up". Isolating herself, does not go out.

the therapy was *not* about (medication, hospitalisation, sectioning, etc). Throughout the therapy the use of Socratic questioning would be emphasised. Attempts would be made to empathise with the patient's unique perspective and feeling of distress and show flexibility at all times, letting the focus of therapy be guided by the patient's wishes. A vulnerability-stress model was to be used such that the patient could understand that vulnerability is a dynamic concept that can be influenced by many factors such as life events, coping mechanisms, physical illness, etc. The therapist would emphasise that he did not have all the answers but useful explanations could be developed in cooperation. While the therapist may not have experienced exactly what the patient had experienced (A), he was willing to look in detail at the patient's human response to these experiences (B and C). An important part of the engagement process would have already taken place during the assessment period.

ABC model

Slowly and thoroughly moving the patient through the model, through Socratic questioning, and clarifying the link between the emotional distress she is experiencing and the beliefs she is holding about the voices, the model was to be used to give the patient a way of organising her confusing experiences:

- Patient to give a rating of the intensity of distress (e.g. 0–10).
- Assess C and divide it into emotional and behavioural aspects.
- Thereafter allow patient to give her own explanation to what events the A factors occurred to cause C. Ensure that the factual events are not "contaminated" by judgements and interpretations. Feed back to the patient that the A–C connection is acknowledged by the therapist.
- Finally assess patient's belief, evaluations and images. Communicate that a personal meaning is lacking in the A–C model. Give a simple example to facilitate understanding.

Goal-setting

Realistic goals for therapy were discussed with the patient using the distressing consequences (C) of the voices to fuel the motivation for change. Four potential options for lowering the level of distress were to be discussed:

(a) escaping from the voices
(b) tolerating them
(c) persuading them to stop
(d) changing her persistent beliefs about them.

Options (a) to (c) had in this case been tried unsuccessfully for over 40 years, therefore it was agreed that option (d) seemed worth trying.

Normalisation

It was agreed to try to develop a "normalising" rationale (Kingdon & Turkington, 1991) with the patient in order to de-catastrophise her experiences. The patient was to be given a leaflet on voices (Kingdon, 1997) for the following reasons: to underline the fact that she is not the only person in the world suffering from this problem (i.e. emphasising universality: Yalom, 1970), that people can experience voices in a whole range of different circumstances (stressful events, hyperventilation, torture, hunger, thirst, going off to sleep, etc.) and to provide her with written material about coping mechanisms. One aim would be to "chip away" at self-stigma by putting her experiences on a continuum with normal experiences (Kingdon & Turkington, 1994). This would allow comparison of voices to a dream-like state, "dreaming awake", "as if part of the brain is still asleep while the rest of you is fully awake".

Critical collaborative analysis

Her voices were to be discussed and it was to be established whether or not anyone else was able to hear them. This might possibly be tested out in the company of more people when a good working alliance has been obtained. She would be asked if she thinks that others may be lying when they deny hearing her voices. If necessary, tape recording of the voices at home could be suggested to help to resolve the issue of whether the voices were internal or external in origin. She could discuss why the voices were directed especially at her and how this is practically possible. Finally, inquiry could be made about whether the patient believes that the voices could be the product of her own mind, perhaps as the result of stress she had experienced and vulnerability.

Challenging beliefs about voices

Gentle, Socratic testing of beliefs about voices to weigh up evidence for and against statements would be used. An assessment would be made of how the beliefs occurred—through inferences, cognitive distortions (e.g. dichotomous thinking, selective inference, emotional reasoning, etc.), reviewing antecedents and slowly moving on to challenging her beliefs. Identification would be made of misattributions and attempts made to re-attribute with the use of appropriate homework tasks.

Developing alternative explanations

Here it is of crucial importance to let the patient develop her own alternatives to her previous maladaptive assumptions about the voices, preferably looking for alternative explanations that are already present in the patient's mind. These explanations might be temporarily or permanently weakened either by external factors or by dysfunctional thinking patterns. If the patient is not forthcoming with alternative explanations, new ideas can be constructed in cooperation with the therapist. Certain seeds might have been sown earlier in the therapy, and these can now be used as building blocks (from leaflets and previous discussions). It would, furthermore, be important to tailor-make the therapy to the patient's relatively limited intellectual capacity by using understandable examples from everyday life and refraining from the use of complicated expressions.

Implementation of treatment plan

Engagement stage

This fundamental part of the treatment process had already been started during the initial history-taking in the development of a strong working alliance that could cope with the challenges of the therapy. This patient proved to be extremely easy to engage. She was immediately friendly, genuinely warm and talkative. Throughout therapy she turned up promptly and the risk of acting out was assessed to be negligible. From the beginning Pat was very willing to talk about the voices that she described as friendly. She would, however, like to get rid of them because she felt that they were becoming a disturbance. She also expressed an interest to get to "the bottom of things" after all these years. Paraphrasing was used extensively at this stage in order for the patient—and the therapist—to feel understood.

She gave a lot of information and it felt useful to organise this into the ABC model. This helped both of us to structure our discussions. The patient asked at an early stage if the therapist had ever experienced voices. When the answer was no, it did not appear to cause any major rift in the alliance. The therapist explained that he was personally familiar with human feelings of low mood and had professional experience of treating people with a similar condition to hers with its consequent feeling of despair. Pat seemed reassured by that.

ABC model

Pat complained of not understanding how her distress (C) could be related to her beliefs and thoughts (B) and not to the voices (A) because "they are real". It was made clear that the therapy did not dismiss her protestation that the voices were causing distress, but merely that her personal interpretation of the voices contributed to her feeling low and inability to go out. As this seemed to be a very central area in the therapy with which the patient had serious difficulties reconciling herself, several examples were used to clarify the importance of B. For example, a man and a woman lie in bed at night and hear a noise downstairs (A). He believes the noise could be due to a burglar (B) and gets very scared (C). His wife knows something he does not know; she forgot to let the cat out earlier and she now believes that the noise is caused by the cat going through the cat-flap (B). She just turns over and sleeps on (C).

The patient was invited to make her own examples with limited success. The model was, however, used as a homework task and the patient did on one occasion (Session 10) manage to write down the A and the C. She would only verbally account for B. She had written down under A that the voices had said that "all doctors know the answer but they will not tell me" (meaning the truth about the origin of the voices). As C she had written down "angry, want to hit him (GP) and disappointed". Through Socratic questioning the conclusion was reached that her understanding of the voices was going through a kind of "personal filter" which caused her more anguish than if the voices had been "left to their own devices"—a defining moment in the therapy was reached! It was mentioned by the patient that the filter may be working for both input and output.

This discovery followed directly from a discussion about how she had noticed that she seemed to remember childhood memories differently from her siblings. She felt that people sometimes experienced her as different because her thoughts also travelled through the same filter before being expressed verbally. The link between the personal filter and B was made. It was, however, noteworthy that this insight had evaporated at the following session where A again seemed glued to C without anything in between! It was a stark reminder of how insight can fluctuate from day to day. The same is the case for intensity of distress but the two parameters do not necessary fluctuate in a synchronised manner. Pat's distress was scored on a scale from 0 to 10 on many occasions and fluctuated significantly, but the trend was downwards over the therapy as a whole.

Goal-setting

1. At our first meeting the patient was already clear about her objective with the therapy: "Get rid of the voices," and she soon talked about finding their origin. This was guided into a more *realistic goal of searching for a better understanding of the voices*. It was discussed with the patient

that a better understanding of the voices in some instances could lead to a reduction in their frequency and intensity.

2. Pat also wanted to get better to enable her to *return to work*.
3. She wanted to be able to *go out more and deal with shopping, socializing, etc.*

During an attempt to prioritise the goals the patient was adamant that if the voices decreased she would automatically achieve goals 2 and 3.

Although clinically low in mood at the onset of therapy, Pat expressed no wish to deal with her depression and remained convinced that the voices were the cause of her problems. We talked about having to take one step at a time in order to achieve her final goal of getting to grips with the voices. As this seemed difficult to grasp we drew a staircase on the board in order to illustrate the process more graphically. The patient accepted this and said: "You have to crawl before you can walk." Following this discussion we talked about the four possible ways of coping with voices (see above). In spite of relating this technique directly to the ABC model the patient clearly struggled with taking it in. She did, however, accept that she had tried to persuade them to stop unsuccessfully—for 44 years. She was also clear about not being able to put up with the voices for the rest of her life. We talked about the possibility of using frustrations as a source of energy to pursue her goals. She nodded pensively and gave an example of how, for years, she had hated the wallpaper in her house and then one weekend redecorated for 48 consecutive hours: "I had had enough... and it really looked good afterwards."

Normalisation approach

This approach was used extensively throughout the therapy rather than at a specific point. It seemed to be important, as one of the patient's core beliefs was that she felt herself to be "the odd one out". Especially during Sessions 3 and 4 we talked about ordinary people's experiences and how little is known about what normal thoughts actually are. She was given examples of when other people can experience unusual things as voices or delusions: during wars, sleep deprivation (just as she had experienced an increase in voices when she lacked sleep), taking drugs and during extreme loneliness. In this context we discussed the stress-vulnerability model (Zubin & Spring, 1977) again. Pat was not used to intellectual pursuits and did not grasp the graphical implication of the stress-vulnerability model that we drew on the board. She could nevertheless easily relate to the fact that her situation worsened when she felt stressed. We talked about her threshold for stress being perhaps lower than other people's threshold because of early experiences, or because she was born with an "anxious streak". Following on from this discussion we drew continua on the board illustrating that her experiences had connections to everyday events. To make the concept of a continuum more understandable, a temperature range was drawn from the coldest to the hottest that she had experienced, which gave her the idea of different degrees of intensity. This exercise was specifically aimed at her dichotomous thinking "I am weird, other people are normal". She seemed to engage very well with this approach. She explained her inability to go out when she felt bad by saying: "It is as if they are all looking at me . . . as if they can see I'm mad and been in psychiatric hospitals." Therefore de-stigmatisation seemed crucial and the normalisation approach was seen as a powerful tool in changing her understanding of self and others. She was the given the leaflet (Kingdon, 1997) as planned, but this was probably more useful as a guide to the therapist than as information for the patient. She attended the first few sessions with her cousin, Moira, and it was hoped that together they could talk about the content of the leaflet. When we returned to the leaflet at a later stage (Moira was no longer attending), Pat was quite dismissive. She said that she had understood that she was not the only one hearing voices but that she could not see much point in the other issues brought up by the leaflet. She told me that she had once seen a programme on television about voices but had turned it off because it bored her. The suggestions for coping mechanisms did not interest her, as her goal was to find the origin of the voices: "One day I'll meet them in the street."

We then discussed all the strange things that happen in our minds when we sleep, and Pat gave many examples of what she was dreaming: "I keep dreaming about my mother, she says weird things and storms around the house to see if I have done the cleaning. She is also keen for me to look after my baby brother." She told these stories with an air of humorous distance. We discussed the possibility that part of her brain was still dreaming even after the rest of her had wakened up. She smiled subtly and said: "It's possible, I am always tired . . . never fully awake."

Critical collaborative analysis

During Session 7 the patient mentioned that the voices had been particularly active and seemed to continue into the session, which was highly unusual for her. She was asked if she thought that the therapist could also hear the voices, to which she responded with a smile: "I'm not sure . . . I think so." I told her that I could not hear the voices but that we could call in a third person if she so wished. She nodded and said that that would do no harm. A young medical student doing his placement in psychiatry was asked to come into the office and listen in silence for a couple of minutes.

As the student was unable to hear anything unusual Pat smiled and said: "With young ears like that?" Pat was therefore gently introduced to the idea that the voices apparently could not be heard by anybody else. She seemed slightly sceptical about this fact and mentioned that her GP might be able to hear something. However, she did not believe he would lie to her and promised to ask him directly again. She had taken a comment he had made more than 30 years ago ("Look for the answer, Pat, and you will find it") to mean that he knew more than he said he did. We talked about the statement and its possible interpretations and came to the conclusion that he might have meant something entirely different. As Pat had believed her version for years this was difficult to accept and it was agreed that she should approach the GP at their next meeting and ask him what he originally had meant.

Pat declined to borrow one of our tape recorders to tape her voices at home as she found that too difficult technically. We did, however, manage to listen to a tape together from Session 7 (the only session where the voices were present) but found no evidence for the voices being audible to others. She accepted this, but was unable to explain why. She was also at a loss to explain why the voices in that case seemed to be directed especially at her. She claimed that she had never thought about this before.

She had thought extensively about how the voices could reach her. Her explanation was not consistent and would change from session to session, even from minute to minute. She was wavering between different explanations:

1. "They implanted a microphone in my tummy when I was in the hospital."
2. "Dr Tyrer (consultant psychiatrist in our hospital in the 1970s) is involved with this."
3. "It has something to do with the Royal South Hants (hospital she was admitted to)... that is where it all started."
4. "They come from the television... even when it is not on."
5. "I thought they were in my mattress, so I cut it open (back in 1958)... but they were not there."

None of these ideas was held with strong conviction but she was, however, adamant that the voices could not be a product of her mind: "How should that be possible... they sound like real people." After an entire session discussing these matters Pat agreed that some of the voices had a conspicuous similarity to her own thoughts: "Dr. N's daughter is going to have a child; will it be a boy or a girl?", "Come on Pat, go and play bingo... you will enjoy it." The last sentence was especially highlighted as this could represent a part of her mind that wanted to play but Pat felt bad about it

Table 3.3 Statement: "Voices are real"

Evidence FOR	Evidence AGAINST
1. They seem real.	1. They respond to tablets. 2. Become worse when I'm ill. 3. Continued even when the Robsons were away in Birmingham. 4. Get better when I socialise. 5. Get better when I see doctor. 6. Worse when mother died. 7. Changes in intensity when my mood changes. 8. Never found any evidence of speakers or chips in the mattress or behind wallpaper.

and therefore disowned the urge. Pat had previously explained that she loved bingo but it was too expensive for her. She accepted that possibility.

Challenging Beliefs about Voices

From Session 6 and onwards the first more systematic challenges took place. We discussed in a Socratic manner the evidence for and against the voices being real. In order to make it more tangible Table 3.3 was written up on the board.

As previously mentioned, the Robsons were the family next door who had lived there throughout her life. Mr and Mrs Robson died 5–10 years ago but their daughter remained. There were indications that this lady might have been mentally unwell herself and Pat had paradoxically provided substantial support for her. Pat's original hallucinations were the voices of the Robsons that she believed to be evil. She felt it was strange that they could keep talking even though she had seen them go off to Birmingham in their car. Even years previously, she had found this fact peculiar. She stated without prompting that the experience had for a short time made her doubt the "realness" of the voices.

Many times we returned to the ABC model to underline that the ideas about the voices were not facts but beliefs—her personal interpretations. One of the items that changed most during the course of the therapy was her belief about the control of the voices, and homework tasks were set with the purpose of giving her the feeling that she had a certain control over them (e.g. attempt to turn voices on by calling them; try to turn them off by phoning Moira, go to bingo, etc). The patient was unable to write this down but reported orally that the tasks had been carried out successfully. Other increasing and decreasing strategies were carried out to build up her feeling of being in control (Chadwick & Birchwood, 1994), and other homework tasks were set, such as filling in a sheet detailing the ABC model, but the voices went "dead quiet on me" whenever she attempted to write them down.

Over the later years Pat had not felt compelled to do as the voices told her. That had, however, been the case when she was young and her only explanation was: "I guess I must be getting used to them." We talked about how circumstances seemed to play an important role in the intensity of the voices. She agreed and gave examples of this (mother's death, physical illness), but was unable to explain why the voices should be so heavily influenced by external circumstances.

Developing alternative explanations

Pat came up with numerous explanations to the origin of the voices (see above) but none of these was strongly held. The possibility that the voices could be a product of her own mind—especially when stressed—were at best responded to with "Hmmm . . . I don't know", and at worst, "No, they are real, I'll meet them some day." After the evidence for and against "the voices are real" were written down, she kept coming back to the fact she had been searching for so many years for a meaning to these experiences and that it could not possibly just be her own thoughts. It was as if it was almost a physically painful process for her to have to consider letting go of assumptions she had held for so long, but she conceded that it would be a lot less scary if the voices just turned out to be products of her own mind.

We also summarised the evidence that was collected throughout the therapy but she did not embrace the suggestions wholeheartedly. It was felt important that she was at least aware that trusted people could hold views that differed from hers. In Session 14 a new approach was developed, drawing a diagram showing a small red area indicating activity in Broca's area of the brain (the "speech centre"). It was explained that this area is active when people hear voices when nobody seems to be around. We went through the list of "evidence" against the voices being real (response to medication, increase when she is ill, etc.) and asked her after every example if it fitted with the new theory. This clearly had a very profound effect on her and she remained thoughtful for a long time as if pieces in the jigsaw were falling into place. She did, however, finally dismiss the idea and said—as if to convince herself—"No, they *are* real."

Achievements

Although Pat did not describe a change in her underlying beliefs, she improved immensely during the course of the therapy that had lasted for

21 sessions. Her rating scales all showed significantly better outcome and the overall clinical impression was much improved. Her scores after three months were:

HoNOS: 3 (from 12), improvement on hallucinations and delusions, physical illness, depressed mood and activities of daily living.

AHRS: 14 (from 24), improvement on controllability, distress, interruption, beliefs of origin and loudness.

DRS: 3 (from 5), improvement on conviction and distress.

It must, however, be taken into consideration that when we first met in February she was recovering from a serious medical condition (pulmonary embolus). Her previous history showed that serious physical illness almost inevitably had led to an increase in the voices. As she recovered physically over the spring period this was considered an important contributing factor to her good progress in therapy.

Another contributing factor was this lady's ability to relate to other people in a warm and trusting manner. Her old notes (dating back to the 1950s) time and again mentioned her pleasant personality. She quite obviously enjoyed the company of others and her sense of humour was well developed. She relished the chance to talk her problem through in depth with someone else. Her compliance with medication was never in doubt and she turned up promptly for every appointment. Long before the therapy started, she had clearly developed her own coping strategies which had improved her situation markedly since her early breakdowns. As she had relied on these strategies and explanations for her experiences, it proved difficult to change her underlying beliefs.

Looking at her initial goals (which did not change during the therapy) her goals about going back to work and being able to go out more were achieved. The voices were still present but were by now causing her considerably less distress.

CONCLUSION

It was my impression throughout the therapy that much of the development of the therapy was dependent on 'non-specific factors' between the two of us—humour, responsiveness, warmth, empathy and genuineness (Rogers, 1959). There is now some evidence that other approaches—such as befriending, where the above-mentioned qualities can be applied, at least in the shorter term—can have an equally positive influence on schizophrenic patients (Sensky et al., 2000). Regarding genuineness, a lesson was learned when the patient asked me in Session 10 who the "top-man" was (she believed that the top-man in the psychiatric services would hold the answers to her questions). I had an idea of her intentions but chose to play ignorant to avoid being side-tracked, and therefore answered: "I don't really know". Her reaction was brisk and she said with a knowing demeanour: "O, yes, you do... you just won't tell me." Momentarily our relationship had suffered an unnecessary blow.

Clinical work must be tailored towards the patient in question. In Session 14 I drew a picture of the brain to introduce her to the idea that part of the brain becomes hyperactive when the voices are active. To my surprise Pat was unaware of where the brain was situated anatomically. The situation was rectified by a little immediate education and the demonstration was extremely helpful, but it also taught me that all our efforts may be lost if we fail to meet the patients where they are. That certainly does not mean that we cannot eventually bring them away from their initial position, but we have to be careful about the way we address them and make sure we are speaking the same language.

The practical experience of doing therapy cannot be overestimated. It is near impossible to guess how your patient will react to certain approaches before they are tried out in practice. The more clinical work we do, the more skilled we will become at picking up common trends in responses, but that should never lead to complacency—it would be a dangerous illusion to believe that we can predict human behaviour with any certainty.

Chapter 4

CASE EXPERIENCE FROM
A REHABILITATION SERVICE

Case 4 (Helena): *Isabel Clarke*

I trained as a clinical psychologist in my mid-forties, having spent a long time in mental-health-related voluntary work while bringing up my family and doing an Open University degree in Psychology. I first became interested in psychosis as a Samaritan, and developed an approach based on helping someone who came to me in that capacity in the 1970s, to distinguish between her psychotic and ordinary style of thinking and experiencing, in order to reduce her distress and help her adaptation. I noted then the different quality of experiencing she described when the psychosis took over, and this is a theme I have followed up.

During my training and in my early years of practice, 1989–1990s, I followed developments in CBT for psychosis closely through conferences and workshops, and developed my own practice, rather tentatively and in isolation. I have since been joined by other colleagues enthusiastic and knowledgeable in CBT for psychosis, and so find myself in a thriving department. While still working in isolation, as well as the different quality of experience, I was struck by the positive aspects of psychotic experience reported by some (but not all) my clients. By relating these observed features to research and writings, such as the body of Schizotypy research (e.g. Claridge, 1997) and the books of Peter Chadwick (e.g. 1997), I developed my own position on psychosis, and its relationship to the more generally valued state of spiritual experience in an edited volume (Clarke, 2001). These ideas are only partially relevant to the current case, where the psychosis is rooted in the experience of childhood abuse, and it is my observation that in such cases there is no positive aspect to the psychotic experience.

A Case Study Guide to Cognitive Behaviour Therapy of Psychosis. Edited by
David Kingdon and Douglas Turkington. © 2002 John Wiley & Sons, Ltd.

FEATURES, CONTEXT, AND APPROACH TO THERAPY

I work in a psychiatric rehabilitation service, catering for people with long-term problems, who need extra support in order to maximise their independence. My work as a therapist is therefore part of the input of a multi-disciplinary team, and this case illustrates this way of delivering CBT for psychosis. Individual therapy is a relatively small part of my contribution to the service. Indeed, my initial face to face contact with Helena came about through her membership of a Voices group I was facilitating, along with one of the nurses in the team. I was already familiar with her situation, as I had been involved in offering consultation over several years. Once individual therapy started, liaison with the team was central to the process. The ways of approaching symptoms that I negotiate with the individual are then shared with the keyworker, with permission, and so employed by the team.

Another feature of this case is that breakdown occurred in middle life, and involved the reactivation of childhood trauma. The most usual course of psychosis involves breakdown at the early life transitions of leaving home, or, in the case of women, entering committed relationship or having children. Helena had passed all these life stages, albeit restricted by agoraphobia and depression. She had brought up two children, gone through three marriages (the third was remarriage of her first husband), before threats to her latest marriage resulted in psychotic breakdown. A feature of her troubles was severe hopelessness, leading to impulses to suicide, which have made the transition from hospital to the community hard to achieve.

This example is therefore, perhaps, untypical and my approach to CBT for psychosis is also non-standard. I belong to a small, but growing, band of therapists who see great potential in the Interacting Cognitive Subsystems model as applied to therapy for psychosis. The theory was first applied clinically to depression (Teasdale & Barnard, 1993). Barnard (in press) has more recently developed the theory to embrace psychosis. The first published work that applies ICS to psychosis comes from Andrew Gumley's team in Stirling (Gumley, White & Power 1999). They report on having used it to good effect in their trial of relapse prevention, and are currently developing it for early intervention. My own approach is slightly different, and I have outlined it in an extended comment on Gumley's paper in the same journal (Clarke, 2002). In a more detailed paper, I have illustrated with a clinical example the application of this theory to cognitive therapy for personality disorders (Clarke, 1999). This chapter will be an opportunity to illustrate what I believe is the considerable potential of this approach in the treatment of psychosis. Following this introduction, I will launch into my chapter with an account of Helena's situation and history up to the point when I became involved. I will then introduce the Interacting Cognitive Subsystems model, as a preliminary to giving an account of the therapy that is currently ongoing.

HELENA

Helena was born in 1949 to a family with two brothers and a sister. Her father was in the army, so the family moved around a lot. She was always underconfident, and more attached to her father than to her mother. However, when she was raped at the age of 8, while waiting for him to come out of his place of work, she felt unable to tell him or anyone else. Whether because of this, or because of the constant moving around, she was a loner at school, and left at 14 without qualifications to do various factory and cleaning jobs. At 16 she married her boyfriend, Neil, and soon became a mother, having a son when she was 17 and a daughter at 20. The role of wife and mother has always been very important to Helena, and she threw herself into it. However, the relationship upon which the role was founded was definitely abusive. Her husband had an alcohol problem, and undermined her constantly mentally and emotionally, as well as attacking her physically when drunk.

Existing outside a relationship has always appeared highly problematic to Helena, and she only divorced Neil when an alternative relationship presented itself, after ten years of marriage. This second marriage also lasted ten years, and her second divorce in 1985 coincided with the death of her father. These events appear to have plunged her into depression, necessitating psychiatric admission, but with no hint of psychotic symptoms at that time. Following her divorce, she remarried Neil, and moved with him to Southampton in 1990. She was admitted to hospital here in 1993, following an overdose, and reported ideas about being constantly watched, and the TV talking about her. There was a period of outpatient follow-up and intermittent admissions, followed by a long admission in 1996. By this time, the marriage had deteriorated; Neil had another relationship, and Helena reacted with suicidal despair that failed to shift with all possible combinations of medication, ECT, etc. that could be devised.

She was transferred to the Rehabilitation Ward to assist the transfer back into the community. I was involved on a supportive and consultation level at that time. Her suicidal impulses were reinforced by abusive voices telling her to kill herself, and progress was impeded by the difficulties of getting any sort of resolution of the relationship with Neil. On the one hand, he was behaving abusively towards her and was openly unfaithful. On the other, once she resolved to divorce him, he would make promises to reform. When she had relented, he would return to his former ways. Eventually she managed to disentangle herself from this impasse when he filed for divorce in 1998. This paved the way for discharge to a 24-hour staffed hostel in the community, and a successful period of community living.

During this period she was able to engage in a number of activities, and to keep herself safe. This success led to plans to move on to a group home, which were effectively scuppered by the reappearance of Neil, and possibly the fear of more independence. She was readmitted to the Rehabilitation Ward, and had been there for two years. The first discharge plan was to follow her wish to relocate to the part of the country where many of her family were living, but this proved impractical. A brief relationship with a fellow patient lifted her mood, but its ending plunged her once more to the depths, with relentless auditory hallucinations urging suicide, and the consequent difficulty of moving towards community placement. It was at about this time that I became more closely involved.

Initial contact and voices group

Helena's keyworker initially asked me to do some work with her, focused on her dependence on particular relationships. From that initial contact it was clear that Helena had the capacity to make good use of cognitive therapy, as she was well able to identify key cognitions. In a short session, we identified that she felt herself to be worthless, and only felt good when someone else was treating her as special. She was receptive to the idea that she needed to work on treating herself well and gently. As we were starting up a Voices Group at that time, and voices were a major problem for her, I used the bit of rapport building achieved in the first session to coax her into joining the group.

The voices groups I run in the Rehabilitation Service are based on the Romme and Escher approach (1993) and are very gentle, with an emphasis on encouraging people to share what meanings they really give to the voices (and other symptoms), as a basis for working towards less distressing ways of making sense of them. This is because people in this service have usually learned, over long contact with the hospital, what they are expected to say, and what responses will best serve their ends in terms of hastening discharge and avoiding extra medication. I am not necessarily suggesting that acceptance of the medical model is a front for a "real" opinion about voices in such cases, as I am of the opinion that there is no problem for most people in holding simultaneously two contradictory explanations of something. For instance, it is perfectly possible to hold the medical model opinion of voices and symptoms at the same time as entertaining other, incompatible, explanations for psychotic symptoms. In the presence of psychosis, explanatory systems and meaning-making become generally more fluid, and people will often "toggle" backwards and forwards between quite distinct positions according to whether the individual is operating more from the shared reality, or from their private, psychotic reality (see further in Clarke, 2001). Part of the focus of the group is in raising awareness of these two possibilities, and encouraging the ability to move into the more adapted, i.e. the less distressing, of the two. Reducing the state of arousal is frequently enough to achieve this.

In Helena's case, we established in the course of the group that high arousal and a powerful experience of the voices did indeed go together, and that simple relaxation breathing, and other calming occupations, were helpful coping strategies. When we came to the point in the group of starting to uncover the idiosyncratic meanings of people's voices, we had something of a breakthrough in her case. She reported that the voice, which she said was the devil, screamed at her to kill herself. She could not identify the voice, but when I asked whether she could recall hearing anyone scream like that, she said yes—she had screamed like that when she was raped, at the age of 8. This enabled us to suggest that instead of being the voice of the devil, this was really the part of her that had never managed to cope with that terrifying and punishing event in the distant past.

The therapy: An Interacting Cognitive Subsystems approach

A full exposition of the Interacting Cognitive Subsystems model can be found elsewhere (Teasdale & Barnard, 1993). In summary, ICS is an information-processing model, based on experimental evidence for different forms of coding information; for instance, immediate and sensory based, verbal and logically based, or a more holistic, meaning-based coding. These and other distinct codes form the basis for nine postulated subsystems: three are sensory and proprioceptive; two involve higher order pattern recognition; two concern the production of response; and two are yet higher order, meaning-based systems on which I will now focus— the propositional and the implicational. Memory is an integral part of the operation of a subsystem, and each stores information in its own memory, using the code particular to that subsystem. Thus, the logical, propositional memory is verbally coded, whereas the implicational memory, which records meaning at a more generic level, is encoded in a rich variety of sensory modalities, and is therefore more immediate and vivid.

Another area illuminated by the research into short-term memory and human-computer interaction on which the theory is based (Barnard, in press) is the need for a transformation process in the interchange of information between one subsystem/coding and another. This interchange of information is constrained by the limitation of the processing capacity. Thus connections are made more immediately within a particular memory store than between the data stored in different memory stores and coded differently. This provides a parsimonious explanation for the memory's ability to connect rapidly vivid memories of events of similar personal significance. An example in Helena's case is the way in which threatening events in current life (dissolution of her marriage) reawakened memories of the trauma of the rape, in the form of the voice. As the memory was derived from the implicational memory store, it was not mediated by the logical awareness that the event occurred a long time ago, or that her own terror and the malevolent intent of her attacker had become jumbled together in a fashion reminiscent of dream logic. Access to propositional memory would be needed to clarify and disentangle the experience.

The other feature of Interacting Cognitive Subsystems that is central to the current argument is the immediate connection between the implicational and body state subsystems, which can signal level of arousal, and the much more indirect route by which information about arousal reaches the propositional subsystem. Good functioning in a human being is characterised by ease of communication between propositional and implicational levels. A state of high arousal disrupts this ease of communication. Such a state occurs where the implicational subsystem picks up a sense of threat to the self, which is passed to the body state subsystem which gets the body ready to meet the threat. In this mode of operation, thinking becomes focused on threat, and the implicational subsystem is not open to new information, or sophisticated appraisal from the propositional subsystem. Where this type of threat becomes habitual, habitual loops of communication between propositional and implicational subsystems develop, which effectively exclude new learning, and which CBT calls schemas. The unpleasant states of arousal accompanying this situation are characteristically avoided, or circumvented in some way. One individual will respond to the emotional overload by withdrawing, and so become depressed; another will become anxious and panicky; a third will drink or take drugs; and yet another will translate all feelings into anger, and so place the problem with "them, out there". In this way, the aversive states of arousal are translated into various forms of psychopathology or deviance, and the communication between the subsystems is further disrupted. As already noted, Helena's voices were worse when she was in a stressed state, and bringing down arousal was an effective coping strategy for her.

I suggest that psychosis represents a more serious instability in the system, in association with variation in arousal levels, and therefore disruption of the usual exchange of information between the subsystems. Crucially, the centrally important communication between the propositional and implicational levels no longer functions smoothly. Barnard (in press) has expounded this process in some detail, where he describes it as follows: "exchanges between two levels of meaning become asynchronous". He explains how this leads to the characteristic symptoms of psychosis. This idea of asynchrony can help one to see how it is that Helena might have had no access to the logical explanation of her voice, and therefore felt powerless in the face of it. I would add to Barnard's exposition that, in my experience, it is the implicational subsystem which becomes dominant in these circumstances, with its monopoly on meaning, which infects everything with that supernatural sense of meaningfulness characteristic of psychotic experience, and aptly described by Peter Chadwick (1997) as "the meaning feeling".

Application to therapy

A central feature of CBT is the need to be able to share a clear, easily grasped, rationale with the person with whom you are working, and obviously the exposition of the Interacting Cognitive Subsystems model given above does not match that description! However, it does lead to some very simple and user-friendly ideas that have been central to Helena's therapy. In summary, if the desynchrony between propositional and implicational levels, mediated by high arousal, is at the root of at least the psychotic symptom part of the problem, getting these to work together is at the heart of the solution. The ideas of shared and non-shared reality, the ability to hold two ideas at once, and the role of state of arousal in mediating access to the more "rational" explanation, as introduced above, all relate directly to this model. Fundamentally, being in the world is seen as a balancing act rather than a given. In most mental health problems the balance becomes tipped, but in psychosis it becomes dangerously destabilised. Recognising the need to keep the balance and exploring effective ways of achieving this become central to the therapy. Teasdale and others have spent some years developing the approach of mindfulness, as a way of consciously attaining this balance, for application to the treatment of depression (see Teasdale et al., 2000, for a multicentre research study applying mindfulness to the prevention of relapse in depression). Linehan (1993) makes it central to her Dialectical Behaviour Therapy approach to borderline personality disorder and adaptations of mindfulness were used in this therapy, both with the Voices group, and in individual work with Helena.

Formulation

The following formulation was shared with the multidisciplinary team, who were struggling with Helena's continuing impulses to commit suicide and the problems of working towards discharge. They found it particularly difficult to cope with her constant talk of her voices and the urge to commit suicide, and the team was split into those who advocated for her, and those who had essentially lost patience. The meeting, which took place five sessions into the weekly therapy, served to increase tolerance and understanding, and so to reunite the team effort. In summary, I identified Helena's core beliefs as self-unacceptability and shame, reinforced by the rape experience. These led to assumptions about her worth being dependent on caring for others, and her survival dependent on others seeing her as worth taking care of. Because of these assumptions, role and relationships had been partially protective against the core beliefs for most of her life, but with the loss of both, the psychotic voice urging her to kill herself joined the earlier symptoms of depression and agoraphobia. The "devil" screaming that she should kill herself can be seen as re-experience of the rape, reactivated from implicational memory, combining the screaming of the terrified child with the contempt, hatred and violence shown towards her by her attacker, with a liberal helping of "the meaning feeling"—the characteristic implicational supernatural glow which led her to identify the voice as the devil.

Helena's assumptions about her survival being conditional on others' caretaking, coupled with the genuine terror of the experience, led her to abdicate responsibility for her safety. My suggested team aims that arose from this formulation were therefore prefaced by the need to reinforce her ability to take such responsibility, which meant the tolerance of some level of risk. I also suggested that staff should limit time spent talking about the voices and balance it with distraction towards positive activity, as building a sense of esteem and efficacy in the present was the way forward. This had the double advantage of helping staff to feel more useful as they engaged her in general conversation and games rather than listening to an essentially repetitive recital which had left them feeling very helpless.

Since then, the team have been successfully helping Helena towards more independence. Ward staff have supported her in a graduated programme which has brought her to the point where she can go out on her own, and resist suicidal urges. She has been encouraged, through initial reluctance, to attend the day hospital as a prelude to discharge. The allocation of an acceptable council flat and the beginnings of a new relationship are external factors which helped Helena to orientate herself more towards the future.

Individual therapy

This has consisted in a mixture of sharing the formulation in easily assimilable portions, and suggesting practical and imaginal exercises to increase Helena's ability to challenge long-held beliefs and ways of doing things in the present—and so to increase the flow of free communication between propositional and implicational subsystems. I have seen her for 16 sessions so far. The work is ongoing, and there is a strong sense of two steps forward, one and a half to two steps backwards about the therapy. However, I am also liaising with her keyworker and the team and, altogether, Helena does seem to be edging towards discharge.

An important aspect of the formulation, as shared with Helena, was helping her to disentangle the respective influences of what we called "feeling thinking" and "thinking thinking", in other words, the dominance of either the implicational or the propositional subsystem in ICS terms. The struggle with the voices produced automatic thoughts about worthlessness, the urge to suicide, and a reluctance to lift her head and look at other people because of her sense of shame and ugliness. We tracked how these ways of thinking led her back into the past; to the shame of the rape, and to her marriage where her husband constantly criticised her and called her ugly. She was able to recognise in the session that, for instance, her husband was not a trustworthy authority on anything, so why should she be influenced by his opinion; that the rape had not been her fault, so she had no need to feel ashamed, and that at least part of her wanted to live and make a home in the new flat, rather than dying. The difficulty was that she easily found herself overwhelmed by "feeling thinking" between sessions. Barnard's concept of "asynchrony" between subsystems can help us to understand this common phenomenon when working with CBT for psychosis (and indeed for other conditions). The individual can accept the logic of the challenge to thoughts or voices in the session, and come up with good challenges spontaneously, but the power of the voices and psychotic thinking is not so easily shaken off in daily life. To deal with this problem, I wrote things down for her, both on paper and on cue cards so that she could remind herself when things were difficult, and also shared these summaries with her keyworker, so that others could help to keep her on track. She was gradually able to make more consistent use of breathing, distraction and thought, challenging herself to distance herself from the voices, and so become less suicidal and be trusted in the community on her own. Whenever a new challenge came along, like the reality of discharge, there was a tendency for the voices to come back strongly.

Once she had mastered breathing and distraction, we tried some mindfulness exercises to help her to stay in the present. She found that concentrating on the complicated knobs on the stereo helped to bring her mind back from past laden, "feeling thinking". The key of her new flat served to remind her of a hopeful future. She is also learning to label judgements as judgements rather than as facts (Linehan, 1993), and so detach from the feelings of shame and ugliness that cut her off from others. Again, thinking too much about the future brings to her mind the idea that it will all go wrong, as it has so often in the past. Bringing herself back to the present through the exercise of mindfulness is a good way of counteracting this particular implicational subsystem pull.

As the therapy is ongoing, I cannot say more on outcome. I am not sure whether the outcome measures I have used (CORE and HAD) will be sensitive to any progress we have made when we do conclude the therapy. In any case, the therapy has been only one part of a true team effort, including dedicated ward staff, medical staff and staff at the day hospital Helena is currently attending—soon to be joined by community support staff when she is discharged. My hope is for a practical outcome in terms of a reasonably stable community placement, and that any setbacks and returns to hospital, which are to be expected in the light of the history of the last few years, will only be minor and short term.

POSTSCRIPT

I am revising this a few months later, and so far the news is good. Helena has managed to remain in her flat without serious crisis, despite the relationship proving frequently more stressful than supportive. She has demonstrated an ability to use the strategies we have devised to help her through the difficult times, and consequently we have moved from weekly or fortnightly to six-weekly appointments in a gradual process of terminating the therapy. I am also in touch with the team supporting her in the community.

Chapter 5

IDENTIFYING THE "AGENT MICE"

Case 5 (Kathy): *Paul Murray*

This is a case study using a brief, manualised CBT intervention targeted on improving insight and generalised symptomatology in schizophrenia. The intervention comprises six structured sessions of psycho-education using a CBT model lasting approximately one hour. The case described was one of the patients with whom I worked when I became involved in the randomised community field study (Turkington et al., 2002) of the Insight into Schizophrenia programme which was compared with treatment as usual. I had qualified as a Registered Mental Nurse in Preston, Lancashire, in 1983 and have worked in acute psychiatry and, latterly, rehabilitation since then in Hertfordshire, Cleveland, Oxford and Southampton. My last NHS post was in a hospital hostel which is part of the rehabilitation service in Southampton before I came to work for Innovex (UK) Ltd. as a nurse adviser delivering the Insight Programme in Southampton and the Isle of Wight, initially as part of the randomised community field study and now in the dissemination of the programme.

This case study is an example of the structure of this brief intervention, although, due to the unpredictable nature of schizophrenia, it is impossible and inappropriate to be rigid. The titles given to each session are ones that are suggested to the client to be included on the agenda.

KATHY

Kathy was referred to me by an occupational therapist working in the community who told me that Kathy was becoming more isolated and complaining of worsening symptoms that included auditory and visual hallucinations. This was the only community support she was receiving at the time.

Kathy is a 42-year-old lady who had been diagnosed with schizophrenia in 1978. Despite six admissions to her local acute psychiatric ward between

A Case Study Guide to Cognitive Behaviour Therapy of Psychosis. Edited by David Kingdon and Douglas Turkington. © 2002 John Wiley & Sons, Ltd.

1975 and 1986 and trying a number of medication regimes, she had remained treatment resistant. There had been a number of incidences when she had contemplated self-harm but no serious attempts had been made. Her medication at the commencement of the intervention was Olanzapine 20 mg nocte and Temazepam 20 mg nocte.

Session 1: Engagement and developing alternative explanations

The first thing that I noticed upon entering Kathy's house was the number of cats that she possessed. There must have been at least half a dozen of different breeds roaming about the house. As I began the session, the cats began climbing all over me, trying to take the pen from my hand. This was becoming a distraction so I asked Kathy if it was possible to use a room where the cats would not disturb us. Unfortunately Kathy was unable to feel comfortable without the cats, so they became a permanent fixture during our sessions.

An agenda was set that started with discussing her diagnosis, exploring critical incidents and developing an agreed problem list. Kathy stated that she had been given a diagnosis of schizophrenia a number of years ago but could not remember anyone explaining to her what this actually meant. When asked what she thought this illness was, she associated it with "violent mad people" and did not see how this was relevant to her. When we started to look at literature that described the symptoms of schizophrenia in such terms as "difficulty in solving problems, making plans and remembering things", she was able to identify with some of these symptoms.

We began to explore her history by drawing a time-line and adding incidents and memories as she talked through her life. Recollections of childhood were sketchy but she described being bullied at school and being made to sit at the back of the class where she was unable to see the blackboard due to poor eyesight, and her father's unwillingness to get her some glasses. Evenings were the time when she was at her most anxious as a child; she could remember lying in bed waiting for her father to return hoping he would be in a "drunk sleepy mood" rather than a "drunk nasty mood" when beatings were common. At 16 she decided that leaving home would be the best option and she recalled long periods of being on her own in a flat, feeling miserable and lonely.

After meeting and marrying the first man who paid her some attention Kathy then started to describe a chain of events that included her husband being shot, a car accident, motorbike accident, a couple of burglaries and her second husband leaving to live with her best friend. When we started to document the emergence of her new or worsening symptoms, Kathy noticed that they were generally at the times when these critical incidents occurred. Kathy detailed a number of symptoms that included auditory and visual hallucinations, paranoia and thought disorder. However she identified her main problem as "French agent mice" with liquorice hats who had been developed for spying purposes by the CIA. They visited her late in the evening and beamed information from her brain back to the CIA. She was 100% convinced of this. Homework was set and Kathy was initially unenthusiastic but agreed to look at the literature about schizophrenia and feedback her thoughts.

Session 2: Developing alternative explanations and formulation

The session began with a review of the homework. Kathy had read the leaflets and decided that there were quite a few symptoms of schizophrenia that she did not know about and it might have helped had these been explained when she first became ill. The cats remained a nuisance, but Kathy explained that they kept the agent mice away from her in the corner of the room.

One of the items on the agenda was to look at how others might get symptoms similar to Kathy's, and normalising techniques were used to introduce her to the stress-vulnerability model. It was at this point, when we linked this to the time-line chart, that Kathy stated that she had never thought about it that way and began to link critical incidents with the onset of symptoms. However this did not account for the French agent mice as they had appeared shortly after she was prescribed her first antipsychotic and in a period of relative calm. A mini-formulation was agreed with Kathy that she probably had a vulnerability to stress, as she remembered that her mother had been admitted to hospital with "nerve problems"; her grandmother had had similar symptoms; and most of her symptoms had emerged at times of stress. It was obvious, however, that it was going to be difficult to move the formulation forward unless the issue with the agent mice was addressed. Homework was set in the form of a diary and she happily agreed to document the time, place and thoughts she was having when the agent mice appeared.

Session 3: Symptom management

The review of the diary set as homework showed that the agent mice always appeared in the evening between 10 p.m. and 11:30 p.m. The mice always stayed in the corner of the room—she presumed that this was due to the cats keeping them there—and she often had a whispering voice or a mechanical sound in her head when the mice arrived. We began to discuss the first time she saw the mice and heard the voices. Kathy remembered that she quickly got into a routine of taking all her medication at night due to the sedation she experienced. She would then go up to her bedroom to take her tablets at 10 p.m. and return downstairs for her last cup of tea and cigarette of the evening. She can remember getting very sleepy and, for a few seconds, thought she saw four mice sitting in the corner of the room. She thought that this could be some sort of explanation for the noises in her head. If these mice were taking information from her mind, that would account for the mechanical sound. It was noticeable that the carpet she had in the room had a patterned effect, so it was not difficult to see that, when sedated, the small whirls of pattern could resemble small mice. We then tried to develop some alternative explanations that might fit her circumstances at the time she developed her current explanation. Using the stress-vulnerability model and her time-line she agreed that stress looked as though it played a part somewhere in her symptoms, although she was still convinced that the mice were real. We explored the possibility of trying to touch the mice as homework (something she had never attempted). She was a little anxious about this until I suggested that if she would try to touch the mice. I would try to contact the CIA as my homework and ask them if they had ever developed an agent mouse. Kathy agreed to this and said she would try. Some weeks earlier I had been looking at the CIA site on the Internet and knew that there was an e-mail address, so we agreed that it was worth a try.

Session 4: Adherence

This session is usually dedicated to issues surrounding medication unless the client wishes otherwise. However, there are few patients who have no issues regarding their medication. Kathy decided that she would like to know how antipsychotic medication works, and this was included in the agenda along with review of homework.

Fortunately the CIA responded to my e-mail, stating that they had never developed such a project. (I did send an attachment stating why I was asking just in case they got the wrong ideas.) Kathy found that the e-mail introduced more doubts about her original explanation. When she had attempted as her homework to try to touch the mice they "just disappeared". A rating of her beliefs at this point showed that she believed that there was a 70% chance that the mice were real and a 40% that they was due to the symptoms of her illness.

The dopamine hypothesis was used as a basis for understanding how antipsychotics might work and Kathy found it easy to comprehend. She recalled incidents where her symptoms had worsened as she became more worried about things, and her ability to cope with situations was reduced when she was not taking medication. She was happy with her current medication except that she found that the weight gain had made it difficult to go out without feeling self-conscious. We agreed that this was something we could consider in the next session. Homework was negotiated and Kathy agreed to try to remember the uncomfortable thoughts she experienced when she left the house.

Session 5: How I see myself and others

As Kathy put on more weight she reached the point of leaving the house only if it was essential, could not be avoided or could not be done by someone else. The thoughts she remembered were of people laughing at her and thinking that she was ugly. We were able to look at how some of the beliefs she held had developed and again try to develop some alternative explanations for what people might think about her and why they might be laughing.

PM: Why do you think these people are laughing at you?
C: Because I am fat.
PM: So what does being fat mean about a person?
C: That they are lazy.
PM: Anything else?
C: That they are ugly.
PM: Are you lazy?
C: No, I work hard on keeping my house nice.
PM: So are all fat people lazy?
C: No.
PM: So, what else may people think when they see a fat person?
C: That they could be pregnant . . .

Using this technique we were able to generate a number of alternative explanations that Kathy wrote down on a card. Her homework was to read through the card when she experienced negative thoughts while out of the house. A rating scale was agreed between us to assess the effect of the rational responses.

Session 6: Relapse prevention

The agenda for the last session was set at relapse prevention and a comprehensive document was put together detailing triggers, key contacts and coping mechanisms. Kathy had found that the rational responses had allowed her to go out and work through the period of intrusive thoughts. This allowed her to complete her shopping instead of dashing home. She was thrilled with this and although her anxiety was rated as high, she was able to complete the tasks she had set herself.

As a way of reinforcing the relapse prevention plan we extended Kathy's time-line into the future and she tried to predict stressful events that may occur in the next few years. The most anxiety-provoking event that Kathy could envisage was that she was moving house in three months' time to be nearer her parents and was able to predict that her symptoms would probably worsen at that time. Kathy was encouraged to make a list of all of the things that could go wrong and developed a set of strategies that she would employ if those things happened. This included such possibilities as "What if the delivery men don't show up?" and "What if I have a bad attack the night before?" She concluded that having such a plan would probably help her to worry less and help to minimise the effect of such a stressful event in her life.

We concluded with an assessment of the effect of the intervention. The belief that the mice were the cause of her symptoms had shifted to 2/10 and that the stress-vulnerability model as an alternative was 8/10. An independent assessment one year later showed that significant auditory and visual hallucinations still remained, although the mice no longer appeared. The house move occurred without incident and Kathy was able go out with a greatly reduced level of anxiety.

CONCLUSION

This chapter has described a brief intervention with a patient with long-standing, distressing and disabling symptoms. The intervention, which was based predominantly on the development of a stress-vulnerability formulation, normalising symptoms and reality testing, was very acceptable to the patient who seems to have gained some benefit. Further intervention might have led to increased gains but it is gratifying to see that even such a short intervention can have a therapeutic effect.

Chapter 6

DEVELOPING A DIALOGUE WITH VOICES

Case 6 (Nicky): *David Kingdon*

My introduction to cognitive behaviour therapy came from reading Aaron Beck's work as a trainee psychiatrist in the late 1970s. Previously I had read about a range of psychotherapies from non-directive therapy (Rogers, 1977), brief psychodynamic psychotherapy (Malan, 1979) and transactional analysis (Berne, 1968) and found them very illuminating. However, Beck's explanations of emotional disorders and way of working with them seemed to draw these together in a coherent and intuitively very satisfying way. I worked on a project led by Dr Peter Tyrer investigating treatment strategies, including CBT, in neurotic disorder (Tyrer et al., 1988) and adapted these techniques for use in psychosis (Kingdon & Turkington, 1991). The importance of understanding how problems developed and how they could be understood was central to this and Laing (Laing & Esterson, 1970) and Foudraine (1971), among others, were influential exponents of this. When I met Nicky, I had been using these techniques for many years but nevertheless her individual presentation was unique and, over the past two years, very challenging. Managing the risks inherent in her symptoms and the distress she experienced was difficult but eventually seems to have been productive.

NICKY

Nicky and I first met when she was an inpatient of a psychiatric colleague. As part of a reorganisation of services, her care was now to be my responsibility. My colleague expressed his concern for Nicky's very distressing and persistent symptoms, i.e. very unpleasant voices and depression. She had also been physically very ill, which complicated her medication management. This, in any event, had not proved very successful against the symptoms she had.

A Case Study Guide to Cognitive Behaviour Therapy of Psychosis. Edited by
David Kingdon and Douglas Turkington. © 2002 John Wiley & Sons, Ltd.

Nicky was then 33 and had been given alternative diagnoses of, initially, depressive psychosis, then later, with the persistence of the voices, schizodepressive illness. These symptoms had developed when she was 25.

Background

She was born in a local country town. Her early childhood was generally happy. However, at 13 years of age, she took an overdose of medication because of feeling low; she "hated school", was being bullied and truanting and also rebelling against her parents. She attended school until she was 16 and passed four GCSEs (basic school examinations). She then did hotel and factory work for 11 years until eventually having to stop because of her illness.

Her family history was unsettled but she generally got on well with her family. Her father, now in his eighties, is well. Although she saw him as being very strict, dominant and religious, she was nevertheless his favourite. Nicky and her mother, now in her mid-seventies, got on well; she was also on good terms with her sisters (one younger and two older) and brothers (one older and one younger). There was no family history of psychosis although one aunt became depressed on a number of occasions, requiring hospital admission.

She has had two significant longer-term relationships: the first, at age 19— (for two years), met with parental disapproval and eventually broke up; the second was from the age of 23 to David, who she married. She had one termination of pregnancy at 17 years of age, miscarriages at ages 24 and 25, and one daughter aged 5 at the time we first met. The termination of pregnancy was because she feared adverse family reaction. She did not discuss this with them and she now regrets the termination occurring.

Development of illness

She became depressed with the birth of her daughter and presented within weeks after childbirth to her general practitioner, and thence for psychiatric assessment. The birth had been difficult but the pregnancy had been wanted. However, since the birth, she had developed suicidal feelings and ideas of worthlessness and had contemplated taking an overdose of antidepressants. Unfortunately her mother had also been seriously ill four months previously, removing one potential source of support. Nicky had become preoccupied with germs and cleaning. She was admitted to a mother and baby unit and treated with ten electroconvulsive treatments.

During this time she described visual hallucinations—shadows of "them" (vague malevolent figures)—and auditory hallucinations telling her that she was bad. She made a partial recovery but was soon readmitted. Pharmacotherapy included lithium carbonate (a mood stabiliser), clomipramine (an antidepressant) and thioridazine (an antipsychotic drug). At the time, she wrote: "I've been very worried about germs again, if I go home I'll hear them growing again. I've lost count of the number of times I'd sit on the kitchen floor and watch them grow" and of the voice: "He made me burn my hand and take tablets—I feel like I was out of control."

Over the subsequent years, the voices frequently returned although for brief periods she was completely free of them. The voices were frequently of a baby, mainly in the evenings, asking 'why?', pleading and crying, telling her to cut or otherwise harm herself. On other occasions, the voices were of an older man, critical of her, but could also be muffled or laughing when her mood was higher. A theme that emerged was that she felt that the termination of pregnancy was wrong. On occasions, she took overdoses in response to the voices or to stop them. At times, her mood would lift but the voices persisted; usually, however, she would become depressed and then the voices would begin. She also developed ideas of persecution: that people were against her, wanting to keep her or get her into hospital, and some ideas of reference from passers-by and people on TV whom she thought were laughing at her. This seriously affected her motivation and drive.

Medication

She was treated with a variety of medication at increasingly high doses. These included various antidepressants including the monoamine oxidase inhibitor, phenelzine, and antipsychotics, including newer atypical drugs. Unfortunately she also had serious physical problems, myocarditis (inflammation of the heart muscle) and hepatitis (inflammation of the liver), treated in a specialist unit in London. A cause for this was not found, although the possibility that it may have been medication related was considered. She also developed irritable bowel syndrome. Clozapine, a drug used in resistant psychosis, was considered but not administered because of these physical complications.

Psychological intervention

Initially, the psychiatrists managing her care thought that psychotherapy, especially for her feelings about the termination, was contraindicated. One entry in her notes says that this should not be attempted "until 6 months stability on medication, providing she is motivated and can then be assessed". However, on consultation with a psychotherapist, it was agreed that such an approach was worth considering and was started relatively early in the course of her illness, initially using dynamic psychotherapy. Nicky accepted this for a number of months but complained that it was persistently "dragging things up from the past" and this was eventually discontinued after a further admission to hospital. Marital therapy was offered to Nicky and her husband, but not accepted. She was later offered psychological intervention using CBT with voices and participated in some individual work with a trainee under supervision and "learned ways to lower voices giving greater control", but she ended this therapy when readmitted to hospital.

We met after she was admitted to hospital, initially floridly psychotic, disinhibited and thought disordered. Over the years medication had, at times, helped to stabilise her symptoms but she continued to have persistent and distressing hallucinations that were derogatory in nature, calling her a prostitute and telling her to harm herself. She had responded to them with overdoses of medication and occasionally with superficial lacerations to her wrists.

As her psychiatrist, I saw her regularly over a period of two to three years as an outpatient and in ward rounds for relatively brief sessions (rarely more than 30 minutes). Over a period of six months, she discussed her understanding of the voices and their development. She talked about how she had become pregnant and had had the pregnancy terminated. Her father had been appalled at this and had made accusations against her, similar in nature to the content of the voices. She herself felt guilty and was unable to discuss the conception of the child, which had resulted from a somewhat coercive relationship with a boyfriend. She would hear the voice of her terminated offspring "Christopher" and the devil, and also see visions of it saying it looked like its father. She seriously contemplated harming her husband and son. Voices commanded her to drown herself and she attempted suicide by using a plastic bag on the ward, but fortunately was rescued by nursing staff. Unfortunately, although initially supportive, her husband's reaction had reduced to telling her to pull herself together. He would become very critical of her care and immediately predict the worst possible outcomes as soon as she developed symptoms, especially hallucinations.

She had delusions of guilt about "killing her baby" and fears of showing love to her daughter as the other baby would be jealous. At this stage she had very limited insight and needed detention under the Mental Health

Act, for which I, as her psychiatrist, had to take responsibility. She did recognise, however, that she was unwell and the apparent conflict between being both therapist and psychiatrist never seemed to intrude on our relationship. It must have affected it, but possibly for the better.

Her voices would say that I was trying to poison her—presumably related to the medication I was prescribing—but she said she "doesn't believe them". On a number of occasions, she asked if I could read her thoughts. We explored this through discussion of why she thought this might be happening. Was it because I was sometimes able to empathise with what she was feeling, or discuss some of the things the voices were saying? We therefore looked at how I might be able to do this, through recognising patterns that the voices showed and recognising non-verbal indications of low mood.

She would visually hallucinate, seeing blood running down the walls, but could readily accept that this was her imagination. Reality testing, by going to the wall and feeling for damp or looking together for the blood, could have been used but her insight was such that this was unnecessary.

Work with the voices involved initially developing a shared understanding of the phenomena—usually at the weekly ward round, although with only a nurse and junior doctor present:

> DK: What did they sound like? Were they like speech—loud and forceful?
> N: Yes.
> DK: Did anyone else hear them?
> N: No.
> DK: Why do you think that is?
> N: Because it is part of my illness.
> DK: OK—What do they say?
> N: Horrible things.
> DK: Why do you think they do that?
> N: Because I'm bad.
> DK: So what can you have done that is so bad, to suffer like this?
> N: I'm a bad mother, I killed my baby.
> DK: Let's take one at a time . . . are you really a bad mother?

We would explore this area sensitively and objectively; she had always cared for her daughter with tenderness and love and done all she could for her. So, on the termination:

> DK: Let's talk about how you got pregnant first.

And this was discussed—young and vulnerable, frightened of the consequences.

> DK: If a young girl came and told you this story, how would you respond?
> N: I'd feel I just wanted to help and support her.
> DK: Would you blame her?
> N: Not at all . . .
> DK: So, why blame yourself? And just because the voices say these things, why do you believe them?

This discussion was repeated two or three times from different perspectives but always with the aim of reducing the self-blame and developing strength in refuting the voices. She began to describe "starting to argue back with the voices about suicide". She talked about the voices as being the devil: "I've seen him as an animal like an evil dragon" but "I know the devil is the darker side of my personality that makes me suicidal".

She returned home on leave as her mood improved, but there was a slight deterioration. Her husband's pressure on her—"You've been in for six weeks and you aren't better"—caused her distress. She fluctuated over the next few months and required further admission because of concern about the voices telling her to harm herself. However, her understanding of the voices was improving; her medication, which had been high but not particularly effective, was reduced substantially; and she started to discuss key issues in her life. She made the decision to separate from her husband but neither wanted to leave the home.

She was receiving support from a clinical psychologist, to whom she had been referred for further exploration of key personal issues, and a community psychiatric nurse. She was also given tremendous support by her sister. She proceeded to divorce her husband, negotiated the matrimonial settlement, and bought a house. She then got a job—two nights per week—in a nursing home. She became increasingly angry, to the extent of getting nightmares, about her husband. From being relatively unassertive, she generally became more assertive. She then developed asthma requiring admission to hospital but learned how to manage it effectively with medication.

The psychiatric medication that she had been given became a discussion point: although taking an antidepressant made sense, she couldn't see the point of the antipsychotic despite discussions how, in most people, it can reduce the likelihood of relapse. So she stopped it, agreeing to restart if the voices reasserted themselves as they had now virtually disappeared.

Single life with a young daughter still had its pressures, and isolation was one of them. She felt that "nobody wants me". Her job was causing her some stress because it involved working two nights a week, and this was disturbing her sleep. She also started attending a voluntary job and was criticised unfairly by her supervisor in front of a number of others precipitating critical voices. She restarted medication with the onset of symptoms but they were quite persistent. The voices had been telling her that she was useless and to hang herself or gas herself with exhaust fumes, and also to harm others. However, she started "asking the voices to prove themselves" and this was shown to be helpful to the extent that she described a "stand up row with the voices" and said "I lost my temper with them". On this occasion, she did not catastrophise about the voices in the same way, nor was her husband there to do so as, unfortunately, had occurred previously. She had begun to understand that the voices related to the termination experience and was able to discuss their content: "I'm not going to listen, I reason with them." She could weigh up evidence about the accuracy of the content, and consider arguments against the "propositions" that the voices made, i.e. that she was evil and should harm herself. She slowly developed a dialogue with them. As her fear of the voices decreased and her mood improved, so their content became less negative and their frequency and intensity reduced.

Her relationship with her ex-husband, who has continued to have contact with her daughter, was difficult at first but has improved. She initially had difficulty talking with others but now is able to be much more spontaneous when meeting people. She has made friends from work and now works during the day. We are to meet again in a few months' time but she has discharged her community nurse and is discharging me gradually. She's spent all but three days out of hospital in the last 18 months in contrast to the pattern in the previous seven years.

SUMMARY

Nicky presented with depressive symptoms and distressing hallucinations. Vulnerability factors included the termination of pregnancy in her teens and the distancing and difficulties with the relationship with her parents. Precipitation of her symptoms occurred when she gave birth and a perpetuating factor was the range of critical comments from her husband. We spent time understanding her symptoms, working on the negative statements that the voices made and her difficulties with assertiveness. Explicit exposition of beliefs about herself were handled very carefully— e.g. "the voices say I'm a bad mother and that I'm evil"—was examined as a hypothesis and negative perceptions balanced rapidly within that session by use of guided discovery to elicit positive counter-balancing arguments. She eventually developed her own—currently successful— way of handling her voices and they have now remitted.

Chapter 7

TACKLING DRUG-RELATED PSYCHOSIS AND ISOLATION

Case 7 (Damien): *David Kingdon*

DAMIEN

Damien was born in 1970 in Southampton. His parents divorced when he was 10 and he has been estranged from his father since. He had two older brothers, one with learning disabilities who lived in a residential home, and another in the army. He had quite a fraught relationship with his mother and his great-aunt, who live nearby. He described his early years as happy, but by the age of 13 he was truanting and was expelled from school when he was 15, although he still gained three "O" levels at the age of 16 after spending some time in care, in a children's home. He then obtained work short-term with a building site for a few months.

He began to abuse drugs, particularly hallucinogenics, from that age. He was convicted of charges of burglary, motoring offences, stealing cars, drug-related offences and actual bodily harm from the age of 16: he tried to rob a post office brandishing a fake knife at the age of 22.

Psychiatric history

At the age of 17 he was assessed as having signs of psychosis by a duty psychiatrist in an accident and emergency department, but he left the building before further action was taken. At 21 he was admitted and a diagnosis of schizophrenia was made. He responded to medication but was said to have been left with residual negative symptoms and soon dropped out of treatment. At 25 he was re-referred in a floridly psychotic state: "angry, volatile" and described as "easily becoming threatening, grimacing and with incongruous laughter", "rapid speech—thought disorder and idiosyncratic use of words". He was admitted to a secure mental health unit after the

A Case Study Guide to Cognitive Behaviour Therapy of Psychosis. Edited by
David Kingdon and Douglas Turkington. © 2002 John Wiley & Sons, Ltd.

involvement of police who were using CS gas and riot shields. In the unit he assaulted two nurses and was reported by another patient as having threatened to stab his consultant.

His mother was noted to take a highly critical stance with him and those working with him. He was eventually discharged with registration on a supervision register subject to a supervised discharge order under the Mental Health Act. (This order requires him to accept follow-up by mental health team members, but it cannot force him to take medication.) He rapidly began to use amphetamines again and indulge in minor criminal activity such that he received summonses about minor thefts. He was transferred to my care at about this time and his predominant problems, confirmed by his mother, appeared to arise from his amphetamine abuse. He refused further medication, orally or as depot injection, and despite regular visits at home, was often difficult to talk to and generally hostile. He began to describe ideas of reference from the television and other people. His behaviour became increasingly disruptive and he became markedly paranoid and thought disordered. In the end, he briefly agreed to admission to hospital voluntarily, but then left and had to be returned compulsorily.

Progress

He believed that all doctors were conspiring against him and that patients talked about him when he left the room (which, in the latter case, was quite accurate but not as frequent as he assumed). He believed that the ward was part of the army and that genetic secrets were held there. He made seemingly pseudophilosophical statements, e.g. "words are a problem not feelings", which may have referred to his difficulty in communicating because of thought disorder. He talked of being abducted, again accurately, although not usually expressed in those terms.

It became clear after admission that amphetamines may have complicated his presentation but were not responsible for it. His thought disorder remained despite confinement to the ward. Urine screening confirmed that he was not taking amphetamines or other illicit substances. He accepted medication and was prescribed increasing amounts with minimal response of his thought disorder but significant sedation and akathisia. Gradually, over a period of 8 to 9 months, he became more settled, but well before his symptoms had abated, he was keen to leave the ward. This was eventually agreed, on a trial basis, with very regular support from an assertive outreach team member, as care coordinator who had training in the management of substance misuse, and with whom he fortunately got on very well.

Outpatient care

As an outpatient, times were difficult with concerns about excessive noise from his TV, and occasional abusive debates with neighbours. He also continued to have problems with the police through minor incidents of theft. Although these went to court, conditions of treatment and probation had usually resulted. He was much less thought disordered and having much less medication. He tolerated discussions of his misdemeanours without leaving abruptly. He professed to be using cannabis occasionally but no other illicit substances, with some lapses when "friends" come to stay.

Psychological intervention

Much of the assistance offered was initially in discussion, along motivational interviewing lines, of his substance misuse and adherence to medication regimes through a negotiated process similar to that described by Barrowclough and colleagues (2001). This was unsuccessful when Damien was an outpatient initially, but was continued when he was on the wards, and this has resulted in continued compliance for the 18 months that he has again been an outpatient. His thought disorder interfered with communication and his impulsivity led to frequent rapid termination of discussions in the early days, but a negotiating, collaborative stance seemed to progressively allow a therapeutic alliance to build.

Discussion of his ideas of reference and paranoia was focused on reality testing: "Who do you think is talking about you?"; "Well, isn't that reasonable if you've just been stamping about the room?"; "So, it also occurs when you go to the shops?"; "Why do you think people might be so interested in you?"

His isolation has been one of his key problems, and has led to his involvement in relationships where he was exploited for money or accommodation, and this continued to be an issue for us and his care coordinator.

Formulation

Work centred initially on making connections between the use of illicit drugs and his mental state and social condition; then on psychotropic medication relevance; and finally on his loneliness and its consequences. Development of a collaborative, negotiating relationship—modelled by

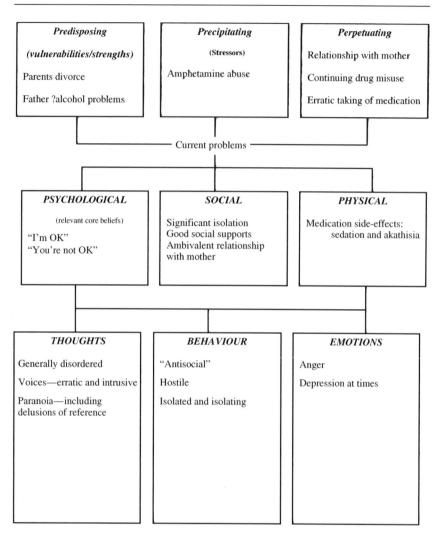

Figure 7.1   Making sense of Damien's problems by diagrammatic formulation

the therapist and care coordinator and persisted with—gradually reduced the number of times he stormed out on discussions or failed to attend.

Work proceeded with his mother who was very concerned about him but had difficulty allowing him independence. This work involved debating tactics with her on how best to help him, having established with her that we understood that this was her intention. Persuasion to use a non-confrontational versus confrontational stance had some success, but inconsistently. A specific team member was eventually found who could spent regular time with her eliciting her concerns and working with them and this has proved invaluable.

Damien had key issues to do with loneliness and, at times, depression at the 'waste' of ten years of his life. However his ability to socialise was only gradually developing and led readily to relationships which damaged rather than supported him. He has made substantial progress over the past couple of years but work continued to sustain this improvement and build on it.

SUMMARY

Damien has presented significant problems of isolation, hostility and psychosis precipitated by amphetamine abuse against a chaotic and disrupted family background. Conventional CBT using regular sessions, socialising to a cognitive model, homework, etc., have not been possible. Adopting a cognitive-behavioural approach to his symptoms and circumstances, however, has allowed us to negotiate, collaborate and gradually understand and formulate his psychotic symptoms (see Figure 7.1) which have ameliorated such that he has been amenable to community support. Family work and support for his mother has been an indispensable component of this.

Chapter 8

"TRAUMATIC PSYCHOSIS": A FORMULATION-BASED APPROACH

Case 8 (Sarah): *Pauline Callcott and Douglas Turkington*

Kingdon and Turkington (1998) suggest four therapeutic subgroups relating to schizophrenia. They emphasise the complicated nature of the phenomenology and have therefore argued for the existence of separate syndromes within the schizophrenia spectrum. These subgroups not only provide a broad spectrum for understanding and normalising individual symptoms; they also help to provide a framework for Cognitive Behaviour Therapy interventions. One of the subgroups relates to psychosis which occurs after trauma. Mueser and colleagues (1998) noted high levels of Post Traumatic Stress Disorder (PTSD) symptoms among individuals with severe mental illness. Ninety-eight per cent of those with a diagnosis of serious mental illness had a history of trauma, with 48% of these meeting criteria for PTSD. Romme and Escher (1989) found that 70% of voice hearers develop their hallucinations following a traumatic event.

Honig et al. (1998) compared the form and content of chronic auditory hallucinations in three cohorts (patients with schizophrenia, patients with dissociative disorder, and non-patient voice hearers). They found that, in most patients, either a traumatic event or an event that activated the memory of an earlier trauma preceded the onset of auditory hallucinations, and that the disability incurred by hearing voices was associated with the re-activation of previous trauma and abuse. Whether the trauma can be seen as a factor in experience that may have made an individual vulnerable to stress and led to the development of schizophrenia, or whether it is seen as a factor to be treated as a separate diagnosis, it would make sense to develop a formulation approach that will increase understanding and, in keeping with a CBT approach, aid collaboration and reduce symptoms.

There is evidence from other studies that CBT provides symptomatic relief (Kingdon & Turkington, 1991; Tarrier et al., 1993, 1998; Kuipers et al., 1997),

A Case Study Guide to Cognitive Behaviour Therapy of Psychosis. Edited by
David Kingdon and Douglas Turkington. © 2002 John Wiley & Sons, Ltd.

but this has not yet been clearly demonstrated in the case of "traumatic psychosis". This chapter describes a single case of CBT and the progress made using cognitive models borrowed from Smucker (1998) and Ehlers and Clark (2000) that assisted in guiding the progress of a formulation approach to therapy.

Prior to describing the process of cognitive therapy that Dr Turkington and I adopted for this case, I (P. C.) will describe my own background. I trained as a Registered Mental Nurse in the mid-1980s and developed an interest in behaviour therapy and the therapeutic relationship with patients. On qualification I worked first of all in a day unit for psychiatric patients and then as a ward manager of an acute psychiatric unit. A social worker introduced me to *Feeling Good—The New Mood Therapy* by David Burns (1980) and using that book I worked with one depressed patient over a course of several sessions employing the techniques described and with both of us reading the book together. I later became involved in audiotaping my sessions with clients via a cognitive therapy training clinic which predated the Newcastle cognitive therapy course. I worked as a community mental health nurse in a primary care setting while completing the cognitive therapy course and saw mainly patients with a diagnosis of anxiety disorders or depression. My training was therefore Beckian, with an emphasis on intensive supervision and academic milestones (Beck et al., 1967). On completion of the course in 1997 I worked as a Clinical Coordinator in a Community Mental Health Team and was able to apply some skills gained in treating patients with a diagnosis of schizophrenia. I initially used formulation-based approaches for depression and anxiety in assisting formulations based on problems and symptoms rather than traditional CBT designed for the treatment of psychosis. I incorporated a normalising rational for understanding CBT for psychosis based on the work of Kingdon and Turkington (1998). I have continued, while working at the Newcastle Cognitive Therapy Centre over the last year, to have supervision for my psychosis work as a clinical pychologist. I have further developed my knowledge of, and experience of working with, CBT models of PTSD with a range of clients with various symptom profiles relating to PTSD.

SARAH

Sarah is a 45-year-old woman with a six-year history of psychosis and a total of 12 admissions to hospital in Edinburgh and Newcastle. Her admissions were for acute psychotic episodes, the last being in January 2001. Her treatment consisted of trifluperazine, 4 mg twice daily, and procyclidine,

5 mg twice daily, regular outpatient appointments and fortnightly visits from a CPN.

Sarah had moved from Edinburgh in May 2000 to live with her 28-year-old son in council accommodation. She had moved to get away from the city, in which her violent ex-husband was a taxi driver. She left a mother and brother in Edinburgh and although she kept regular phone contact had not returned there since her move. She had a son from her first marriage which she described as happy but "they were married too young" (both 17).

When I began to see Sarah she described a high level of daily distress. She heard voices saying "I'm going to kill you" and "I will find you" on a daily basis, and sometimes up to 15 times a day. She described having catastrophic images of violent incidents that might happen, such as seeing her son being attacked by her ex-husband, or real incidents such as when she had been verbally threatened with the image of her ex-husband's face appearing unexpectedly. With these images the associated worry was that "it might happen" and the belief that he was still pursuing her. Her usual coping strategy was distraction and trying to push the thought or image away. This resulted in heightened awareness, scanning of the environment for potential dangers and a heightened level of tension and a startle response.

The excessive ruminations often resulted in vivid images of violent incidents that might occur. Specifically these would involve her ex-husband acting on threats he had made to her son or other members of the family, the images of which became graphic and very disturbing. If distraction and thought/image suppression didn't work, which seldom did, Sarah was unable to sleep and with lack of sleep came generalised paranoia and other psychotic symptoms leading to admission to hospital.

The first goal of engagement with Sarah was to develop a shared understanding of her symptoms. Her physical and emotional reaction to the voices could be linked using a thought–behaviour–emotion and physical sensation framework. Sarah's catastrophic appraisal of intrusive voices or images was often "He is out to get me" or "I'm going mad again". Over the 12 sessions we worked at this first appraisal of these phenomena. Sarah had been admitted to hospital just before therapy commenced and we began to look at the hypothesis that her appraisal of her symptoms as a sign of madness only served to increase arousal and maintains a cycle of symptoms.

Initially Sarah was able to see a pattern, but was cautious about making any changes to this existing pattern because of her understandable fear of breakdown and readmission. We were fortunate in that Sarah had maintained good links with the hospital-based team, and although her paranoia had extended to them in the past she currently saw them as a useful safety net on which to fall back should her psychosis return. From this lead we used the background of a stress-vulnerability model to develop an understanding of how the first incident of psychosis developed. This is vital in the development of a shared formulation derived from the antecedents of psychosis.

I asked Sarah to describe in detail the events leading up to her first psychotic episode. Sarah had been in bed after fracturing a couple of ribs in a fall at work. She was taking painkillers and was worried about her son because of threats her husband had made towards him. She had also been sleep deprived, which may have heightened her vulnerability (Oswald, 1974). Her husband had an ongoing dispute with neighbours, which was currently reaching a peak. Sarah heard the mumble of menacing voices and at first put it down to her dressing gown zip rasping on the door.

We were therefore able to develop an initial trigger for the psychotic phenomena. Once physiologically aroused by the fear, because of what was happening coupled with ongoing stress, Sarah was able to see how the symptoms could be perpetuated. A normalising rationale explains symptoms as understandable in light of experiences and this allowed Sarah to see why she could become ill at that particular time. Examples of psychosis occurring as a result of physical and mental stress assisted in explaining this process. Symptom management focused initially on providing a framework for understanding what might be maintaining and perpetuating the voices and other symptoms, and later on exploring what current strategies were useful and what might be maintaining symptoms.

A baseline recording revealed 3–5 occurrences a day of voices or images. Sarah was asked to rate her level of distress on a scale of 1–10 associated with the thought or image. We did not focus on the content of the voice as this could usually be traced to a threat by her husband in the past. The charts (Figure 8.1) show the link, monitored by daily diaries between emotions and voices. There were peaks in fear, paranoia and feeling down at times of increased voices. The period between 16 and 23 May was a particularly difficult time for Sarah with marked links between increased voices, paranoia and fear. We used the session to challenge what Sarah made of the voices and how much that changed the strength of belief in the logical process that Sarah used to dispute the voices. This was phrased as "although logic tells me that he is unlikely to follow me to Newcastle, I still believe he will".

We began testing the hypothesis that Sarah's symptoms could be explained by an understanding based on a model of post-traumatic stress. Initial ratings showed that Sarah scored highly on a list of post-traumatic symptoms. As well as hearing her abuser's voice, she had intrusive images of traumatic past events—for example, of when her ex-husband had attacked her or her son, or more often when he threatened to do so. These images were not always of real events but were often vivid images that *appeared* to be actual events.

Behaviours that were sometimes effective included distraction and avoidance. Sarah kept herself busy seeing friends, knitting, etc., and often took to her bed or avoided going out when distress was high. She stopped her son talking about the past although he often wanted to do so as he was trying to come to terms with a difficult time in his life. It soon became apparent that avoidance of social contact was based on negative experiences when she went out and the fear of triggering symptoms. One example of this was when she saw someone wearing a coat like her ex-husband's; this could lead to increased anxiety, and menacing voices attributed to an external source. If reasoning was ineffective, catastrophic thoughts and images ensued of what might happen if her husband turned up.

Sarah accepted the explanation that her hypervigilance and heightened startle response might lead to her noticing and perhaps misinterpreting clues in her environment. As a good example of this, she would look up and think that she noticed his image in the mirror behind her. She would not try to disprove what she saw but would let this develop in her imagination as an extremely frightening perception. Attempts not to think of the thoughts, images and voices had therefore a minimal effect and might even be increasing the likelihood that they would recur. Coupled with withdrawal and avoidance, Sarah was able to see how the symptoms might be perpetuated. Ehlers and Clark's (2000) model of chronic PTSD specifies three maintaining factors: excessive negative appraisals of the trauma; the nature of the trauma (which explains the re-experiencing of symptoms); the patient's appraisals which drive a series of dysfunctional behaviours and cognitive strategies (such as thought suppression, rumination, distraction). These are intended to reduce the sense of current threat, but maintain the problem by preventing change in trauma memory and appraisals and lead to an increase in symptoms.

A distinction was drawn between behaviour that Sarah felt maintained her stability, such as medication, contact with hospital services, and how they interfaced with the maintaining symptoms such as keeping to the same routine, no trips away and social withdrawal if feeling stressed. Sarah stated that the use of logic at the initial stages of voice hearing had given her the "inner strength" to nip anxiety symptoms in the bud. This, however, did not always work. To test the emerging hypothesis that avoidance might be

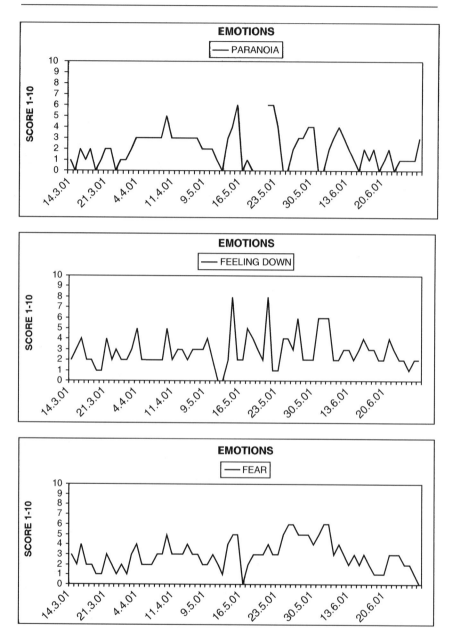

Figure 8.1 Charts of emotions and voices.

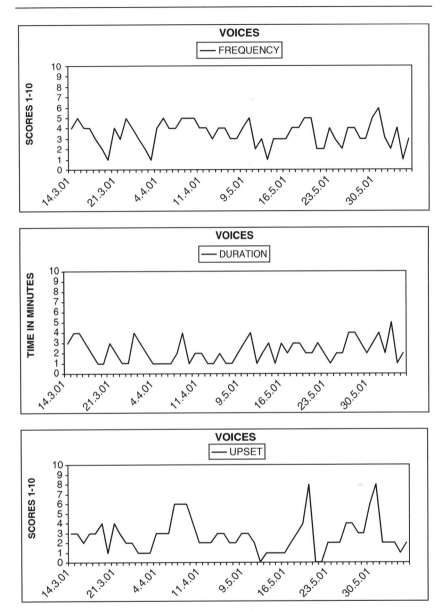

Figure 8.1 (*continued*).

maintaining symptoms, we agreed that if Sarah could talk in greater depth about the images and thoughts in the session this should dissipate some of the fear associated with the image/voice. This is in keeping with the CBT rationale for PTSD treatment, based on habituation principles (Richards &

Lovell, 1999). "Hotspots"—peak levels of fear—may need further exposure if habituation is to occur.

Ehlers and Clark (2000) described three goals of therapy. First, personal negative appraisals are identified and changed. Therapeutic techniques include reliving of the event to identify emotional "hot spots" and associated meanings, Socratic questioning, behavioural experiments and imagery modification. Second, the trauma memory is elaborated through imaginal reliving and the patient learns to discriminate triggers of re-experiencing symptoms from what was actually happening during trauma. Third, the patient is encouraged to drop maintaining behaviours and cognitive strategies. The therapy involves relating past, and imagined, events in the first person and building up detail as it progresses in order to unpack the meaning of events and to habituate to the fear triggered by thoughts of the event. Tapes were made of these sessions and Sarah was asked to play them between sessions using a subjective unit of distress scale in order to monitor her distress at listening to the detail. Various incidents kept in diary form were explored during the session, with the distortions noted. Triggers to the voices provided incidents with which to test this hypothesis. For example, Sarah was asked to explore the image of her ex-husband in the mirror instead of her normal strategy of pushing the image out of her mind with the usual consequence of the fear of it returning. Sarah was asked to stay with the image and describe it in detail. She was able to see the distortions in the image. It was headless with its face contorted—in other words, a disembodied image of a head rather than a photofit image of her ex-husband. Fear dissipated with this realisation and, consequently, instead of avoiding mirrors and windows in the dark, Sarah was able to carry on with her normal activities.

A further strategy of resisting avoidance was applied to voices and catastrophic thoughts associated with the voices. Letting them have their say and then resisting any self-criticism, or calling herself "stupid" for having the voices, changed the meaning of having voices. In line with a developing formulation we were able to identify that, because of the years of living daily in an abusive marriage, Sarah had developed the predominant conditional assumption that "in order to survive I must stay in control". The sheer impact of additional stress as the result of a dispute with neighbours, coupled with the physical consequences of broken ribs, had tipped the balance so that Sarah was no longer in control. A pattern developed that maintained this lack of control. Sarah's diagnosis of psychosis further lowered her confidence in her own abilities to control the symptoms and maintained the symptoms.

Sarah's·engagement in psychiatric services, however, served as a basis for being able to work with what might appear to be a frightening process.

She knew that she could be admitted if talking about her fears in depth increased her distress. By developing a questioning stance ("let's stand back and see what happens") rather than trying to maintain control by pushing out thoughts and images, Sarah was able to test the assumption that 'in order to survive I must stay in control'.

Sarah has recently been readmitted to hospital, and this could be explained within the formulation. Causative triggers—e.g. her son moving a girl-friend into her flat, and intervening in a neighbour's argument—brought back memories of violent incidents. On the day of admission to hospital Sarah had seen a car outside which looked like her ex-husband's. She saw a man sitting in it writing and, although she tried to resist checking, she continued to look. The voices returned, which she was not able to label as worries with the recurrent appraisal: 'I'm going mad again, it's never going to stop." This increased physiological arousal caused her mood to dip and Sarah consequently overdosed on procyclidine and trifluperazine. She contacted the local psychiatric emergency team and was admitted to hospital.

The procyclidine overdose resulted in extreme confusion. She was subsequently embarrassed by her behaviour in the local hospital where she had to be restrained and medicated as she had been searching lockers and trying to serve in the hospital shop. This confused phase was replaced by paranoia. She was relieved to be told of the effects of a procyclidine overdose, and can see how the catastrophic thinking around the recurrence of intrusive thoughts and images as 'voices', and thus a sign of madness, had led to her wishing to end her life. We are now working on the hypothesis that this catastrophic appraisal of intrusive thought, as a 'voice', might be locking her into a diagnosis of serious mental illness that is restricting her own sense of control over her life. A period of paranoia and the confusion following the procyclidine overdose have led to an increase in antipsychotic medication as well as the addition of an antidepressant. This sits uneasily with developing a hypothesis that tests the label of psychosis, but is not wholly inconsistent as medication has value in 'buffering' at stressful times. However, we have returned to the same starting point as our first session. This meant looking at developing an individual formulation for Sarah that makes sense, allowing for engagement in psychiatric services that support her in making new appraisals of her symptoms.

Symptom profiles

- Dysfunctional Assumptions Scale (Weissman & Beck, 1978): In March, the DAS score of 88 indicated a score below clinical depression levels. This did not change significantly when repeated in July. There were higher scores for the need for approval and love that may relate to the impact on Sarah of a traumatising relationship or her predisposition to develop such a relationship.

• Impact of Events Scale (Horowitz, Wilner & Alvarez, 1979): From March to July there were changes on the symptom profiles from these events occurring often too rarely, and not at all. The main shifts on the 15-item scale indicated a reduction in symptoms of PTSD and a reduction in avoidance strategies.

• Beck Depression Inventory (Beck & Greer, 1987): At the beginning of treatment this was 32; in July, it measured 14.

CONCLUSIONS

Factors that provide a rationale for formulation-driven CBT include the evidence of thematic links between early psychosocial stressors and the content of psychotic symptoms (Raune, Kuipers & Bebbington, 1999). Similarly, the content of psychotic symptoms and the process of their development, rather than merely the fact of their existence, seem crucial for understanding the patient. Individual case formulation facilitates engagement, guides interventions and heals alliance ruptures (Moorhead & Turkington, 2000). Indeed, it has recently been advocated that unless a therapist is able to show a clear linkage between personal experience, schema and psychotic symptom emergence, the accuracy of the formulation is questionable (Brabban & Turkington, 2001). Understandability of psychotic symptoms, both in their content and in their development and maintenance, has implications for change. If understanding can be reached the patient will become more active in the change process and is less likely to blame himself or herself for the problem.

Models drawn from CBT of trauma, including Smucker (1999), served as a useful framework with Sarah. Time spent developing a formulation around stress-vulnerability as a factor in developing psychosis, engaged the patient enough for her to be prepared to take risks. Pacing of sessions, allowing longer time for exposure to trauma, prevented avoidance during the session. CBT (as an add-on to existing services), assisted collaboration and simple behavioural experiments created a change in Sarah's symptoms, and symptom profiles over the course of therapy allowed the patient to see the gains she was making.

Chapter 9

COMMUNICATIONS FROM MY PARENTS

Case 9 (Carole): *Ronald Siddle*

I was initially trained as a psychiatric nurse. I left school at 15 having just sat my GCE "O" levels and was persuaded by a friend to apply to the local psychiatric hospital as a cadet nurse. After two years of working in the various departments of the hospital I started training as a student nurse. Towards the end of the RMN training I applied for the shortened post-registration RGN course and was able to finish that training in about a year and a half. Swiftly returning to the safety of psychiatry I spent a year or so as a staff nurse before getting a relief charge nurse post. When I was allocated to a ward full time I tried to do what I could with the patients. Unfortunately it was an uphill struggle with schizophrenia and institutionalisation making psychological work difficult. Of course at that time (1980s) even though there was some evidence of effective therapeutic strategies, I did not know them, and was in any case trying to influence things at a more basic level. The ideal wards to work on in the psychiatric hospital where I worked, were the admission wards, and eventually I was allocated to one of these. Though the management was still necessary, the patients were less chronic and I tried to develop my counselling skills. I had not even heard of CBT, but attended a few short (non-accredited) counselling courses and tried to help the patients. I was a casualty of the nurses' clinical grading structure and left the system, which I thought was spoiled by nepotism and managers.

I began working in the department of clinical psychology as a nurse behaviour therapist. My initial training was in-house from the clinical psychologists and the other nurse behaviour therapists. The focus was upon problem behaviours and there was an emphasis upon working with staff to eliminate troublesome behaviours in the longer stay patients of the hospital. I became frustrated at this manipulation of staff and patients and

A Case Study Guide to Cognitive Behaviour Therapy of Psychosis. Edited by
David Kingdon and Douglas Turkington. © 2002 John Wiley & Sons, Ltd.

wanted to do something more direct. I also realised the importance of thoughts to my actions and knew that I had to find out more about the Cognitive Behaviour Therapy (CBT) that was being mentioned. Our department was fortunate that two of the clinical psychologists were training to be supervisors on the CBT training course at the cognitive therapy centre at Newcastle, and was able to learn about CBT from them. I then attended a certificate course in theory and practice of counselling with the intention of ensuring that my interpersonal skills were adequate. I knew from the outset that I did not want to be a counsellor since I did not believe that patients had the inherent ability to solve their own problems, and I also knew that people needed help and training to challenge their thoughts and beliefs. Consequently, I almost failed the course by submitting a tape in which I was doing far more than reflecting and summarising. I persuaded my manager that I ought to try for the CBT course at Newcastle, and she agreed thinking (I believe) that I would never be accepted.

I did get a place on the course and was allocated Douglas Turkington as my supervisor. Though we did not discuss schizophrenia we got on well and I enjoyed the course, although the days were long. I was simultaneously doing an OU course in child psychology, which was helpful, though it added to the stresses of the assignments.

After the required period of supervised practice I applied and was accredited. During that period I had been working initially in a Community Mental Health Team and then on a research study working with schizophrenia. This was the Wellcome funded RCT (Sensky et al., 2000) and I was supervised during this time by the editor (D.T.) and a clinical psychologist who was also involved in the study. I maintained an interest in working with non-psychotic patients for my one session a week, which was spent in the Community Mental Health Centre that had seconded me to the study.

As the Wellcome funded trial was drawing to a close, I went to a conference in Maastricht where I met one of the grantholders, Gill Haddock, for the SoCRATES study (Lewis et al., in press). She asked me if I would be interested in working on a trial investigating CBT in early schizophrenia. I saw this as an opportunity to enhance my skills as well as a personal opportunity to do a Ph.D. and move to the south (Manchester). When I was interviewed and offered the job at a higher grade than I was applying for, I could hardly believe my luck. This was because I was asked also to undertake a managerial and supervisory role in addition to the therapy. These enhanced roles allowed me additional opportunities to acquire new skills and develop my existing ones. It was a busy time, but rewarding.

As the SoCRATES study was coming to an end I started looking for a job. The short-term contracts of university employment were a little stressful, and I wanted a period of stability. To not have to beg for rooms, and to be a fully fledged member of a department, I applied to the hospitals in which I had enjoyed working while doing the SoCRATES study and was fortunate enough to find a position in the Clinical Psychology department as a Cognitive Behaviour Therapist. My current role is for three sessions per week to be with patients from primary care teams in two GP surgeries. I get a research day and the remainder is spent working with patients from the adult mental health speciality. These patients have various problems, though many who find their way to my list have schizophrenia or other psychotic illnesses.

CAROLE

Carole was referred to the psychology service by her psychiatrist. The referral letter told of a woman with a schizophrenia diagnosis who heard the voices of her mother and father talking to her. Carole believed that the voices she heard were actually caused by her parents despite the death of her father. The psychiatrist had begun to challenge these ideas, though she thought that CBT would be of help with the lady. In particular, the psychiatrist hoped that Carole could learn to cope with her voices better. The psychiatrist described Carole as having "remarkable insight" and a well-preserved personality.

Session 1

The aim of the first session was to engage Carole in a collaborative investigation of her difficulties. There was a focus upon establishing a clear problem list from Carole's perspective (as opposed to a comprehensive symptom list) and I wanted to clarify and, if appropriate, shape up Carole's aims in therapy. Often patients have a desire to make the voices disappear, though this is unlikely to happen since voices are, as far as is reasonably established, attributions of thoughts as if they were external perceptions. Given that it is unlikely that CBT or any therapy could or would wish to eliminate cognitions, it is better to attempt to shift attributions for the voices from "communications from my parents" as in Carole's case, to "my brain playing tricks again", or some such attribution of cause.

Carole volunteered that her voices started when she was 13 years of age. They continued to trouble her for four or five years and stopped for some time, only to resume four or five years ago. She had been troubled by the voices ever since, and reported getting extremely depressed as a consequence.

In asking a few relevant demographic questions it was confirmed that Carole had a diagnosis of schizophrenia (and was comfortable with the label), and was prescribed the following medications:

Clopenthixol 200 mg IM weekly
Trifluoperazine 20 mg BD
Chlorpromazine as required.

Carole reported that her medications were effective in that they helped her to calm down and contributed to the voices being less persecutory. Around the time that her depot medication was due, Carole reported that her voices got worse and afterwards they got better. She had been an inpatient in the past, had nine siblings and her father had had a history of what Carole believed was manic-depressive psychosis.

If she did not have the voices Carole believed that she would be less depressed and life would be much better. The voices were assessed. The male voice appeared to come from behind her, very close but outside of her head. It was of normal volume but was capable of shouting, and spoke BBC English with a "plum in the mouth" accent. Typically this voice would be heard one or two hours before going to bed. It would try to control her, telling her to do harmful things to herself, and sometimes she obeyed the voice. At first Carole thought that this voice was a spirit, though her current causal attribution was that this was a chemical imbalance.

At this point, because of concerns about her safety, and a clear indication that Carole would be less depressed if she was not troubled by the voice, it was decided to try to introduce some doubt into the validity of the voice as well as trying to increase her coping skills. Initially an experimental approach was suggested which allowed her to hurt herself, though in a safer manner. She was asked, as a homework assignment, to try to crush an ice cube in her hand when the temptation to harm herself was great. This would perhaps satisfy her need to hurt herself, and would not cause any serious damage.

The hallucinations were discussed in a matter-of-fact manner, and normalising examples were included to help Carole to recognise that voices occur in other people and that anyone could develop such symptoms should they be subject to enough stress. Subvocalising as a coping strategy for voices was described as this helps to shift attributions towards the explanation that the "brain is playing tricks", in preference to the "real perceptions" explanation. In doing this explanation a slight digression into the differences between "top down" and "bottom up" cognitive processing were discussed. The rationale for this short course in basic cognitive psychology is that by realising that her expectations may affect her subsequent perceptions (real and otherwise) she will be more likely eventually to realise that her brain has a capacity for error, especially when under stress.

In discussing the nature of Carole's problems she volunteered a particularly traumatic event which she associated with the recommencement of her voices. I later found out that Carole had experienced voices from the age of 13, though they had stopped for a time. Ten years earlier, while she was living in India, Carole was having some domestic troubles. She had separated from her husband, but he had returned to the family home and kidnapped the children. From that point onwards Carole had been troubled by the voices. The point of asking about the onset of her symptoms in the midst of a series of queries about the nature of the voices was that it was hoped that Carole would recognise that this clearly stressful event had brought about the start of the voices. This fact would later be alluded to, in altering attributions of cause regarding the voices.

I assessed that Carole was intelligent, articulate and psychologically minded. Accordingly, although this would not usually be done so soon in therapy, and in view of her dangerous response to the voices, I thought it worth while to spend a little time in this first session trying to introduce doubt into the validity of the voices. I tried to summarise what we had discussed, and in summarising the information about the voices I encouraged a bit of guided discovery. This was intended to enhance the possibility that she would doubt the voices' validity and thus not act upon them in a self-injurious manner. Carole was asked how many times she had been threatened by the voices over the past years. She estimated that this would be in excess of 500 instances. She was asked if the voices themselves had ever actually harmed her. Carole realised that, despite over 500 threats, there had not been a single instance of actual threat from the voices, other than as a consequence of her acting on instructions from them. She was asked how her symptoms varied with medication, and this was summarised as: the voices are not removed with medication but are certainly more frequent without it. Carole was informed in a matter of fact way that, under stress and on occasions even without stress, the human brain makes errors. She was informed of the research which shows that under stress it was normal to hear voices, and she was reminded that her voices began during a period of acute stress. To try to extend the gains made, Carole was asked if she thought that others would be able to hear the voices. She had noticed that others didn't seem to respond as if they heard the voices, and was willing to try a homework assignment involving an attempt to record the voices onto a cassette tape when she was next troubled by them. The other homework experiments that Carole was to embark upon were an evaluation of the impact of singing along to a Bob Marley song when the voices were bad, and using the crushed ice cube technique if she felt the need to harm herself.

Carole found the session helpful. It would normally not be sensible to set so many homework experiments, but she was keen and could see a rationale for each.

Session 2

Carole had found the homework helpful. Her voices had been really bad on the Sunday after the first session, and she had been sure that they were loud enough to show up on the tape. When they did not show up on the tape, she at first feared that she was going mad, but then realised that they were unlikely to show up. This helped her to shift her causal attributions such that she became 100% sure that the voices were from her brain (while previously she revealed that she was only 30% sure that the brain was at fault).

The ice cube experiment worked well. When, on Sunday, the voices had been bad she took two ice cubes and crushed them in her hands. It had been painful, and she had then taken another two, and done the same thing again. Fortunately this intervention at a time of crisis had prevented Carole from harming herself any further. Again on Sunday Carole had tried subvocalising as opposed to her usual strategy of shouting at the voices. Because she had a passion for Bob Marley songs, this subvocalising of his songs served as a distracter as well as interrupting the voices. When the voices were at their peak the subvocalising was not of help, but when the voices were less intense the subvocalising diminished them by 70%. Carole was really upbeat about the value of the experiments.

Building upon these coping strategies a list of rational responses (RRs) was generated in the session. The RRs were designed to help to shift Carole's attributions of the voices when they troubled her. The kind of things that were discussed, and written on a card for Carole to carry, are shown in Figure 9.1.

The voices did not show up on tape

Subvocalising helped

The ice cubes helped

I can (and have) resisted the voices in the past

Despite years of threats and abuse these voices haven't actually harmed me

Figure 9.1 Rational response card given to Carol.

During the development of the rational responses, the possible similarity between her thoughts and the contents of the voices were discussed. Carole added some details about the onset of her voices. She had developed voices from the age of 13 years. At that time she was living with her mother who she believed tried to kill her by pushing her head under water in the sink. These voices then disappeared when she met and married her husband, only to return when he kidnapped the children.

In order to ensure that the main problem experienced by Carole was fully investigated, a cognitive assessment of the voices was carried out using the semi-structured interview developed by Chadwick and Birchwood (1994).

Carole revealed during this assessment that she heard two regular voices and occasionally the voice of a stranger. These voices, which appeared to come through her ears, have used her name and were attributed to external factors. These attributions arose from the content of the voices. Her dad's voice reassured her that he still loved her and that she ought not to worry about her mum, though her mum's voice was extremely critical. Mum's voice typically said things such as "should have drowned her at birth . . . she's worthless, etc.". Mum's voice also told Carole to cut her wrists and end the fairly long-standing relationship that she had developed with Paul, a new male friend. Carole identified that, if we were to get rid of her voices completely, she might miss the voice of her dad. Getting ready for bed was a typical antecedent for the onset of her voices. When they came on she felt either calm if it was her dad's voice or tormented if it was her mum's. She would typically fret, and become uneasy, adjusting her clothing and fidgeting. Though she tried to ignore the voices and to stop them talking, she had been unsuccessful on the whole. Carole ended up listening to the voices because she not only felt that she had to, but also because she wanted to. Carole believed the voices to be powerful; they stopped her from doing some things such as having a bath and were trying to harm her by making her distressed.

The homework for Session 2 was to take the rational response card home and to read it at bedtime when the voices were present. She was also asked to test the notion identified during the development of the rational responses, which is that the content of her voices are similar to her own thoughts in many instances. Carole expected a lot of similarity between the thoughts and voice content.

Carole found the session to be helpful and, particularly, that her thoughts may have a lot to do with her voices. Despite the discussion about some upsetting incidents Carole had not found our discussions to be anxiety provoking, and she was keen to continue in therapy.

Session 3

In reviewing the Session 2 homework Carole found that in 75% of entries there was a similarity between the content of the voices and her own thoughts. Even in the 25% of cases where there was no direct similarity, Carole was able to see that the differences related to merely a difference in topic under consideration, rather than a completely different opinion to her own. This helped to support the notion that her brain was doing this to her, rather than some external person, regardless of how real the voices sounded.

Carole also found the rational responses helpful. In fact she made herself two copies of the card so that she could leave one in her handbag, have one in the bedroom, and the original. She read the cards when she was concerned that the voices were threatening to hurt her, and found that the most helpful was the response about the voices never actually harming her despite many threats.

Carole revealed that since the second session she had been doing all sorts of things that she would not normally do. This had included going swimming and having friends around. Inspired by the progress she had been making Carole had decided to try to get rid of some of her "emotional baggage", and was eventually going to get a divorce from her husband.

To try to enhance Carole's understanding of her symptoms and, in the process, to help her to see the additional benefits of medication (as a stress reducer if for no other purpose) the stress-vulnerability hypothesis was discussed. The rationale was that if Carole understood that many people experience hallucinations when subject to sufficient stress—and, of course, she recognised that *she* had been subject to stress—it was hoped that she would be even more sure that her voices were caused by her brain making errors, rather than her parents giving her instructions via some as yet unknown mechanism.

At Carole's request a rational response tape was created with the voice of the therapist outlining the statements and adding some supplementary information. Carole was keen to have this tape and wanted to edit it by adding a sample of her favourite Bob Marley songs so that she could simultaneously have rational responses, subvocalisation, and, of course, a bit of distraction and pleasure. Carole had identified during this session that bath times were especially worrying, with the voices often becoming really bad when she tried to bathe. She was asked to take the tape on a Walkman personal tape-recorder into the bathroom and, instead of having an anxious and hurried bath, listen to the tape and try to enjoy a relaxing languid bath. Anticipating this to be difficult, it was discussed that even if this was not possible she ought to remind herself of the RRs and remain in the room to prove to herself that she could resist the voices even in this difficult scenario.

Session 4

Four weeks had now passed since we first met. Carole reported that she was unwell physically with an abscess, though her voices were much better and attributed much of the benefit to the homework tasks. She had tried having a bath while listening to the rational response tape and some Bob Marley music. There had been only one voice, which called out her name, but nothing else. She had tried to summon the voices without any success, and this had helped her to feel as though she had a measure of control over them.

Since Carole was feeling so much better she was a little reluctant to go much further with therapy. We agreed to spend the remainder of Session 4 discussing "staying well" strategies. A staying well plan, a minor crisis plan, and a crisis plan were discussed.

Staying well plan

Firstly, Carole was asked about the symptoms she felt before the onset of the voices. A list of typical early warning symptoms was discussed and Carole identified 19 of these which had preceded the auditory hallucinations that had become so troublesome for her. She also identified that of these 19 symptoms she was only suffering from one at the moment.

Carole was asked to state the aspects of the CBT that had been the most helpful for her. She picked out the ice cubes, trying to record the voices and subvocalisation. A staying well plan was developed to try to help her to minimise the likelihood of further relapses. This plan involved encouraging Carole to continue with her medication and keep doctors' appointments. She should try to keep busy, mixing her activities between essential tasks, activities that would give her a sense of achievement, and tasks that would give her some pleasure. Carole identified that she may need to minimise stressors, which included "allowing her" to avoid people whom she knew would upset her. The need to monitor early warning symptoms was discussed, and Carole agreed to do herself some "self-therapy" on a fortnightly basis. During these "self-therapy" sessions Carole was to monitor her early warning signs and review what has happened during the fortnight. She was asked to imagine the questions that I would have asked her, had I been present, and Carole was able to anticipate my style of questioning after these four sessions. A personalised checklist of early warning signs was written out for Carole so that she simply needed to check the list to see if any of her symptoms had been evident during the fortnight.

Carole agreed to share the details of her plans with the health and mental health professionals involved in her care.

Minor crisis plan

If Carole observed that her early warning checklist had more than two ticks, indicating that two symptoms had emerged, or if she had a recurrence of frequent hallucinations, she was to implement this minor crisis plan.

The first thing on the plan was to ensure that Carole had carried out the requirements of the staying well plan. Assuming that these actions had been carried out, Carole was to consider taking the "as required" dose of chlorpromazine that had been prescribed for her by her psychiatrist. Carole was also to begin implementing the CBT techniques that she had found so helpful. She thought that she would derive benefit from listening to the rational response tape, beginning to use subvocalisation if troubled by the voices, and use the ice cubes if the voices were upsetting her to the point that she wanted to harm herself. In relation to her activity schedule, Carole agreed that if she was suffering a bit of a crisis it would be helpful for her to increase the amount of pleasurable activities she did, rather than her natural tendency to reduce them. Carole also thought it would be helpful for her to talk to someone about her problems at this point, rather than keep them to herself.

Crisis plan

In the event that Carole had a significant increase in her early warning signs, or the strategies discussed earlier were not successful within a week, Carole had a crisis plan. This plan involved establishing that the actions detailed earlier in the other plans were carried out. It was also decided at this point that expert assistance might be required. Carole agreed, therefore, to contact her keyworker in the first instance or, if that was not possible, she had a list of people she could contact who knew of her difficulties and the plans. In the meantime, to try to increase her doubting of the validity of the voices, Carole was to try once again to record the voices onto a cassette tape.

Carole agreed to implement these plans and was given a booster appointment a month later.

Session 5

Carole had experienced a few voices during the intervening month, though not many. Her attributions had shifted and she reported being much more relaxed. Even when the voices were present Carole was able to resist them and get into the bath. She was pleased that she had withstood her voices and that her discomfort had not been bad enough to make her want her "as required" medication. When she had been checking her early warning list she had discovered a couple of symptoms, but she had been able to tackle these with ease and had shared her plans with her friends and mental health workers.

At the conclusion of this session Carole preferred no additional appointments, but was happy for me to retain her notes for 18 months in case she had a further setback that she could not cope with.

Nine months later I was asked by Carole's keyworker to resume involvement. Carole had experienced a recurrence of her psychotic symptoms, which she was unable to deal with herself.

Session 6

Carole's mother had died unexpectedly and the voices had been terrible. Though they were telling her to harm herself she had not been cutting herself. Other changes to Carole's regimen included a change in medication. Since we had first met and she was prescribed chlorpromazine, Trifluoperazine and Clopenthixol, Carole's medication had altered. She had subsequently been prescribed Amisulpiride, though was now prescribed Risperidone. Though Carole was not taking any anticonvulsant medication when she first attended for therapy, some had been prescribed in the intervening months. Subsequently the anticonvulsant medication had also been altered and Carole had subsequently and "inexplicably" started to wake during the night having wet the bed. Carole was very embarrassed about this and had resorted to an attempt at avoiding sleeping as a strategy to minimise the incontinence. The studies of the 1970s relating to sleep deprivation and hallucinations were recounted, and I empathised with Carole. She began to realise that it was possible that her incontinence was caused by epilepsy, though she ought also to get herself checked by her GP in case she had some kind of urinary infection.

At Carole's request we went over some of the evidence relating to the voices, which we had discussed earlier in therapy. She had recently tried, without success, to record the voices and was still resisting the voices with the aid of ice cubes when was told to hurt herself. Carole still used subvocalisation as a means of reducing the intensity of the voices.

At the end of the session Carole was 50% sure that her voices were produced by her own brain playing tricks on her. Although this was less than her belief at Session 4 or 5 it is an improvement on the intensity of her belief when she came into the room for Session 6.

Carole agreed to go to see her GP and to resume her plans; in particular she was keen to begin listening to her Bob Marley tapes again. She took away the session tape and when she got home was keen to listen again to the things we had discussed.

Session 7

When seen at follow-up, Carole reported that her voices had completely disappeared, as had her anxiety symptoms, and she had regained her sense of humour. The incontinence of urine which had so distressed her had been attributed to a side effect of the risperidone, and she had resumed chlorpromazine. The incontinence cleared up immediately.

She had purchased a portable tape-recorder and was listening to the session tape and rational response tape on a regular basis, and was keeping herself busy. Carole had resumed swimming, was playing squash on a regular basis and doing some voluntary work. She was keen to have the "insurance" of follow-up CBT sessions, and these were arranged at six-monthly intervals. Carole was assured that she could have a telephone session or cancel the session if she wished, and also that she could bring the appointment forward if she felt that was necessary.

DISCUSSION

This case involved an intelligent and articulate woman, who had a number of awful experiences in her childhood. These experiences helped to shape her beliefs about herself, and when stressed she would hear voices criticising her, which would say the same kinds of things about her as she thought herself. Therapy was brief and focused upon challenging the attributions that she made regarding the hallucinations that she experienced. Despite a swift abatement of symptoms, Carole experienced a setback perhaps due to the changes in medication, though no doubt exacerbated by the death of her mother. It is also worth recognising that the cognitive behavior therapist is unlikely to be aware of all of the factors in a patient's situation. In this instance epilepsy had been diagnosed and treated, and significant changes in medication had occurred. By retaining Carole's notes and "planning" for a setback she was helped to get back on track sooner than might otherwise have been the case.

Carole was shown the initial draft of this case study to ensure that she was giving informed consent, and because I thought it might help her to understand what the therapist was thinking of, when conducting CBT with her. She found it helpful to read the case study and was pleased to realise that she presented as articulate. Carole found the parts of the case study about the evidence regarding the voices especially useful, as was the discussion about the ice cube intervention. She had no reservations about the case study being published since she could see that her identity had been disguised by changes to biographical details that were not especially relevant to the case.

Chapter 10

TWO EXAMPLES OF PARANOIA

Cases 10 (Mary) and 11 (Karen): *Nick Maguire*

I trained as a clinical psychologist at Southampton University, qualifying in 1999. My particular interest during training was the treatment of psychosis using Cognitive Behaviour Therapy (CBT), supervised by Professor Paul Chadwick. My thesis extended this interest, firstly within a theoretical paper describing cognitive and evolutionary aspects of paranoia, and secondly an experiment to empirically investigate the theoretical and clinical observations that there are two distinct forms of paranoid thinking.

I am currently working as a locality team psychologist, dealing with people with severe and enduring mental health problems, i.e. psychosis and personality disorder, all within a CBT framework, although I recently undertook the Dialectical Behaviour Therapy course for more specialist work with personality disorders. I am also currently extending the CBT model to the treatment of those with homelessness and alcohol/substance abuse problems. This project is being evaluated, and some results should soon be available.

Two case studies presented here were treated using CBT, and are also interesting in that they presented only one psychotic symptom—paranoia—representing paranoid thinking in the absence of a diagnosis of psychosis. Paranoid ideation is most commonly associated with diagnoses of psychotic disorders, e.g. paranoid schizophrenia. Indeed, it is considered one of the primary first rank symptoms of such disorders in both DSM-IV (APA, 1993) and ICD-10 (WHO, 1990) classificatory systems. However, there is a body of empirical research that places paranoia on a continuum with non-clinical populations (Fenigstein, 1996, 1997) In addition, another position evidenced by empirical research indicates that it is useful to consider psychotic symptoms of paranoia, voices and delusional beliefs individually, rather than purely as indicators of an overarching syndrome (e.g. Bentall, 1990; Chadwick & Trower, 1996).

A Case Study Guide to Cognitive Behaviour Therapy of Psychosis. Edited by
David Kingdon and Douglas Turkington. © 2002 John Wiley & Sons, Ltd.

Paranoia and delusions: Process and product

Thinking psychologically about psychotic symptoms, a useful distinction can be made between paranoid thinking (characterised by particular cognitive distortions) and delusional ideation. The former can be considered to be a perceptual process, involving attending to stimuli salient to the individual because they are threatening. Delusions are considered as the explanatory hypotheses developed by the individual to account for the strange perceptions. This conceptualisation is a development of that proposed by Maher (1988), and stresses the evolutionary use of cognitive distortions such as selective abstraction that are associated with paranoia (see Gilbert, 1998). Paranoia is therefore the cognitive process of continued attention to threatening stimuli, and delusional beliefs are the product of this continued attention. Both cases were treated according to this simple model describing the relationship between paranoia and delusions. The treatment that follows is therefore cognitive behavioural.

Both of the people presented hear received diagnoses associated with paranoia and delusions. However, paranoid thinking was the only *clear* symptom of psychosis manifested, as it is arguable whether their beliefs were delusional. The beliefs formed to account for the paranoid perceptions—although involving some degree of malevolence—were not inconsistent with cultural possibilities, i.e. they were conceivable. They both illustrate the usefulness of the distinction outlined above, in terms of the conceptualisation of the perceptual abnormalities, the maintaining factors in terms of selective abstraction, and the explanations developed to account for the perceptions. In addition, core or schematic beliefs were implicated in both formulations in terms of the aetiology of the perceptions.

There are, therefore, several interesting conceptual points highlighted by these two cases. The first is, as discussed, the presence of paranoia (in terms of cognitive processes) in the absence of other first-rank symptoms of psychosis. The second, related, point illustrates the difficulties in defining "delusional" beliefs. As will be seen, the beliefs formed by the two individuals not only made sense in terms of their particular set of life experiences, but they were plausible inferences. This reflects an emerging literature challenging a discontinuity between "normal" and "delusional" beliefs. This is along two dimensions: that investigating delusional thinking in the normal population (Peters, Joseph & Garety, 1999; Verdoux et al., 1998) and the criticism of the construct of delusional thinking in psychotic populations (Peralta & Cuesta, 1998). The third point concerns treatment. Both cases illustrated the importance of "metacognition", i.e. the ability to reflect on what one is thinking, and this will be discussed in more detail with respect to the cases themselves.

Both cases have been anonymised in terms of their names and details.

MARY

Mary was a 62-year-old lady, married to her second husband. She was referred by her consultant psychiatrist because she believed that her husband was being unfaithful to her, and that he was at some point going to throw her out of the house. This was causing her a great deal of anxiety, and putting a strain on their relationship, as she sometimes became angry and abusive towards him. Although these beliefs could have been well founded, the psychiatrist and community nurses believed that this was not the case, having interviewed both Mary and her husband.

There was some query over her memory, and the question of early onset dementia had been raised. There was, however, no evidence of this other than the husband's perception that Mary was becoming slightly more forgetful.

Her treatment at the time of assessment consisted of Sulpiride, designed to reduce her levels of anxiety and paranoia. She was receiving regular out-patient appointments with a consultant psychiatrist in addition to weekly support from community psychiatric nurses (CPNs).

Initial assessment

The first three sessions were spent gathering information about Mary's perception about her situation and her husband's perspective. The first two sessions were spent with Mary alone; the third was a joint session with her husband. Mary presented as a smartly dressed older woman, with a pleasant, calm manner. She was well spoken and quite articulate. She had a firm view of the problems that she faced, and described them with no apparent affect.

Background and history

Mary had had a difficult childhood. She was chronically neglected by her parents, her father having been alcoholic and her mother "cold". Her mother apparently had an affair when she was young, and Mary described having been sent to live with her aunts before she was 8 years old. They apparently did not want her, and sent her back to her mother. She then described having taken on many of the household chores throughout her childhood. When her parents separated at around this time, she and her mother spent much of their time moving from place to place looking for work and lodgings. As a result, Mary grew up fearing insecurity and vulnerability.

Mary left home at the age of 17 to get married to her first husband. While they were married he had a number of affairs, he physically and emotionally abused her, and was financially irresponsible, again making her feel vulnerable and insecure. He developed a depressive illness towards the end of their marriage, necessitating some time in a psychiatric hospital. She separated from her first husband when she was 48, and met her second five years later. She described this man as rather controlling at times, but extremely caring and loving.

Development of the problem

Mary's difficulties appeared to have started about a year before her presentation to the services. She initially painted a rather confused picture, involving her husband and his daughter. She had at some time believed that her husband was going to evict her from the house that they shared, which he had bought. She no longer believed this so strongly, but was convinced that the daughter would throw her out of the house if her father died. This, she reported, was because the daughter was resentful of Mary replacing the daughter's own mother who had passed away. Mary had a number of overheard and third party conversations that seemed to back this up, involving comments made by the daughter and some confusion about whether her name was on the deeds of the house. The husband reported that this had been dealt with by a solicitor in the presence of Mary, and that there was no impropriety or confusion. He appeared to have gone to some lengths to make Mary feel secure within their marriage, but was becoming worn out with his efforts and Mary's apparent refusal to believe what he said. Alone, Mary also reported that she believed that her husband was having an affair. Particularly anxiety provoking were her reports of mobile phone calls that went dead when she answered them, and money disappearing out of her purse inexplicably. This, she assumed, was her husband taking money to spend on his mistress.

The Sulpiride somewhat reduced the general affect associated with her beliefs, although they still peaked occasionally, resulting in distressing rows between Mary and her husband. Her conviction in the beliefs, however, was not affected by the medication, and remained high at around 80–90%.

Formulation

When initially formulating this case, it was important to hold open the possibility that many of Mary's fears concerning her husband could actually be true. Indeed, there was a variation in opinion on behalf of the mental health professionals involved over time as to whether the beliefs could be true or not. Certainly Mary's husband did have a slightly confrontational style, and was described as controlling by Mary and health professionals alike. However, it became increasingly apparent, particularly during the joint assessment sessions, that Mary's husband had made strenuous efforts to allay her fears, and appeared to be extremely supportive.

In terms of predisposing factors, Mary's early experience of vulnerability and not having a safe, stable home was implicated. Mary's worst image of herself was as a homeless "bag lady", wandering the streets. It is theorised that this vulnerability was encoded at a significant stage in her life, and formed part of her core beliefs about herself and the world. Thus most of her life was spent trying to avoid the confirmation of such beliefs.

In terms of onset, a set of circumstances prevailed setting the conditions for her having to face these fears. When faced with perceptions of the possibility that this prediction may come true, she became extremely anxious and hypervigilant for confirmatory evidence. This also served as a maintaining factor, in that Mary only attended to information that confirmed her beliefs, discounting evidence that may have been disconfirmatory (the process of selective abstraction). There were a number of stimuli that did not fit Mary's expectations (and therefore necessitated explanation), i.e. strange telephone calls and money disappearing from her purse. It is possibly these "abnormal perceptual phenomena" on which Mary fixed, forming her "delusional" inferences of infidelity around them.

An initially unanswered question in this case was that concerning Mary's cognitive state. The issue of early onset dementia was raised by the Community Mental Health Nurses, although the only evidence cited appeared to be occasional lapses in memory. This memory loss could, of course, have contributed to the information available to her when forming explanatory hypotheses around the abnormal perceptual phenomena. She may have been more likely to remember affectively charged events than those that did not raise affect, i.e. those events that confirmed her fears.

Action plan

1. Enable her to consider her experiences in terms of *beliefs*, rather than facts.
2. Validate the affect around her beliefs and how she came to these beliefs in terms of her early experience.
3. Make the link between her perceptions, her beliefs and her affect explicit (within the ABC framework). Formulate the role of core (schematic) beliefs and maintaining factors diagrammatically.
4. Treat these beliefs as hypotheses and draw up alternative hypotheses to explain her perceptions.
5. Seek evidence to confirm or disconfirm these hypotheses (behavioural experiments).

Intervention

The first step in the intervention was particularly tricky with Mary, as it was important not to invalidate her fears about her husband's infidelity. Two techniques were particularly important here. The first was to validate her affect, i.e. to express an understanding of the emotions surrounding the events. The second was to implicitly link that to her previous experience.

T: So what seems to be happening now?

M: Well, George's daughter obviously wants the house to herself. That's why she said that. She can get all the money then, leaving me with nothing.

T: How did you feel when you heard that?

M: Sick. Really bad. Worried. And angry.

T: I can understand that. It must have been made even worse given your experiences with your mum—is that right?

M: Yes. That was a frightening time. Not knowing where we were going to end up that night.

M: George keeps stealing money from my purse. I don't know why he's doing it. He only needs to ask and I'd give it to him. I don't understand why he needs to steal.

T: Any ideas as to what's going on there?

M: It must be because he's spending it on some other woman.

T: What does George say about this?

M: Oh, he denies it, of course.

T: Right. So money seems to be disappearing from your purse, and you believe that George is taking it?

M: Yes.

T: And your explanation for that is that he must be spending it on another woman, otherwise he'd tell you. Is that right?

M: Yes.

T: Does this situation remind you of any of your early experiences?

M: Oh yes. We were always running short of money when I was a child. And my first husband was always having affairs. We never had any money then, either.

T: Do you remember any feelings of insecurity around those times?

M: Of course!

T: So is it possible that your memories of those experiences have stayed with you, and that as a result you may pay particular attention to things that are happening now that look the same?

M: Maybe. I hadn't really thought about it like that.

Here a link is being made between Mary's current experience and her schematic beliefs. This serves the dual purpose of providing a rationale for what she believes, and also why she believes it, relieving her of possible stigma around her beliefs. The subtext is that it is entirely understandable how Mary has come to believe what she has, and it does not necessarily mean that she is "mad".

Psychometric testing

In order to test the hypothesis that Mary's cognitive state may have deteriorated and that paranoia may be associated with this (Ballard et al., 1991), the CAMDEX test (Roth et al., 1986) was used. This part of the intervention/assessment was designed to rule out global dementia, and also to test for specific cognitive strengths and weaknesses. It had the advantage of having specific short- and long-term memory subscales. The test results revealed no indication of global cognitive underperformance that may have been indicative of deterioration. However, her short-term memory was below the normal range, backing up anecdotal evidence that she sometimes forgot events that had happened recently.

This test was explained to Mary in terms of needing to test cognitive functions such as memory. The results were shared with Mary in the session following that of the test.

Hypothesis generation

It was important to concentrate on one very tangible idea in the first instance, rather than try to address all of the ideas and inferences drawn by Mary. Therefore, when drawing up alternative hypotheses, we dealt with the issue of the disappearing money. It was intended at this stage that any doubt raised in her mind might then be exploited to generate other hypotheses for other anxiety-provoking beliefs.

As a result of the results of the psychometric test a new hypothesis to explain Mary's perceptions was developed. We raised the possibility that she had spent the money in her purse and had then forgotten about it. Mary was obviously initially sceptical, but agreed to hold it as a "working hypothesis". This was aided by formulating the two inferences within the ABC framework:

A	B	C
Money disappears from purse.	Husband must be stealing it. Forgot I spent it.	Worry, anxiety, fear, vulnerability. No problem.

Evidence gathering

It was important for Mary to convince herself that this second hypothesis could be valid. We therefore set a homework task to monitor any events that she forgot about, enlisting the help of her husband with this. This was set up as a genuine enquiry, with one possible outcome that she remembered everything.

After the second week of gathering evidence, Mary came back to therapy with an interesting finding. She described how in the previous week she had gone to pay a bill using her cheque book. However, when she came to write the cheque, she found that she had already paid the bill as the cheque stub was already completed in her hand, although she had no recollection of this. This incident opened up a discussion about what other things Mary could have forgotten, and the explanations that she developed to account for this. This, in turn, precipitated a shift in Mary's thinking over the subsequent two or three sessions, in which she reinterpreted many of her previous experiences in the light of the new information. Her affect associated with these beliefs fell as her conviction in the alternative beliefs rose. The other beliefs associated with her safety and vulnerability also disappeared at this time. This evidence, together with the findings of the cognitive tests was enough to convince Mary that many, if not all of her beliefs about her husband's infidelity, were unfounded, which relieved her greatly.

Outcome

Two forms of measure were used to assess the outcome of this case: normative and idiosyncratic. The normative measure used was the Hospital Anxiety and Depression Scale (Zigmond & Snaith, 1983). Before and after results from these measures indicated that anxiety had reduced from 10 to 0, and depression from 6 to 0. Her conviction associated with her belief that her husband was being unfaithful fell from 80% early in the intervention to 0 afterwards, and her perception of associated anxiety fell from 80% to 20%.

KAREN

Karen was referred by her consultant psychiatrist because of paranoia and ideas of reference which he thought were mildly or bordering on psychotic. She was reluctant to take antipsychotic medication, and was thought by her psychiatrist to be able to make use of a CBT approach.

Initial assessment

Karen presented as an extremely articulate and well-dressed lady in her late forties. She did not appear at all anxious about the assessment procedure, and was keen to explore a psychological approach.

Background and history

Karen had a relatively stable upbringing as a child and adolescent. She was well educated, with MA degrees in theology and education. She described having been driven to complete these degrees in order to address feminist issues. She was also artistic and imaginative, with an appreciation for literature and art. Karen described herself as an independent, strong woman, but also very caring. These attributes she traced to her mother.

At the time of therapy, she was separated, but not divorced from her husband. She described her current relationship with him as amicable and supportive. Karen also had one daughter, who was about to leave to go to university.

Development of the problem

There were a number of critical times and incidents implicated in Karen's difficulties. Firstly, her husband had emotionally abandoned her when she was pregnant with her daughter, which precipitated their separation. She thought that he was probably depressed at the time. More importantly to Karen, in 1987 she had had an operation in which the anaesthetic had not been properly administered. This had resulted in a terrifying, painful experience of being paralysed, but fully conscious and aware of pain at the time of the operation. The hospital concerned had never admitted responsibility or apologised, which Karen felt deeply bitter about.

Lastly, and most salient, Karen had experienced an episode of actual persecution, related to her having reported an employer to the police for suspected abuse. Shortly after this, her car was attacked by a man known to associate with her ex-employer. The man was also seen lurking around her new place of work a few weeks later. Interestingly, this piece of information did not come to light until several weeks after the assessment period, until we had started to talk about beliefs around persecution. This incident was around the same time as the anaesthetic accident.

Karen traced the beginning of her fears back to a year or so after the difficult time around 1987. She first started to notice and feel anxious about "rough-looking" men, cues being tattoos, earrings and shaven heads. She also began to notice foreign-looking people, particularly Chinese. The anxiety associated with these stimuli was severe enough for her to avoid crowded or busy places altogether, and much of her time was spent thinking about issues such as personal safety, drug rings and organised crime. These thoughts caused her a great deal of anxiety, and affected her social functioning.

Formulation

We formulated Karen's difficulties within a cognitive-behavioural framework, again focusing on the understandable conclusions to which she had arrived, given the experiences that she had suffered. We diagrammatically identified the important factors in the generation of persecutory ideas. These were: (1) her imaginative and creative disposition, which contributed to her inclination to create scenarios in her mind from the most skeletal of stimuli; (2) her experience of the anaesthetic accident, which, as well as being extremely traumatic, confounded her core beliefs of herself as strong, independent and not at all vulnerable; and (3) her experience of having actually been persecuted by an "unknown" agent, ensuring that she became vigilant for other possible sources of threat.

Her experiences of actual threat set Karen on a "conclusion-driven search"; i.e. she selectively abstracted stimuli that appealed to her sense of threat.

The most salient stimuli for Karen were people who appeared "different", i.e. those who were not Caucasian. There were, of course, many people from ethnic minorities in her hometown, but Karen fixed on those from Chinese origin, having read a report about a Chinese organised crime syndicate, the Triads. It seemed to Karen that there were increasing numbers of people of this sort, and that at times they followed her, or signalled to each other that she should be followed or harmed. Her resulting avoidance of these situations ensured that these beliefs were never disconfirmed. She also had many stimuli about which she could form these ideas. The beliefs that she formed, identified within an ABC framework, were as follows:

"They're going to harm someone."
"They are part of an underworld subculture."

These beliefs were anxiety-provoking in themselves, but by using downward chaining (i.e. asking what a particular belief means), Karen identified further beliefs and evaluations that caused her feelings of helplessness. These were:

"Education must be lacking."
"As an educationalist, I should be able to do something about it."
"I can't."

This process of identifying thoughts is represented in Table 10.1.

Therefore, not only were the perceptions anxiety-provoking, but the underlying interpersonal negative evaluations (identified using downward chaining) resulted in a feeling of hopelessness. In terms of a maintaining factor, she appeared extremely conscious of her surroundings, and noticed

Table 10.1   Thought identification process

Antecedent event	Belief		Consequence
See Chinese person	Inferences	They're different	Anxiety, hopelessness
		They're going to harm someone	
		They are part of a subculture	
		Education must be lacking	
		I should be able to do something about it	
		I can't	
	Evaluation	I must be inadequate	

the slightest strange or bizarre behaviours, which are of course not uncommon in a large city centre.

Action plan

1. Conceptualise relationship between thoughts, feelings and behaviour within an ABC model (Chadwick, Birchwood & Trower, 1996), paying particular attention to considering thoughts as beliefs rather than facts.
2. Normalise her experience of paranoia in terms of her previous experience, thereby reducing affect surrounding this experience.
3. Formulate the role of core (schematic) beliefs and maintaining factors diagrammatically.
4. Treat these beliefs as hypotheses and draw up alternative hypotheses to explain her perceptions.
5. Seek evidence to confirm or disconfirm these hypotheses (behavioural experiments).

Intervention

The first part of the intervention focused on this formulation and psycho-educational aspects of paranoia. We discussed the functional nature of continued attention to threat and how, for humans in unpredictable situations, it was necessary for survival. This, together with the idea that given her experiences it was understandable that she was hypervigilant for threat, relieved Karen greatly. She revealed that she had been told by a psychiatrist that she "*was* paranoid", which worried and angered her. She equated this with a psychotic diagnosis, increasing her anxiety about her state, and angering her because she was at that time convinced of her beliefs. The idea that paranoia was in some senses adaptive, and on a continuum, reduced her anxieties about treatment. Karen easily understood the model, and readily worked with it in specific situations. However, she initially did not generalise this new understanding to all situations, and those beliefs around threatening stimuli remained fixed. In addition to the psycho-educational aspects of the intervention, Karen was asked to start to capture the data each time she experienced feelings of anxiety in the vicinity of strangers, and to catch the thoughts that preceded these feelings.

It was extremely important for Karen to be able to generate alternative explanations for her beliefs, and account for her apparently strange perceptions. To this end, specific examples of disturbing experiences were generated, and her beliefs about what she thought was going on were

Table 10.2

Antecedent event	Belief		Consequence
See man across street looking at her	Inferences:	1. They're doing it deliberately to ruffle me (80%) 2. It's a coincidence (50%)	Anxiety, anger

made explicit. In addition, her conviction was rated 0 to 100%. She was then asked to generate alternative explanations, and again rate the conviction. An example of this, using the ABC framework, is represented in Table 10.2.

She was then asked to consider the evidence for each belief, which of course was difficult for her as there was no concrete evidential base. This search for "evidence" raised doubt in her mind, and indeed she found the statement 'What's the evidence?' extremely useful when considering her thoughts. Each new threatening experience was framed according to this model, until she was able to do it herself.

As homework she used the ABC framework to describe other thoughts and evidence, and by the eighth treatment session, was starting to formulate her continued attention to strange men as a downward spiral. Thus her metacognition was developing, and she was starting to be able to describe *how* she was thinking. After this, Karen seemed to make a sudden shift in her thinking, and was more able and willing to challenge her anxiety-provoking beliefs about being watched. This also generalised to other beliefs about difficult incidents around her home, such as a car being abandoned outside her house.

Lastly, she was able to reformulate her anxieties in terms of her previous experiences (i.e. the anaesthetic accident, her previous employer), and fully understand the impact of those experiences. It seemed that only after she had started to convince herself that her beliefs were just that, i.e. beliefs, could she re-examine her experiences this new light. Before this happened, the formulation, although collaboratively generated, remained rather abstract.

We tackled Karen's reduced social functioning by using the problem-solving method to identify activities that she would enjoy and would not be too onerous or difficult to begin. She highlighted rambling as an interest in which she used to participate, and that would be easy to restart. The first step was to use the Internet to find local rambling clubs. We acknowledged that this could be an avoidant strategy, in that she was staying away from crowded situations that provided stimuli for her particular beliefs. Therefore, we set tasks that would necessitate her going to the "worst" place for stimuli of that type, which was the local shopping centre. This exposure programme was done in stages.

Outcome

Karen made extremely good progress, to the extent that her reported anxiety reduced significantly, and her social functioning increased to her premorbid levels. Her conviction in the beliefs that there were people following her fell from 80% to 0. She reported that she very much liked the cognitive model, and expressed an interest on working further, particularly around the traumatic experiences surrounding her anaesthetic accident. She wanted to work on this with a private therapist outside of her hometown, so we used the listing of accredited therapists to highlight some possibilities.

SUMMARY

These two cases represent the cognitive behavioural treatment of paranoid thinking in the absence of any other psychotic symptoms. They illustrate the usefulness of the conceptualisation of paranoia as a cognitive process characterised by continued attention to threatening stimuli and selective abstraction, which may or may not result in the formation of delusional beliefs. Both cases also provide some evidence for the consideration of delusional beliefs as continuous with "normal" ones (Peters, Joseph & Garety, 1999) and the usefulness of separating the process of paranoid cognitive processes from the resultant beliefs.

Chapter 11

MANAGING EXPECTATIONS

Case 12 (Jane): *Jeremy Pelton*

The following case involved work with both Jane, a patient with a 16-year history of mental health problems, and her parents. I met her while I was training in CBT for psychosis. I had first entered the mental health arena as a nursing assistant in 1980. This was a summer job to see me over my university years. After finishing university and not being able to find another job I continued on as a nursing assistant for nearly two years until my then nursing officer gave me a prod in the direction of my RMN training. I trained at Cherry Knowle Hospital in Sunderland, qualifying in 1986. For the first three years I worked in acute admissions and day hospital, working mainly with anxiety and depression. In 1990 I then moved into the community as a CPN and worked within a rehabilitation team, with a caseload of patients with schizophrenia who had been discharged into the community. It was during this time that I developed an interest in PSI and CBT, completing a PSI course in Sheffield and Hazel Nelson's CBT course in London. I then went on to formalise my CBT training at Manchester University with Gillian Haddock, Christine Barrowclough and Nick Tarrier. I developed an interest in early interventions in psychosis and enjoyed working within a CBT framework with patients and their families.

In 1999 I became involved in the Insight into Schizophrenia study as a research therapist where I received training and clinical supervision as part of that project. I am currently a nurse manager setting up new sites for the Insight project, doing reviews of established sites, supervising, training and organising accreditation.

JANE

Jane is a 30-year-old woman currently on a depot injection, a mood stabiliser, an antidepressant, oral neuroleptics as required, and anticholinergic medication prescribed by the consultant psychiatrist. Prior to her last

A Case Study Guide to Cognitive Behaviour Therapy of Psychosis. **Edited by**
David Kingdon and Douglas Turkington. © 2002 John Wiley & Sons, Ltd.

admission Jane had been maintained in the community by her parents and the consultant psychiatrist, and there had been brief interventions by both social workers and community psychiatric nurses. Following her last admission after a particularly severe relapse it was decided to refer Jane to the Enduring Mental Health Service. She has been with this service for two and a half years and it has always been an objective of her care plan to introduce her to CBT as both her consultant and her community psychiatric nurse considered it would be beneficial.

Presenting problems

Jane was in hospital from July 1994 to September 1995, which was the last in a number of relapses (see personal history) that ended in a lengthy hospital stay. On admission Jane had been very paranoid generally to young children and football supporters and specifically to her parents. On discharge Jane was referred to the community psychiatric nurse (CPN) department, and was allocated to a keyworker. Although it was felt that Jane's improvement was being maintained by the medication, it was felt that there was still an amount of distress in her life and that her social functioning was suffering as a result. Jane presented with both delusional and hallucinatory symptoms, and at an outpatients review cognitive approaches were considered to help to alleviate the distress and modify the symptoms. In January Jane commenced cognitive-behaviour therapy and the process and the format were negotiated with her. Jane was very keen to try this new approach and a consent form was signed covering taping, confidentiality and supervision.

Psychometric assessment

Three psychometric tools were used to assess Jane. Firstly, the modified KGV Scale (Krawiecka, Goldberg & Vaughan, 1977) highlighted the severity of any psychological phenomena present. This is a 14-point assessment tool, six areas being elicited by questioning and eight by observation. Secondly, the Social Functioning Scale (SFS: Birchwood et al., 1990) examined Jane's social capability and highlighted any areas of concern. Finally, the Liverpool University Neuroleptic Side Effect Rating Scale (LUNSERS; Day et al., 1995) is a self-report scale for side effects of neuroleptic medication.

KGV Scale

Jane scored highly in four sections: depression, anxiety, hallucinations and delusions (Table 11.1). During the assessment interview it became clear

Table 11.1   KGV results

	Session 1	Session 15
Anxiety	4	2
Depressed mood	3	2
Suicidality	1	0
Elevated mood	1	0
Hallucinations	3	1
Delusions	4	2
Flattened affect	1	0
Incongruous affect	0	0
Overactivity	0	0
Psychomotor retardation	0	0
Incoherence and irrelevance	0	0
Poverty of speech	1	0
Abnormal movements	0	0
Cooperation	1	0
Total	**19**	**7**

that her affective symptoms were secondary to her delusions and hallucinations, which were initiated and exacerbated by stress. Her hallucinations were reported to be only evident on a minority of days in the month and usually followed a degree of sleep deprivation. The suicidal ideation although episodically present was assessed as a minor risk as Jane confirmed neither an intent nor a plan. Her short periods of elation appeared to be related to her schizo-affective disorder and again seemed to be linked to environmental stress.

Social Functioning Scale

Jane lived in a group home and scored highly in the Social Withdrawal section but also in the Relationships section as she had a tight circle of friends within the home. She had a number of social activities available but due to her negative symptoms and the anxiety caused by her delusions she was unable to access them without being accompanied by a care worker and being motivated to do so. She was capable of being independent but lacked the confidence to function at her optimum ability due to her low self-esteem. Jane has never worked as she has been in the mental health services since she left school.

LUNSERS

Jane scored very highly on this Side Effect Rating Scale. However, on examination some of the side effects could be attributed to her thyroid disorder and the medication being administered to correct it. Other side effects were synonymous with anxiety and depression and they would be observed to see if they lessened as her symptoms were alleviated. It was also observed that she wasn't taking her anticholinergic medication as prescribed, and once she increased her compliance this score decreased. Finally, there were a number of side effects that she took for granted and was prepared to put up with in contrast to her psychotic symptoms.

Personal history

Jane is the younger of two daughters. Her father was a successful business-man in shipbuilding, and although now semi-retired travels the country attending meetings and problem-solving. Her mother never worked. Jane's sister was always a high achiever and Jane often felt she was struggling to keep up with her family's expectations. Jane described a fairly happy childhood until her teenage years. Her parents were both very caring and she felt she had a good relationship with them. She was never very happy at school and missed a lot of primary school through sickness, tonsillitis and recurring chest infections. She always had friends at school and until the age of 15 was often the centre of attention and seen as the organiser.

Jane viewed her mid-teens as a time of change. Within a short period of time she went from being "one of the gang" to being cast as an outsider. It is uncertain what triggered this and how much of it was down to mis-interpretation by Jane. She tried desperately to be liked even to a point of ridiculing herself. A number of conditional and unconditional assump-tions were activated at this period of her life.

Jane's first admission to a psychiatric hospital came in 1984 at just 17 years old. At first her problems were mainly psychosomatic and Jane was seen to be hypochondriacal. She often complained of pains in her chest and thought she was going to die. She became very withdrawn and lost contact with her school friends. Eventually she had to leave school after a series of panic attacks and was referred to the psychiatric services for assessment and treatment. It was only prior to her first admission that Jane exhibited psychotic symptoms when she became very paranoid and thought that her parents were trying to poison her. She consequently stopped eating and on admission to hospital was tube and drip fed.

She was diagnosed as having schizophrenia at 18 and this was eventually modified to schizo-affective later in her illness. She spent most of 1985–89 in and out of hospital before having her longest period of remission to date. During this time out of hospital she lost the weight that she had gained while she was ill and became quite successful at golf, winning trophies and local championships. Her last admission was in 1994.

Since her discharge in 1995 Jane's biggest achievement was to leave home and to move into a group home. She was spending four nights at the group home with the residents, then returned home for the other three to spend time with her family. She was reluctant to cut all ties with her parental home as she still regarded this as a place of safety. There was, however, a problem at the group home: one resident was quite dominant and Jane viewed this as being reminiscent of childhood.

Jane tended to take change very slowly and was wary of too many new challenges, as this has often been a trigger for past relapses. It was sometimes hard to distinguish between her negative symptoms and her avoidance due to anxiety.

Jane still had personality traits of hypochondriasis and was hypervigilant to both somatic and psychological symptoms, often catastrophising and fearing the worst. She was recently diagnosed as having thyroid problems, which accounted for some of her biological and psychological symptoms. Jane's cognitive formulation is presented in Figure 11.1.

Current thinking, affect and behaviour

Cognitions

Jane often complained of the following thoughts:

- There's something wrong with me, I'm a "weirdo"
- People are after me
- People look and laugh at me
- Something's going to happen to me
- Nobody likes me
- I am going to die
- I am going to relapse.

Affect

Jane often complained of both depression and anxiety, and at times talked about being "afraid for her life". She also described being "emotionless" and unable to cry.

Behaviour

As a consequence of Jane's thoughts and feeling she often withdrew and avoided situations which fuelled her anxiety. At home she would close the blinds and stay away from the windows to avoid anyone seeing her. Her drinking had increased as a coping mechanism and she complained of

Early experiences
- Over-achieving brother—
  Five years older
  (now living in America)
- Strict father; Jane remembers
  resenting him
- Missed a lot of school due to
  physical illness
- 13 years old: name calling
  (content unknown) and
  bullying
- 16 years old: trip to London
  (drink spiked)
- 17 years old: possible abuse

**Dysfunctional assumptions
and delusions**
- I have to please people or I will
  get hurt
- If things go wrong it's my fault
- If I don't meet other people's
  standards I am a failure

Critical incidents
- Thyroid problems
- Leaving home: Group home
- Father-like figure at sheltered
  accommodation

Negative automatic thoughts
- There's something wrong with
  me: "weirdo"
- People are after me
- People look and laugh at me
- Something's going to happen
  to me
- Nobody likes me
- "I am going to die"
- "I am going to relapse"

Behaviour
- Withdrawal
- Avoidance
- Closes blinds/stays away from
  windows
- ↑Drinking
- ↑Lethargy
- ↓Motivation

Emotion
- Depression
- Anxiety
- "Emotionless"
- Frightened

Physiological
- ↓Sleep
- ↑Appetite
- Anxiety type symptoms

Figure 11.1 Cognitive formulation.

lethargy and a general lack of motivation. Her parents always highlighted
this as her main problem.

Themes

While completing the above assessments and the cognitive formulation a
number of themes became evident:

- Resentment—initially success of sister and firmness of father, and then
  being "under control" of father-like figure in group home.
- Rejection—by father and friends at time of need.
- Acceptance—the need to be accepted by the above.

- Failure—to meet her own and her families expectations.
- Blame—blaming herself for events prior to her first episode of psychosis.
- Responsibility—for the events prior to his first episode of psychosis.

Dysfunctional assumptions

Jane's dysfunctional assumptions all stemmed from the themes above with a strong emphasis on responsibility, failure and blame. This has been hypothesised to stem from her early childhood experiences with both her family and her school friends.

Problem list

During the assessment Jane highlighted the following problem list in descending priority:

- Feeling frightened and stressed
- Poor sleep pattern
- Inability to sit in parents' sitting room with blinds open
- Unable to lead "normal" life—e.g. going to town centre, shopping, etc.
- Worry of further relapse.

Aims and course of therapy

The aims of therapy were as follows:

- To establish a good rapport conducive to working collaboratively.
- To introduce a cognitive therapy model.
- To introduce a stress-vulnerability model and relate to Jane's symptoms.
- To introduce a normalising rationale.
- To teach Jane cognitive behaviour techniques to help to alleviate her high level of anxiety and build her confidence thereby increasing her quality of life.
- To reach a mutual understanding regarding the influence of events during her childhood upon her beliefs about herself and the world (conditional and unconditional schema).
- To use Socratic questioning to challenge and explore areas peripheral to her delusions.
- To look at evidence to support her delusions and then identify and test out alternative explanations.
- To use cognitive techniques to treat symptoms of depression which are predicted to arise as the delusional belief falters.
- To introduce relapse prevention and promote a blueprint for future use.

Course of treatment

At the time of writing Jane has been seen on 15 occasions, of which three were for assessment. Jane was seen on a weekly basis with sessions usually lasting between 45 to 60 minutes.

From the start of therapy it was essential to ensure that a good rapport was established. This is seen as of paramount importance when using cognitive behaviour therapy with this client group (Fowler, Garety & Kuipers, 1995). It was also vital to ensure that the therapy style was neither confrontational nor totally compliant with Jane's view of the world (Kingdon & Turkington, 1994).

The fact that Jane had been known prior to the commencement of this therapy was an advantage in establishing the therapeutic relationship. It was, however, initially awkward at times when setting the new parameters of the relationship and the structure of the sessions. This was completely new to Jane and she tested these parameters throughout the initial settings. Therapeutically the structure and the nature of the cognitive behaviour techniques allowed Jane to open up and disclose, and probably more was learned about her in the three assessment sessions than in the previous two and a half years.

Jane had a good deal of insight into her symptoms and freely discussed her previous psychotic episodes. She felt that she could recognise her early warning signs, but if they were not caught quickly relapse was fast and insight soon went.

In the early sessions Jane was introduced to the stress-vulnerability model (Zubin & Spring, 1977). It was explained that certain individuals were more vulnerable to stress than others, and that this determined their stress threshold. Once this threshold is breached the person is more susceptible to her symptoms and possible relapse. This was put across using the analogy of a bucket being filled with water and overflowing, with the water representing stressors and the bucket representing an individual's capacity to contain the stress (each person having a different sized bucket). Jane was able to identify a number of stressful life events or stressors that could have contributed to her "illness". As homework for that session she agreed to create a life chart highlighting the stressful events mentioned above, putting them in chronological order and hopefully adding others.

The result of this homework was a very revealing life map which covered Jane's childhood, her period prior to her "breakdown" and a psychiatric history to the present day. With Socratic questioning Jane disclosed three events that she had never talked about before. Firstly, a period of name-calling at school that originated from a cartoon character; secondly, a weekend in London when she had her drink spiked; and, finally, when a care worker had made sexual suggestions and advances to her. Jane understandably found this very difficult to talk about, but following the session she expressed relief at having aired them. She curiously rated the name-calling as the most stressful and upsetting, and it was assumed that this somehow linked into her schema and had exacerbated her symptoms. Unfortunately after discussing this event over a few sessions Jane requested that we leave it to a future session, but to date the discussion has not been resumed (see Further treatment below).

This seemed to be a suitable point at which to introduce Jane to Beck's four-factor cognitive model (Beck et al., 1979) and to use some examples from her assessment and homework to personalise the model to her. Jane soon became socialised to the model and was able to distinguish between thoughts and feelings and how they may affect her behaviour. She spent two weeks completing a modified daily record of dysfunctional thoughts and the homework was used to generate themes for the following session.

Beck (1967) wrote about the importance of having an explanation of the symptoms of anxiety and depression, and described this as fundamental to the application of cognitive therapy in these conditions. Kingdon and Turkington (1991) reported the success of the same "normalising" strategies when working with schizophrenia. Nelson (1997) also reported on the importance of lessening the impact and distress of delusions and hallucinations prior to treatment. One of Jane's highlighted problems was her lack of sleep, and on assessment this could be linked to the above stress vulnerability and her psychotic symptoms, as illustrated in Figure 11.2.

Jane's increase in psychotic symptoms could then be normalised through discussion of the effects of sleep deprivation (Oswald, 1984) and this initially reduced the associated anxiety. The situations that caused the initial stress could then be explored using the cognitive model. Jane kept a diary of such situations and recorded the associated thoughts and feelings. During the following sessions various alternatives were generated and evidence for and against debated. At first Jane found it difficult to comprehend the alternatives without seeing them in black and white, so these were written on flash cards. Jane was encouraged to keep a daily diary so that if she could rationalise her anxieties if she had a bad night and hence promote a good night's sleep.

Jane was also encouraged to develop a list of her stressful events (see Table 11.2) prioritising them on levels of anxiety (marked out of ten). This

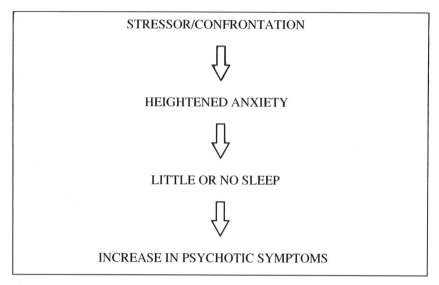

Figure 11.2   Stress-vulnerability diagram.

would enable her to visualise the problems and allow a care plan to be negotiated. One of Jane's strengths was her interest in, and ability to do, homework/tasks set in the sessions and it allowed her to report on events in detail.

The list in Table 11.2 was discussed and it was decided to work from the bottom up. Jane would use her keyworker from the group home, her community support worker and her family to help her to tackle the bottom four events. She would feed back to the therapy sessions, commenting on progress, thoughts and feelings associated with the situations and coping strategies used when confronting these anxieties.

Table 11.2   Prioritised list of stressful events

No.	Situation	Rating
1.	Sitting in parents' sitting room with blinds open	10/10
2.	Using public transport	8/10
3.	Being in a situation where there is a bad atmosphere	8/10
4.	Bad news, such as serious world events or tragedy	8/10
5.	Meeting people who are not known	7/10
6.	Going to the city centre	6/10
7.	Going among is a lot of people	6/10
8.	Going out of the front door	4/10

One of Jane's other highlighted problems was her constant fear of relapse. This was linked to constant hypervigilance on her part and being able to catastrophise on the first sign of any symptom. To help Jane with this fear, the session revisited the rationale of normalisation and educated Jane on the variable course of her "illness" and coping strategies to prevent catastrophisation. Jane's insight was highlighted as a positive attribute, and the importance of a relapse blueprint was stressed. This blueprint was designed collaboratively and included:

- early warning signs: Nelson (1997) discusses the importance of therapists encouraging the recognition and labelling of symptoms;
- associated coping strategies: Tarrier (1992) advocates the use of coping strategy enhancement, patients' own coping strategies were enhanced and used if appropriate, if none were present—or if those were present but not functional, new strategies would be taught;
- an action plan for Jane to implement: Birchwood, Todd and Jackson (1998) highlight the potential therapeutic value of self-monitoring by the patient and allowing him or her to facilitate control and prevention.

Jane also thought it would be a good idea to share this action plan with her parents and the staff of the group home. Once this network was in place Jane felt more comfortable with the possibility of relapse and, again, seeing the plan in black and white acted both as reassurance and as a prompt for necessary action.

One other area that was covered in therapy was that of her negative symptoms and her activity schedule. Jane was encouraged to report on her weekly tasks as homework, highlighting activities that she enjoyed and those that she found a chore. Gaps in the week were also emphasised and short- and long-term goals collaboratively drawn up. A realistic action plan was negotiated and a safety net of a back-up plan was put in place to lower Jane's anxieties. Jane incorporated her list of anxieties into her weekly programme hence providing a timetable for her carers to work with.

Difficulties encountered

There have been surprisingly few difficulties during therapy sessions. Initially it was felt that Jane was perhaps being too eager to please, and this might be clouding issues. However, once she settled into the sessions this soon resolved. One of the main problems had been an overbearing resident who appeared to be trying to sabotage any improvement in Jane. This was often an item that Jane placed on the agenda and will need addressing in the future when she is more confident and more efficient coping strategies are in place.

Outcome so far

As can seen in Table 11.1 in the psychometric assessment section, there has been a positive outcome so far. Jane's anxiety and depression have lowered considerably and this can most likely be linked to the reduction in her hallucinations and delusions. Her hallucinations are hardly evident at present and when they do occur the associated distress has reduced considerably. Her delusions are still evident but none of them is held with full conviction. Again the associated distress has lowered. Both Jane and her parents feel that she is better than she has been for a long time. She is functioning at a level where she reports doing things for the first time since she became "ill".

Further treatment

Future sessions will continue along current themes. Jane continues to work with her stressful events and confrontation and although finding it easier to apply the cognitive model she still requires time to deal with some of the more difficult issues. One area that appears to be dormant at present is the schema work surrounding her three early experiences. In particular, there is work to done with the name-calling and the cognitions and beliefs around that time. Jane continues to be aware that they are there, but as of yet is reluctant to accept them on the agenda.

Evaluation

After only 15 sessions Jane had shown considerable gains. Several factors seem to have influenced this result:

• Jane was able to accept the stress-vulnerability model, which was used to explain the exacerbation of her psychotic symptoms. In particular she was pleased to be able to normalise the way she had felt and that this had been recognised and appreciated.
• Jane accepted the rationale of cognitive behaviour therapy and has since been able to identify specific thoughts and associated emotions and put theory into practice.
• The collaborative nature of cognitive behaviour therapy was particularly useful to her. Having an opportunity to feedback on sessions allowed her to have some say in the structure and to flag up pertinent points to herself in the process. Jane felt that she benefited from the structure that the sessions provided and has indicated that she would like to continue with cognitive work in the future. She seemed to be able to pick up on the logical nature by which these theories were hypothesised and tested

out and was always keen to participate. Jane was an intelligent woman and it seems that since leaving school this was the first time that she had been "challenged".

- It has been difficult to assess the appropriate level to work at, at what stage, whether to work with negative automatic thoughts or to jump ahead and work with schema which appeared so central to the delusion. In contrast with anxiety and depression, which seemed to follow a natural progression, working with psychosis needed a more open approach and the therapist's plans can often go 'out the window' depending on the patient's priority.
- The enthusiasm which Jane exhibited greatly facilitated the therapy. The learning process was, however, on both sides and the therapeutic relationship was probably at its most effective.

WORK WITH JANE'S FAMILY

Jane's family consists of three focal people: father, mother and Jane. There is another sister but she has married and settled in America. Dad is a semi-retired shipbuilding consultant, mother is a housewife and Jane has a 14-year psychiatric career. Both parents are in their early sixties and Jane is 31.

Reason for referral

Jane's family was referred for intervention by their community psychiatric nurse because of a dilemma in Jane's ongoing rehabilitation programme. Jane had been out of hospital for two and a half years, and the last two years had been split between sheltered accommodation and her parents' home. Jane's parents had opposing views on the next step; father thought it should be independent living while mother worried about losing contact with her daughter.

Provisional hypothesis and rationale for procedures used

When the above case was discussed it was felt that Jane's family would be suitable for family work as there was a high degree of contact between the patient and her parents (>35 hours) and there appeared to be a certain amount of high expressed emotion. It was agreed that assessment should begin with a view to offering a number of family sessions on completion. Depending on the outcome of the assessment, differing amounts of education, stress management and goal-setting would be negotiated. The aim of the family work would be to lower any distress within the family, offer education to cover any deficits in knowledge and attitude towards schizophrenia and begin to lower contact between Jane and her parents (for further details, see Barrowclough & Tarrier, 1992: Falloon et al., 1993: Leff & Vaughn, 1985).

Assessment (formal and informal) and formulation

Jane and her parents were assessed formally using a number of psychometric tests (see Table 11.1) and informally through observation and interview. Four psychometric tools were used to assess Jane's parents: the Relative Assessment Interview (Barrowclough & Tarrier, 1992), the Knowledge About Schizophrenia Interview, the General Health Questionnaire (Goldberg & Williams, 1988) and the Family Questionnaire (Barrowclough & Tarrier, 1992).

Relative Assessment Interview

Following the assessment of both parents the information obtained was formulated into six areas (see Table 11.3). The RAI showed that there was high contact between Jane and her parents, in particular her mother. There was a certain amount of irritability in the family but this was usually between Jane and her father and was mainly centred around Jane not doing much. Her father would "nag" her into doing an activity and Jane would often become irritable after being coerced into something she didn't want to do. Her father's critical approach was in contrast to the emotional over-involvement of the mother who, on her admission, tends to "smother" Jane. It appears that quite a few of the family's problems surround this stress and conflict and their coping strategies.

Knowledge About Schizophrenia Interview

Both of Jane's parents scored highly on the above scale, and showed a good awareness of her diagnosis, her medication/side-effects, associated symptoms and prognosis. However, I felt that there was a certain lack of application of this knowledge and that although they understood about negative symptoms they still attributed Jane's lack of motivation and lethargy to laziness and personality (even though there was no evidence of these prior to her illness).

General Health Questionnaire

Jane had just recently had a minor relapse and although she was kept out of hospital it meant that she was with her parents for a longer period of time. This reflected in both of their GHQs as they both scored quite highly

Table 11.3   Summary of the parent's problems, needs and strengths
(as obtained from the interviews, GHQ and FQ Assessments)

Understanding the illness
- Good understanding of positive symptoms
- Good knowledge/understanding of medication
- Scored well on diagnosis and prognosis
- Showed a good understanding of Jane's negative symptoms (but ? application)

Distress and situations triggering distress
- Confrontation with Jane over laziness/sitting around doing nothing
- Jane turning up at parent's house unannounced after confrontation at group home
- Jane's restlessness while at parents
- Jane's attention-seeking behaviour
- ? Onset of relapse—hypervigilance and catastrophisation
- What's happening at group home?

Coping strategies
- Able to identify areas of concern and approach appropriate agencies for help
- Ability to talk over problems between themselves
- Both parents are active members of carers groups
- Regular contact with mental health services

Restrictions to lifestyles
- Haven't seen daughter in America since 1995. Poor access to grandchildren
- Unable to go on holiday either with Jane or without her
- Often stay in at night rather than go out if Jane is around
- Social life not as good as has it has been in the past
- Have moved house in the past due to Jane's beliefs
- Stopped going out with friends—"put all energies into Jane"

Dissatisfactions with Jane's behaviour
- Smoking—although Jane smokes in her room she leaves the door open
- Appearance—unwashed and hair unkempt
- Poor motivation and sitting around doing nothing
- Turning up at the house unannounced
- Pacing around the house/agitation
- Irritable—lack of sleep

Strengths
- Caring supportive family
- Always there when Jane needs them
- Good insight into mental illness—aware of who to contact when help is needed
- Interest in mental illness—involvement in voluntary agencies

and were shown to be more stressed than usual and unable to function at their optimum ability.

Family Questionnaire

A number of behaviours were highlighted in the FQ, though it was evident from the questionnaires that Jane's parents seemed to believe that they were coping with these. However, through interview it transpires that they have completely differing views on how these behaviours should be dealt with, and this can lead to conflict not only with Jane but also between themselves.

The formation of an appropriate family intervention treatment strategy

Following the above comprehensive assessment and the subsequent formulation, the family were invited to a feedback session to discuss the outcome of the session and the possibility of negotiating further sessions. Following discussion with both Jane and her parents it was decided that she would not be present at the initial sessions but would join the sessions at strategic points throughout the therapy. The family work would hence consist of patient-focused sessions, parent-focused sessions and feedback/planning sessions involving both parties.

Session 1: Feedback and future planning

The family were welcomed to the session and thanked for the time during the assessment. The co-therapist was introduced and his role, compared to the main therapists, was explained. The nature of the family work was reinforced by discussing the boundaries, expectations and goals of both the parents and the therapists:

• Lower stress/distress
• Create hope
• Non-confrontational approaches
• Enhance and modify coping strategies
• Patient-focused and parent-focused interventions.

Formal feedback and areas of concern from assessment were discussed with the parents with particular attention to the following areas:

• Understanding the illness
• Distress and situations triggering distress
• Coping strategies
• Restrictions to lifestyles
• Dissatisfaction with behaviour
• Strengths.

The family was invited to feedback and offer any other concerns, and a problem list was negotiated and areas of work highlighted.

PROBLEM LIST

1. Jane's lack of motivation/laziness
2. Fear of relapse/consequence of relapse
3. Lack of time and space for parents
4. Frustration/annoyance at Jane's behaviour
5. Reduce the distress both in Jane's life but also the parents.

The family and therapists then negotiated the way forward, and it was agreed to hold weekly sessions at first, followed by fortnightly and eventually monthly sessions. The frequency would be reviewed on a regular basis and altered to suit the needs of the family. Initially the sessions would first focus on education, the sessions would then turn towards stress management, and the later sessions would be on goal-setting. The family was informed that there would be time at the beginning and the end of each session for feedback on process and progress. The collaborative nature of the family work was discussed and again the focus reinforced.

Homework was set for the next session and the family was supplied with some literature on schizophrenia. They were requested to read it by the next session and highlight anything that they didn't understand or felt was particularly relevant to them.

Management proposals

Following the first session the therapists planned the following:

- The next session would focus on education, with particular reference to negative symptoms. Any concerns highlighted by the family would also be discussed.
- The therapists would use the stress-vulnerability model to link education to stress management, and self-monitoring of stressors would be introduced.
- Jane would become involved with the sessions at this point: firstly, to discuss negative symptoms from her perspective; secondly, to link her symptoms to the stress-vulnerability model; and finally to begin to discuss the stressors within the family environment.
- Sessions would then focus on problem-solving and coping strategies around the above stressors, functional coping strategies would be enhanced while dysfunctional coping strategies would be modified.
- Jane would also be involved at the start of goal-setting, and activity scheduling would be used as both a patient-focused as well as a family focused strategy. The aim was to involve Jane in a more active weekly programme of activities, and to enable the parents to structure some valuable time for themselves.

Session 2: Education (1)

The aim of this session was to cover the literature that I had given the family and discuss any concerns. Unfortunately Jane had decided to hand her notice in to the sheltered accommodation and since things had been a little fraught within the family the homework from last week had not been completed. However it gave us ample opportunity to discuss the implications of Jane's actions and how the parents were reacting. It was interesting to notice how the mother and father differed here; mother's reaction was of instant relief while father's was of bitter disappointment—reinforcing the high expectations and failure that Jane often commented on. The father's goal was to plan for Jane's independence so that she would be catered for if any thing happened to either of her parents. Jane's mother, however, was happy to keep her at home where she knew she was all right. These differences were highlighted by the therapists and following discussion with the family it was decided to put them on the agenda for a later session looking at goal-setting. The latter part of the session focused on negative symptoms. We discussed some of Jane's behaviours with which the parents were dissatisfied and looked at possible causes. The mother thought that it was possibly due to the illness, but the father, although showing a good understanding of negative symptoms, put it down to his daughter being "damn lazy". As the father became quite agitated and defensive when we were discussing Jane's behaviour and different coping strategies, we therefore agreed to defer any further discussion to the next session after the family had had another chance to read the literature.

Session 3: Education (2) and introduction to stress management

When we reviewed the previous week the parents seemed to be happier with events and felt that Jane had settled back at home, and since her decision to leave the sheltered accommodation she had become less agitated and distressed. The family had had a chance to read and discuss the literature this time and had highlighted any areas of concern. Two items that they highlighted were the role of the new atypical neuroleptic medication with schizophrenia and again negative symptoms. We agreed to split the session into two, the first part looking at education and the above two topics, the second part introducing stress vulnerability and its role within both the family and in schizophrenia. The family was more receptive in this session and it was hypothesised by the therapists that this is likely to be due to the growing therapeutic relationship/rapport.

The family queried why their daughter was not on the new atypical medication as they were written about very favourably in the literature. A number of reasons were explored with the family, with both parties generating alternatives. The most reasonable appeared to be that if the consultant psychiatrist felt that a patient was stable on one medication, there may be reluctance to 'rock the boat' by introducing another. It was agreed that their concerns should be addressed at the next care programme approach review when the consultant would be present. When we looked at discussing negative symptoms again, the father was more receptive this week than in the previous session. We worked a more visual four-factor model;

	Negative symptoms	
Side-effects	(All four interact)	Depression
	Personality	

The above model was accepted by the father, especially when it was explained that the negative symptoms can exaggerate aspects of his personality and that these may be further clouded by depression and the tranquillising effects of the medication.

When introducing the stress-vulnerability model to the family it was done in a diagrammatic form (see Figure 11.2). The rationale was given via a handout and the way that stressors/conflicts can affect functional and dysfunctional families was shown Table 11.2. An overview of coping strategy enhancement was also explained using a handout. The family was very receptive to the stress-vulnerability model and could relate it to both Jane and her immediate environment. (The handouts are available from the author on request.)

Finally the concept of keeping stress diaries was discussed and offered as a homework task for that week. It was explained that the entries could then be used towards future agenda items and work with coping strategies, as mentioned above (see Table 11.4).

Session 4: Stress management and introduction to goal-setting

The fourth session began with an overview of the week, which again appeared to have gone quite well with Jane settling in at home and looking like she was continuing to make an effort. The family had highlighted two concerns on their stress diaries, these being Jane's sleep pattern and her diet.

Both events had happened in the last week and had ended up with conflict among the family. The parents were worried about her sleep pattern and diet and thought that they may be signs of an imminent relapse. Both events could be normalised and a rationale was discussed with the parents. The

Table 11.4 Example of a stress diary

Date/time	Event	Feeling/s
Monday	Jane prepared a meal for herself and then left the mess for her mother to clear up. Father ends up having a go at Jane.	Stress/frustration

two events may have been linked with relapse in the past, but if there was no supporting evidence surrounding them other reasons need to be explored. It was explained to the family that one of the future sessions would be covering relapse prevention and relapse blueprints, and early warning signs would be discussed then.

The rest of the session was negotiated with the family and on their request Jane was invited into the session for the last 30 minutes. This was recognised as not being ideal as work was still to be completed on stress management. However, Jane's individual work was running faster than the family work, and she was looking at activity scheduling to see how it would fit in with the family. It was acknowledged by the therapists that sessions would not always go to schedule and that this opportunity could be taken to introduce goal-setting and activity-scheduling. It was stressed that it would be beneficial to backtrack and cover any unfinished business in future sessions. Jane had agreed to activity-scheduling in her individual sessions but needed to work with her parents to devise a blueprint should the daily plan fall by the wayside. The parents and Jane generated some alternative solutions to the problem and the pros and cons were considered before agreeing on the most suitable. The family agreed to try it over the next week as homework, and feedback at the next session. The parents would also continue to complete the stress diary for future use.

Future sessions

Immediate future sessions will continue with stress management. There will always be a need to return to education occasionally but mainly it will be heading forward towards goal-setting. Jane's activity-scheduling will continue to be encouraged and work will go ahead on her individual work with her therapist and support worker. The parents will also be encouraged to start to plan their own activities when appropriate support networks are in place with Jane. Reassurance and support will have to be available and incidents evaluated as and when necessary. Finally, the family work will examine relapse and the fears around it, early warning signs will be highlighted and a relapse blueprint will be drawn up between Jane, her parents and the mental health services.

Evaluation/critical review

The first few sessions with Jane's family seemed too good to be true as there seemed nothing to really work on, and on the surface everything seemed "rosy". However, once this surface was scratched and the family felt that they could "let down their guard" the sessions started to generate some good therapeutic issues. At first the father appeared defensive and at times got quite agitated when he felt that his coping skills and approaches were being questioned—even though both the therapist and the co-therapist went out of their way at times to be diplomatic. However, during the third session his attitude appeared to change and he started to warm to the family work. It was hypothesised that the change was brought about by the work on negative symptoms and stress vulnerability, and as this proved to be very new to him he felt that he was getting something out of the sessions.

Even though only four sessions had been completed, a certain amount of ground had been covered, the family had eventually engaged, and common goals had been highlighted and agreed upon. The family did have a very caring attitude towards their daughter and were keen to make sure that she received what was best for her. The family showed that they were survivors. Mother and father have just celebrated 40 years of marriage, and the fact that they have coped with Jane one way or other over the last 14 years is a credit to their perseverance and commitment. With the right support the initial goals are achievable and the levels of distress/stress within the family will visibly decrease. The problem in the future will be down to resources and the provision of suitable sheltered accommodation for Jane. Both Jane and her parents recognise the need for staff support, at least in the short term. If her individual coping strategies improve and she learns to deal with stressors/conflict effectively, the future does look brighter and her father might get some way towards his wish!

Chapter 12

COGNITIVE BEHAVIOUR THERAPY FOR PSYCHOSIS IN CONDITIONS OF HIGH SECURITY

Cases 13 (Malcolm) and 14 (Colin): *Andy Benn*

This chapter[*] presents two case studies involving the use of cognitive behaviour therapy with patients detained in conditions of high security. The aim of this chapter is to examine the feasibility of applying cognitive behaviour therapy in this setting. While clinical trials have demonstrated the utility of cognitive behaviour therapy in various settings (see Chapter 16), there are no published clinical trials of this work in conditions of high security and few case studies (Ewers, Leadley & Kinderman, 2000). The chapter also highlights the useful contribution that cognitive behaviour therapy can make to risk reduction in situations where there are clear links between offending and psychosis. Readers are referred elsewhere for a more general discussion of prevalence, triggers, and determinants of offending and psychosis (Hodgins, 2000). The service aims for this setting will be outlined, alongside a discussion of key issues in engaging people with psychosis in this particular setting.

I currently work as a Clinical Psychologist at Rampton Hospital, part of the Forensic Directorate of Nottinghamshire Health Care Trust, and I first became interested in cognitive behaviour therapy for psychosis when I worked there as an Assistant Psychologist in 1987. I investigated coping with auditory hallucinations in a forensic psychiatric population for an M.Sc. thesis completed in 1990. My work at Rampton hospital continued up until I joined the SoCRATES project in 1996 (Lewis et al., in press) as a therapist. I returned to work at Rampton Hospital in 1998 to contribute to the introduction of psychosocial interventions in a multi-site initiative.

---

[*]The views expressed in this chapter do not represent the views of Rampton Hospital or Nottinghamshire Health Care NHS Trust.

A Case Study Guide to Cognitive Behaviour Therapy of Psychosis. Edited by David Kingdon and Douglas Turkington. © 2002 John Wiley & Sons, Ltd.

From 2002 I will have additional responsibility for the development of psychosocial interventions in the Mental Health Directorate at the hospital.

SERVICE SETTING

There are three high-security hospitals (high secure psychiatric services) in England: Ashworth, Broadmoor, and Rampton. These hospitals have been described as "a service for patients with the most severe psychiatric illness, and who are potentially or actually dangerous" (Kaye, 2001, p. 2). Despite historical and contemporary arguments for the closure of the Special Hospitals (see Gunn & Maden, 1999, for a summary), the need for high secure psychiatric services is not in dispute. Maden and colleagues (1995) comment that "whilst medium secure units occupy a central role in any comprehensive psychiatric service, they are not a replacement for maximum secure hospitals". These services care for approximately 1,250 patients directed there from courts, transferred from prisons and also from medium security psychiatric facilities. The question of how to organise and provide high secure psychiatric services has driven reforms in management, care, and security over the past 30 years. Kaye (2001) summarises efforts to modernise and integrate high security hospitals into mainstream forensic services.

Patients admitted to high security hospitals must have a legally defined "mental disorder", represent "a grave and immediate danger" to themselves or others, and be unmanageable in conditions of less security. Almost all patients admitted to high security are detained under sections of the Mental Health Act (1983), the remainder under criminal law acts. Multiprofessional panels ensure that referrals meet the strict admission criteria prior to accepting transfers from prison and medium secure services.

Key service tasks

High-security psychiatric services perform several broad functions simultaneously. The services *contain* mentally disordered offenders who cannot be managed in less secure facilities. Within the services additional high support wards exist to provide care to patients who cannot be managed within other areas of the high secure environment. Alongside the containment function the services aim over the long term to reduce risk of harm to both the public and the patients themselves, and to improve patients' mental health and social functioning. These goals are met by multidisciplinary teams operating individual care plans, and services offering a variety of offence and mental health focused interventions on an individual or group basis. Within the services interventions are therefore focused broadly on risk behaviour (e.g. aggression, violence, self-injury, and suicide/para-suicidal behaviour), mental health problems (e.g. psychosis, affective disorders) and social functioning (e.g. social isolation and social inclusion, communication, and interpersonal problem-solving). Remission of symptoms is *not* required for transfer to conditions of less security (Maden et al., 1995), merely the reduction of risk from being "grave and immediate".

This chapter concerns cognitive behaviour therapy for psychosis in cases where the management of patients' mental health problems is central to risk management. Cognitive behaviour interventions for delusions are relevant to high secure service provision "with the aim of reducing the likelihood of them [the delusions] being acted upon" (Ewers, Leadley & Kinderman, 2000). Attempts to analyse the relationship between psychosis and offending have proved difficult (Juniger, 2001; Taylor, Garety & Buchaman, 1994) though direct relationships between symptoms and offending appear to be more common in violent non-sexual offences than in sexual offences (Smith & Taylor, 1999; Taylor, Less & Williams, 1998). Any relationship between psychotic symptoms and offending needs to be identified on an individual basis during assessment in order that appropriate intervention can be agreed upon. In practice, a clear link between psychotic symptoms and offending adds the need for risk reduction to the existing clinical need to reduce distress associated with symptoms. However, in cases where these symptoms are not distressing (see Case 13: Malcolm), alternative motivators need to be identified to encourage the patient to engage with mental health professionals in order to address symptoms.

Although compliance with medication is an issue among high-security hospital patients (and relevant to both cases described below), as it is with people with psychosis and chronic illnesses in general (McPhillips & Sensky, 1998; Swinton & Ahmed, 1999), the focus for this chapter is on the psychological management of psychosis.

Challenges to engagement

Patient engagement within high secure psychiatric services in general is central to security in high secure hospitals. The identification and management of risk through "the professional relationships between staff and patients and the differing elements of the treatment programmes" is referred to as relational security (Kinsley, 1998). Strong working alliances between staff and patients with schizophrenia are associated with better

outcomes (Frank & Gunderson, 1990; Gehrs & Goering, 1994). Supportive interpersonal skills, including empathic listening, the ability to explore
meaning in symptoms and responding to patients' concerns, are central
to engagement (Gehrs & Goering, 1994). Gentle persistence with attempts
to engage patients, warmth, appropriate humour, and a willingness to
explore patient misinterpretations of therapist behaviour are also helpful
(Kingdon & Turkington, 1994; Kingdon, 1998). Kingdon warned against
attempting to do too much in each session and to ensure that patients
discuss their own issues in order to build up the working relationship.
Useful advice concerning the engagement of mentally disordered offenders is available elsewhere (including guidelines on motivating offenders
with mental health problems, Gresswell & Kruppa, 1994). Before stating
the case vignettes, this chapter will explore some of the more common obstacles that I have encountered in engaging patients with psychosis in a
high secure setting.

RESPONSES TO AND PERCEPTIONS OF DETENTION

Many patients initially react with frustration and anger to their involuntar-
ily detention. Those emotions can periodically re-emerge often in response
to slow progress through the hospital towards discharge. Additionally, perceived "setbacks" may include failure to gain discharge at Mental Health
Review Tribunals, or risk assessments from their own Clinical Team or outside agencies that conclude that there is a continuing need for detention
in a high secure setting. A similar situation may arise during the waiting
time for transfer to medium secure services despite acceptance for those
services.

Admission to high secure psychiatric services can carry with it the additional implication of "long-term" detention, giving rise to feelings of
hopelessness and helplessness. Court Orders for detention in high secure
psychiatric facilities (under Section 37 of the Mental Health Act), together
with discharge dependent on endorsement by the Home Office Mental
Health Unit (Section 41), can carry the *"Without Limit of Time"* tag from
the courts, depending on the particular offence and patient. Furthermore,
prior knowledge of high-security hospitals, of former patients, or of the
various inquiries into conditions or abusive care may prime new patients
to fear the environment in which they are to be detained, the other patients
they may meet, or the care or "treatment" they will receive. Poor understanding or acceptance of the need for detention can generate feelings of
injustice at the detention and a sense of "unfairness". These factors, combined with poor anger control, confrontative and violent coping styles, can
trigger disagreements with staff, and at times result in violent behaviour.

Hodgins (2000) has reviewed further the prevention and management of violence by people with mental health problems in secure settings.

POOR INSIGHT INTO MENTAL HEALTH PROBLEMS

When the above issues arise in combination with poor insight into mental health problems (persecutory beliefs, for example), patients may misinterpret their detention as an attack or confirmation of an attack against them that is unjustified. Consequent anger and violence may be directed against staff and other patients, should they be viewed as agents in the detention process. The blame for detention may be lodged along contemporary cultural lines according to individual patient beliefs. Hence blame has been attributed to: partners, children, parents and extended family; friends, neighbours, and unknown people; at Government generally or particular individuals; Civil or Military Intelligence; Foreign or International organisations; supernatural beings (God, Devil, devils, spirits and so forth) and alien beings. The conviction of unjust detention can continue even when positive psychotic symptoms are no longer active or distressing (see above).

MINIMISATION AND POOR INSIGHT INTO RISK

Cognitive distortions minimising risk and overconfidence about their ability to survive without symptom, social functioning or offence relapses are common among this population. These distortions need to be addressed in order that "they may be taught to recognize risky situations and that a concrete plan for dealing with those situations be devised" (Bloom, Mueser & Muller-Isberner, 2000).

Patients with psychosis may have difficulty tolerating the affect associated with remorse, or indeed be emotionally blunt as part of their negative symptoms. Affect associated with remorse may be experienced as aversive, and avoided as a potential stressor that might trigger symptoms. Such presentations can be difficult to distinguish from lack of concern for the consequences of past action. Ensuring active efforts to identify and manage stressors and risk situations helps to confirm that the patient regards risk management and reduction as an internal goal.

Patients may have difficulty reconciling their actions while "ill" with their usual self. One patient told me, "It was me who killed him, but it wasn't *me*, if you see what I mean". These attitudes are similar to cognitive distortions blaming alcohol, drug abuse, and anger/rage for offending. The oversimplified rationale, "I killed because I was ill", cannot be accepted as evidence of adequate understanding of the relationship between the patients' mental health problems and offending. Such explanations omit key variables and factors linking the "mental illness" or symptoms with the offence. Interventions based on theoretical models of schizophrenia (Nuechterlien & Dawson, 1984) and symptoms (Fowler, Garety & Kuipers, 1995; Haddock & Slade, 1996; Kingdon & Turkington, 1994) aim to educate and enable people with psychosis to identify, understand, and cope with their mental health problems. Offence-focused work with patients enables them to manage the risk factors associated with their offending. The importance of patients understanding their mental health problems and offending cannot be underestimated. Actively coping with stressors, symptoms, emotions, unhelpful thinking, building and maintaining supportive social relationships, skills in interpersonal problem-solving and communicating and co-operating with psychiatric services (including medication adherence), are the foundation for effective risk management. Problems with these issues are cited as obstacles to discharge or to transfer to conditions of lesser security (Maden et al., 1995).

Most patients want to leave or be discharged from Rampton. Motivation to present as "problem free", or denial of symptoms, can be high. In the main, this can be understood in terms of a desire to be free combined with the belief that discharge is largely based on the presentation of symptoms. This is not the case (Maden et al., 1995) but is understandable since the presence of a "mental disorder" within the terms of the Mental Health Act (1983) is required for detention. Providing information and educational approaches are helpful in clarifying this misunderstanding.

Differentiating genuine change in level of risk from continuing high risk is fraught with difficulty. Patients can become skilled in "knowing what to say" (see Orr, 1998, for a humorous example of 'Ten Tribunal Tips'). Decisions and clinical judgements about changes in level of risk cannot rely solely on patient self-report. Patients' insistence and judgements that they are *not* in need of treatment in high security require careful evaluation by Clinical Teams. Observations of behaviour across a range of settings contribute to clinical decision-making about risk. Patients' responses to increasing levels of freedom and responsibility are tested within high security to ensure the stability of any change. Patients have the opportunity to demonstrate problem-free behaviour when with single escorts, on parole within the hospital grounds, and on escorted trips out of high security.

SKILL ATROPHY

However, for some patients particularly in the "pre-discharge" areas, the need for treatment in conditions of high security is indeed questionable.

Many patients who are detained in high security have already been accepted for transfer to, or are awaiting assessment or acceptance from, medium security services (Maden et al., 1995). Here, then, the issue is to maintain their motivation to prevent the atrophy of the very mental health and offence related risk management skills that have contributed to the reduction of the risks they present.

Skill atrophy is a common problem where skill rehearsal opportunities are limited. Discussion of hypothetical risk-laden situations is a useful strategy to maintain risk management skills. Skill maintenance exercises can be completed periodically. Exercise sheets outlining a realistic problem situation, or symptom profile based on known vulnerabilities, stressors and risk situation, are drawn up by the Clinical Team. Patients are asked to think through how they would deal with the situation and prepare for a meeting with a member of the Clinical Team. In this meeting, the patient's planned response to the hypothetical events are identified and discussed. Well-planned and realistic descriptions of coping, combined with competent rehearsal of skills in role-play vignettes, are encouraged and reinforced by the Clinical Team. Expressions of uncertainty about how to tackle the situation, poor planning, unrealistic descriptions of coping, and less competent rehearsal of skills are noted, so that further skill-building and rehearsal can be undertaken. An example of such a skill maintenance intervention is given later in the chapter (Case 14: Colin).

ASSESSMENT

A key aim of assessment is to understand the various factors contributing to the offence in sufficient detail to decide on interventions to reduce and manage the risks presented. A functional analysis of behaviour helps to understand the purpose of the offending in context. For many of the patients with whom I have worked, violent offending has occurred in the context of attempts to escape or avoid harm, persecution and torment, often with fatal consequences. In one of the case vignettes described below (Colin) the index offence resulted in death, motivated by persecutory delusions and an attempt to prevent further harm.

SUITABILITY OF COGNITIVE BEHAVIOUR THERAPY FOR PSYCHOSIS IN CONDITIONS OF HIGH SECURITY

The literature on cognitive behaviour therapy for psychosis in forensic settings is meagre (Ewers, Leadley & Kinderman, 2000). However, there are two ways in which cognitive behaviour interventions are relevant to the management of psychosis in conditions of high security. Such interventions are relevant to both improving mental health and reducing risk of offending (where there is a link between a patient's psychosis and his or her offending).

Cognitive behaviour therapies have been shown to be beneficial in the treatment of chronic positive symptoms of psychosis, and intelligence and symptom severity do not appear to be associated with outcome (Garety, Fowler & Kuipers, 2000). Cognitive behaviour therapies have been demonstrated as beneficial in the treatment of patients resistant to conventional antipsychotic medication (Sensky et al., 2000). Provisional evidence from Italy suggests that the outcome of depression in people with a diagnosis of schizophrenia taking atypical antipsychotic medication is improved using combined cognitive behaviour therapy and social skills compared to combined individual supportive therapy and atypical antipsychotic medication (Pinto et al., 1999).

Where psychosis is linked to offending, in such a way that the offence is unlikely to have occurred had psychosis not been present, then psychosis is a mediating variable in risk of re-offending (Smith & Taylor, 1999). However, there are many patients who have a history of violent offending prior to the onset of psychosis, many of them with co-morbid substance misuse problems. In such cases the focus of intervention by necessity includes reducing violent behaviour, improving coping skills, managing psychosis and substance abuse. Given the above, it should not be surprising that cognitive behaviour therapies are viewed as useful and are being employed in conditions of high security.

Both cases in this chapter involve patients prescribed atypical antipsychotic medication. Recent evidence (Dalal et al., 1999; Swinton & Ahmed, 1999) suggests that atypical antipsychotics are beneficial in many instances of 'medication-resistant' schizophrenia and can lead to more speedy transfer from high security. My own work with Malcolm and Colin took place in the context of close multi-professional working.

MALCOLM

Malcolm is a 34-year-old man with a diagnosis of paranoid schizophrenia. He was admitted into high secure psychiatric care as a transfer from medium secure psychiatric care following absconsions and hostage-taking. His admission to medium security had been made by Court Order following a conviction for attempted murder. Assessment revealed a complex persecutory belief system (Delusions Rating Scale (DRS) = 18;

Haddock et al., 1999) and a separate grandiose belief system (DRS = 17). While Malcolm reported distress when thinking about unseen adversaries, there was no evidence of subjective distress about being specially chosen. Similarly, Malcolm's omnipotent and benevolent auditory hallucinations (Auditory Hallucinations Rating Scale (AHRS) = 14; Haddock et al., 1999) were not experienced by him as distressing. Malcolm had a history of depression and suicidal ideation. His current self-esteem, measured using the Culture-Free Self-Esteem Inventory (Battle, 1980) was rated as "low" (18, 25th percentile; Bartram, Lindley & Foster, 1991). He believed his "voice" was that of an "alien mentor-protector" who had promised him imminent rescue from his secure care. His psychological formulation involved low self-esteem, auditory hallucinations reflecting a wish to be free, and a compensatory grandiose belief of being an "intergalactic chosen one". He was certain he would be rescued and trusted implicitly in his "voice".

Multidisciplinary risk assessment concluded that Malcolm was at increased risk of suicide and/or hostage-taking in a bid to escape. Two clinical hypotheses were apparent. Firstly, since his hopes of rescue were delusional there was the possibility that he would be disappointed, perhaps experience low mood, and think his situation hopeless once the deadline for his rescue passed. Alternatively, it was possible that he might make an attempt to escape, perhaps taking a hostage in an attempt to secure his release. The multidisciplinary plan included: regular reviews of his mental state with the nursing team; individual work with his named nurse focused on increasing his self-esteem; and cognitive behaviour therapy targeting his auditory hallucinations and grandiose delusions.

Intervention with positive symptoms

With the working assumption that auditory hallucinations can be conceptualised as misattributed inner-speech, Malcolm was asked to compare what his "voice" said with his current concerns (Birchwood & Iqbal, 1998). His comparisons highlighted themes of desire for freedom and promise of rescue, low self-esteem and being the "chosen one", motivation to pursue powerful goals outside of secure psychiatric care, and that he was above containment by virtue of his "status". This comparison process is shown in Table 12.1.

Malcolm's current concerns (wanting to be free, believing himself to be worthless and to have lost everything, and having urgent goals outside of Rampton Hospital) were understandable in the context of his detention. Discussion of the similarities between themes in his positive symptoms

Table 12.1 A Comparison of Malcolm's "Voice" and beliefs

Themes in positive symptoms	Own thoughts
Rescue from confinement	I want to be free
Being specially chosen	I'm worth nothing, I've lost everything
Status precludes confinement	I can't be held here, I'm above these earthly matters
I have lots of wives in Europe	I need to find my wives urgently

(the content of his "voice" and beliefs) and his own thoughts highlighted several key issues. Malcolm commented that he was puzzled by thinking himself worthless and all he had ever gained and achieved had been lost, and at the same time feeling excited because he had special status in the universe. He said these two were "like extreme opposites, very different... I don't understand, but that's how it feels". Secondly, he noted that he wanted to be free from the confinement of high security and that what his "voice" told him was akin to having his wish fulfilled. He said that his imminent departure from Rampton Hospital by "tele-transportation" gave him great hope for his future. Finally, Malcolm told me of a quest he had to find up to 14 wives he had married a few years previously while in Spain. He acknowledged that this was unusual but urgently wanted to return to Spain to recommence his search for records and confirmation of his many marriages. Malcolm attached great importance to this goal and said it was "unfair" for him to be prevented from pursuing his search.

Three areas of work were agreed with Malcolm during the lead up to his anticipated "tele-transportation". Our shared understanding of his situation highlighted the need to address his low self-esteem, his understanding both of his "voice" and inferences made about the "voice", and his adjustment to his detention.

Reduction of negative self-evaluation

The coexistence of negative self-evaluation and a grandiose belief (of being specially chosen) was the starting point for developing a shared understanding of Malcolm's problems and potential ways forward. Malcolm's Named Nurse worked with him closely to help him to identify unhelpful extremities in his self-evaluations, to find more moderate and realistic self-appraisals and also to identify sources of rebuilding a more reality based self-image. The Clinical Team's formulation was that Malcolm was

Table 12.2   An ABC analysis of Malcolm's "Voice"

Antecedents	Beliefs and interpretations	Consequences
Seeing a calendar, thinking about being "inside" and urgently needing to be "outside"— feeling tension	I need to find my wives	Voice: "You'll be rescued." "Don't worry you'll be out of here"—tension reduction
Voice: "You'll be rescued." "Don't worry you'll be out of here"—tension reduction	I'm leaving here soon	Search for meaning of experiences: "Who is speaking to me? Why me?"—puzzlement
Search for meaning of experiences: "Who is speaking to me? Why me?"—puzzlement	I have been contacted to be rescued by an alien, I must have been specially chosen	Hope. Elevated sense of status

reacting to his confinement and loss of his previous life, and that his hallucinations involved compensatory themes that enabled him to feel hopeful and special.

Understanding and making inferences about "voices"

Three issues were relevant here: understanding his experience as a "voice" hearer; the process of making inferences about his experience; and the meaning of the content of the "voice". The stress-vulnerability model was introduced to the client. Malcolm understood and accepted the idea that stress could trigger a range of psychological problems, and he recounted a previous period of depression brought on by job loss and a relationship break up. An ABC analysis was completed for particular instances when Malcolm experienced his "voice". A sample of this analysis is shown in Table 12.2.

As the deadline for rescue approached and the exploration of his experiences, interpretations and alternative interpretation of those experiences continued, I enquired of Malcolm how he would feel, what he might think and what he might do if he remained in the hospital after his expected departure date. Reality-testing exercises require that possible outcomes and interpretation of what the outcomes mean are agreed upon in advance. Malcolm and I generated a list of possible outcomes and agreed that either he would still be in Rampton after his deadline or he would not be. Since

Malcolm fully anticipated leaving, he said there was no need to make an appointment to see me the following week. I urged him to agree to an appointment for the following week so that we could continue our work should he still remain at the hospital. He agreed to a further appointment with the rationale that if he was still in the hospital the following week he would be greatly disappointed and would probably want to talk about his feelings.

The following explanations for why he may remain in Rampton past his "rescue" deadline were generated: his rescuer had abandoned him; his rescuer had been interrupted; there had been a breakdown of the "tele-transportation" system; the "voice" was something different to how he had been viewing it and his hopes for rescue had been in vain. Malcolm, who was frank about how disappointed he would be, agreed that he may get extremely low in mood but thought it unlikely that he would become suicidal. He told me he was unsure about which explanation would best fit if he was not rescued. His "voice" had been occurring less frequently in recent weeks and he had been increasingly relying upon his own beliefs and hopes rather than the reassurance of his "voice".

Given Malcolm's previous absconsions from medium security, I asked about whether he had contemplated trying to escape from high security. He told me that he had thought about escape, but that as far as he knew his only remaining chance of getting out of Rampton Hospital were with help from his rescuer, via a discharge by a Mental Health Review Tribunal, or transfer by order of his doctor. Ward staff continued to monitor his ward behaviour and proximity to female staff in vigilance for potential hostage-taking during this period.

With these methods in mind, I asked Malcolm to consider how he would normally cope with disappointment. We identified how he had previously prepared for important occasions that he very much wanted to happen, but did not take place. Malcolm recalled two important occasions in which he had previously coped with great disappointment (being turned down for a date, failing to gain a desired job). We collaboratively evaluated the methods he had used to moderate the impact of these events, and these formed the basis of the strategy to prepare himself for the potential disappointment as a consequence of not being rescued. The list included the following:

1. Reminding himself that there are established means of leaving the hospital (i.e. discharge by Mental Health Review Tribunal, recommendations by his Clinical Team) and that his "rescuer" is not his sole hope.

2. Acceptance of disappointment as a natural consequence of failing to have expectations met and not a "catastrophe".
3. Accepting that not all wishes come true.
4. Reminding himself how he survived past disappointments, learned from his experiences and tried again more successfully later in time.

These points were put on a discreet card that he taped on the inside of his door to remind himself of his skills in coping with disappointment. The rationale for Item 1 was to encourage Malcolm's reliance on reality-based ways of being discharged from high security, which he had mentioned during our discussion about "ways out of Rampton".

Adjusting to detention in a high-security psychiatric hospital

A psycho-education approach was taken with the issue of adjustment. Malcolm's experience of admission to high security was discussed. His fears about being attacked and living with a group of men who themselves had mental health problems were explored. Malcolm had few expectations of what he would need to do while at the hospital. He asked how long he would be at the hospital, but accepted that it was difficult to be precise about a time scale, given that the average length of stay is approximately seven years. He was informed that the broad aims of the hospital were to improve mental health and social functioning, and to reduce the risk of re-offending.

Outcomes

Malcolm made no attempt to escape when the deadline for his "rescue" passed. He did feel disappointed about remaining in Rampton but commented that his Clinical Team had prepared him well for his "non-event". He reported that since he had been the only person expecting him to leave, he was aware that "something is not right" in his thinking about his situation. He had used his self-help list for coping with disappointment on a regular basis and said that he had half expected not to be "tele-transported" out of the hospital. Reassessment of his positive symptoms suggested a shift in his auditory hallucinations (AHRS = 9) with marked changes in his belief about the origin of the "voice", and the disruption to his daily life. While Malcolm's grandiose belief rating had diminished (DRS = 6), his persecutory beliefs did not appear to have changed (DRS = 19). He did not report experiencing a shift towards low mood, nor having thoughts on harming himself. His self-esteem work with his Named Nurse appeared to have successfully challenged his ideas about having "lost everything". He spoke vividly of past achievements and the importance of reminding himself about these, and was also able to list several personal qualities that he valued and anticipated would help him to cope while he remained in Rampton Hospital. Malcolm's mental state improved during the period described and a potential increase in the risks he posed to himself and others was managed successfully. However, his persecutory beliefs remained. These were not the focus of intervention during the period described and are subject to ongoing work. Changes in his persecutory beliefs are required before Malcolm's risk is likely to diminish sufficiently for him to be transferred to conditions of less security. His engagement with cognitive behaviour therapy, his ability to entertain possible interpretations other than his own, and his openness about his thinking processes appear to bode well for his progress with understanding and coping with his mental health problems.

COLIN

Colin had been in Rampton Hospital for nine years before I met him. His index offence was one of manslaughter—the killing of his landlord. Colin had no previous offence history. He had emigrated to the United Kingdom four years prior to his index offence, primarily motivated by better employment prospects. Although he found employment he was socially isolated and experienced periods of low mood that went untreated due to his reluctance to seek help. Six months prior to the index offence, Colin began to feel physically unwell, which he associated with milk stored in the refrigerator he shared with his landlord and other lodgers. Colin developed the delusion that his landlord was poisoning the milk. After confronting his landlord with the allegation that he was putting poison into the milk, a fight ensued, in which he overcame his landlord and killed him. Despite assertive treatment with antipsychotic medication over a period of nine years, Colin's belief that he had been poisoned continued. This medication-resistant delusion was regarded as a key risk factor preventing transfer to a medium security hospital. Several times during his detention at Rampton Hospital Colin had expressed the belief that he was again being poisoned. Careful management of staff explanations in a supportive atmosphere had prevented potential assaults against staff. In particular, the clinical teams view was that the absence of racist comments had ensured that Colin did not form the belief that staff were against him. However, his continuing beliefs about his former landlord and periodic suspicions that hospital staff were attempting to poison him maintained the Clinical Team's view that Colin continued to pose a grave and immediate danger to others.

Assessment

A therapeutic relationship was quickly established with Colin. He was particularly interested in discussing his beliefs and commented that while many staff had previously asked him about his offence and beliefs, no one had asked him how he had obtained his beliefs or enquired about the foundations of his beliefs. It appears that he had been repeatedly assessed, treated with antipsychotic medication, but exploration of the basis for his beliefs had not occurred.

Colin revealed key details of his history, including being subjected to racist comments periodically by his landlord. A discussion between him and a co-lodger had reinforced Colin's suspicions about the landlord—the co-lodger had essentially agreed that Colin was being poisoned by their landlord. Colin's central beliefs were agreed on and subsequently rated using the DRS (DRS = 14).

Formulation

In the lead up to the index offence, Colin was experiencing a series of physical symptoms including nausea, excessive perspiration and headaches. He was socially isolated and had no close confidants with whom to discuss his concerns and worries. When he attempted to discuss his suspicions about being poisoned with a co-lodger, his co-lodger essentially confirmed his suspicions. Colin had formed an understandable contextual belief that his landlord was *against* him by ruminating on the meaning of his landlord's racist comments. This formulation was developed with reference to Maher's (1988, pp. 15–33) hypotheses concerning the origin of some delusional beliefs as a consequence of misinterpretation of undiagnosed medical problems and cognitive biases in psychosis (Bentall & Kinderman, 1998). Colin had an undiagnosed milk sensitivity and the sensations he interpreted as evidence of poisoning appeared to be symptoms of an allergic reaction to milk.

Intervention

The intervention process sought to identify the evidence that Colin used to support his beliefs and to search for disconfirmatory evidence. Colin's particular delusional beliefs appear to have been maintained partly by being his best explanation of his experiences and also the absence of any viable alternative explanation for his nausea. Colin was asked what puzzled him about the chain of events leading to his offence, and these were explored. He identified the following issues:

- what did his landlord have to gain by poisoning him?
- his landlord was "mean" and rarely spent money unnecessarily
- his landlord often complained about lodgers staying for only a short time and preferred long-term lodgers like Colin.

I encouraged Colin to view his uncertainties as valid and needing to be fitted into his understanding of his experiences. Reviewing the source of support for his beliefs (comments by his co-lodger) highlighted further uncertainties. Colin did not generally regard his co-lodger as reliable. He was an alcoholic, would steal from others in their accommodation, and at other times would make accusations against other co-lodgers about things he had lost or possibly sold. Discussion and careful weighing of the evidence led to a diminution in Colin's certainty of his beliefs about his landlord (DRS = 4). The incorporation of Colin's milk sensitivity into the formulation gave him a plausible alternative explanation to being poisoned. His avoidance of milk-based products while he was at Rampton Hospital was discussed, and Colin expressed surprise as to why he had not previously made a connection between his sensitivity to milk and his belief that his landlord had poisoned him.

Progress

Colin remained stable over the remaining time that he was detained in conditions of high security. During the period he awaited transfer to medium secure services, I continued working with him to ensure consolidation of his recent improvements. Primarily the aims were threefold. Firstly, I wanted to ensure that he was self-monitoring for early warning signs of his mental health problems returning. Secondly, Colin needed to demonstrate that he was able to communicate clearly to staff any changes in his mental health status. Finally, Colin was required to demonstrate that he could manage minor fluctuations in his mental health when support was unavailable. I hold the working assumption that multiple coping strategies for tackling problem situations increase patients' opportunities for successfully managing those situations.

Given the stability of Colin's mental health, the Clinical Team agreed that a series of analogue exercises involving changes in mental health would highlight skills deficits in terms of self-monitoring, communication with staff, and coping skills. An example of such an exercise with a specific problem is given in Box 12.1.

Using analogue exercises to maintain skills

Box 12.1   Staying Well Exercise

Dear Colin

Please read through the following exercise and think about what you could do to tackle the problems described. Make some notes for a discussion and make an appointment with one of your Ward Nurses to discuss and practise dealing with the situation.

Imagine yourself feeling sad compared to usual. You've noticed yourself not wanting to get up in the morning and not talking with other Patients and Staff. You noticed Staff laughing in the office and think they were laughing at you. While you've been sitting quietly with others you've listened out for other people "taking the mickey" and are worrying about what people are saying about you.

It may help to make notes on the following:

1. Why this might be a problem that needs action?
2. What you would say to yourself to help cope with the situation?
3. Who would you talk to and what you might say to them?
4. What other action you might need to take?

---

1.   Why might this be a problem that needs action?

Colin spotted that the situation that he chose for his exercise was related to his own symptoms. He said that if the situation happened to him he would need to do something because "I might be going down hill again". Colin was prompted to be more specific about what he was using as a signal that his mental health problems were deteriorating. He identified "feeling sad" as a key signal that a problem was present. Further, he said that he had hurt people previously when his symptoms were active, so he needed to act quickly to help to ensure that he did not act on any persecutory beliefs. He did not spontaneously recognise that his paranoid worries might make him feel fearful of other people. This was noted, agreed as an important topic, and dealt with later (see section 4 below).

2.   What you would say to yourself to help cope with the situation?

Colin identified that his usual reaction to worries was to catastrophise, or "think the worst". Helpfully, he said he thought he could counter some of his worries, including "it's all starting up again", "this is going to be bad", and "I need to get a knife so I feel safe". He talked through how he would counter-balance such worries by reminding himself of more realistic interpretations of emerging symptoms. These included, "I've noticed the worries quickly so I can get help before they get any worse", and "I can cope with ups and downs, I'm not alone, staff and my friends can support me". With prompting he was able to recall alternative safety behaviours from a list he had previously generated. These behaviours included suggesting time out of workshops when sharp tools were available and enlisting support from a trusted patient friend. Role-play rehearsal involved inviting a patient friend to a game of draughts "to take my mind off things". During this role-play exercise Colin was asked to weigh the pros and cons of asking for support to help to distract him from his problems versus asking for help to cope with those problems. He was able to identify a different patient who could either help to distract him from problems or help him to engage in coping efforts. Colin's comment about not wanting to "feel like a complete idiot" highlighted a need to review his critical self-evaluations, the role of these in his self-esteem and his mood. These issues were addressed in a later meeting.

3.   Who would you talk to and what you might say to them?

Colin had already identified the need to speak to any nurse to outline his situation. A discussion clarified that he would need to convey that he was concerned about his symptoms returning. Colin recognised that he may need to speak to a nurse *urgently* because, in the past, he had become extremely paranoid within a few days of initial worries about what others were thinking about him. Role-play rehearsal concerned assertively asking for time with a nurse. He was required to respond to potential problems in asking for help. These included being asked not to interrupt a Clinical Team discussion in the office about another patient, being asked if the query could wait until after lunch-time, and being offered discretionary medication by staff without any discussion of possible causes of the recent low mood and worries about being talked about.

4.   What other action you might need to take?

Colin was uncertain about any other approaches he could take to help to manage the hypothetical situation. Colin's approach to tackling his hypothetical problem (described above) was praised as realistic and manageable and he was also praised for particular skills shown during his role-plays. A note made earlier in the exercise suggested that he had not initially recognised the possibility that he may feel fearful of attack. He was asked to identify how he might feel if he had worries about others talking about him or laughing about him. He said he may be "scared of attack" in this situation, and possibly feel "uptight and tense". Subsequently he suggested that he could use a relaxation tape (which he had previously found beneficial) to reduce his tension. Colin was asked to go through his relaxation exercises and re-read his self-help materials. He was asked to complete an entry in his ABC diary to practise identifying key beliefs, images, automatic thoughts and consequences, particularly emotions and actions. He was also asked to re-read his list of early warning signs to remind himself of which signs and symptoms to monitor.

Skill maintenance and rehearsal exercises can also be used for other symptoms, triggers for anger and violence, depending on the individual patient's need. The exercises above are particularly helpful during periods of positive mental health functioning when the patient may use self-monitoring skills less or become complacent about the need for active coping. The patient's response to such exercises can help to gauge the progress or efficacy of his or her coping skills or indicate need for further skills building. Additionally, such exercises can identify both Clinical Team and patient overconfidence in coping skills that are not supported by evidence of effectiveness. Though the demand on the patient is high, the outcome for intervention and risk management is helpful. The exercises also offer patients an opportunity to show a grasp of coping skills relevant to the management of their mental health and risk to others within the limited confines of their environment.

Outcome

Colin made no subsequent allegations of poisoning by staff. In subsequent assessments by the Clinical Team, Colin explained what he had learned about his misinterpretation of his physical symptoms and conveyed his revised beliefs about the activities of his landlord. He experienced a period of low mood associated with expressions of remorse for having killed his landlord. This was regarded by the Clinical Team as a normal and understandable reaction to the development of insight into his illness and acceptance that he had killed his landlord in the mistaken belief that he had been poisoned by him. Within 14 months of the conclusion of our therapeutic work on his delusional beliefs, he had been accepted into medium secure care.

DISCUSSION

In the long term, patients with a legal classification of mental illness (under the Mental Health Act 1983) fare better with regard to re-offending than patients with a legal classification of psychopathic disorder (Steels et al, 1998). However, actuarial risk assessments contribute little in comparison to judgements about risk made on the basis of more detailed formulations of the relationship between mental health problems, social functioning and risk. Assessments made during cognitive behaviour therapy are able to contribute to risk management by identifying stressors and factors that increase risk, and, during intervention, by using methods that can improve the management of those risks. Effective self-management and coping skills and interventions facilitated by staff are required for successful risk management. Clinical data from cognitive behaviour therapy case-work can provide compelling evidence supporting changes (or lack of change) in the level of risk that patients present. Realistic accounts of previously misinterpreted events provide more certainty about genuine insight than accounts which merely conclude "I was ill then". Patients who report minor temporary increases in the severity of their problem, or a disturbance caused by potentially remitting symptoms, allow a more confident assessment of risk by the Clinical Team than the unlikely and unrealistic generalisation "I'm cured now, I don't have any problems". Regular and demonstrable self-monitoring with credible diary entries suggests that the patient is taking the management of his or her mental health problems seriously regardless of whether the patient is motivated by fear of symptoms and distress returning or by the desire to secure release. Rehearsal of coping with symptoms and social stressors augurs well for problem recognition, improved coping skills and generalisation of coping across settings.

Providing ready access to psychosocial interventions remains problematic (Tarrier et al., 1998). High secure psychiatric services face similar issues to community services in making effective interventions for enduring mental health problems more widely available. However, attempts to overcome these obstacles are in progress (Carton, 1999). Two medium secure units and one high secure unit are currently engaged in training staff in assessment, formulation, and coping strategies enhancement using the stress-vulnerability heuristic (Nuechterlien & Dawson, 1984) model as a guiding framework. The focus for intervention concerns the reduction of personal vulnerability factors, improving coping with environmental stressors, and increasing the use of personal protectors and environmental support. Skill development is being achieved through training, supervision, and reflection on theory and practice. Several of the first graduates who completed training now contribute to training and supervision on the course. Benefits to patients, in terms of their care plans being more clearly focused on either improving mental health or social functioning, are becoming evident.

Although the evidence base for the efficacy of cognitive behaviour therapy for psychosis in secure settings is extremely poor, combining interventions shown to be of value in community settings with individual formulation permits the development of feasible interventions within conditions of high security. The assumption that the risk of offending can be reduced by treating mental health problems is not new. Psychosocial interventions for psychosis have an increasingly impressive outcome data set, and it would be worth while researching the efficacy of cognitive behaviour therapy combined with atypical antipsychotic medication in a high secure setting. However, the institutional context involving a wide range of treatment services, the coexistence of offending, substance abuse problems, and dual diagnoses would require a complicated research design. Individualised formulation-based approaches to cognitive behaviour therapy in psychosis have advantages over the protocol-based approaches commonly used in research trials (Bentall & Haddock, 2000). Individualised approaches are constructed on the basis of client history and presenting difficulties, and are necessarily less time-limited. Research-oriented treatment protocols may limit the focus of interventions (for example, to positive psychotic symptoms) and neglect other key issues relevant to the case formulation (acceptance of responsibility for offending, for example). The treatment of medication-resistant schizophrenia with atypical antipsychotics has been evaluated in conditions of high secure psychiatric settings with promising outcomes. The study of longer-term outcomes is problematic and most intervention trials have only a modest follow-up period. Tracking individuals through the different levels of security and ensuring that relevant interventions are available should improve outcomes still further. A long-term study of the impact of psychosocial interventions on a range of re-offending, mental health, and social functioning outcomes is required.

PART II

TRAINING, SUPERVISION AND IMPLEMENTATION

Chapter 13

TRAINING IN CBT FOR PSYCHOSIS

David Kingdon and Jeremy Pelton

Over the past few years, opportunities for training have increased in the UK from a situation where many mental health professionals working with schizophrenia had little or no access to courses that allowed them to develop a psychological angle to their work. Previously there were a number of books and articles being published on the broad range of psychosocial interventions and, more specifically, cognitive behaviour therapy, but there was no opportunity to develop skills unless you worked alongside the specialist practitioners and researchers within the area. The established courses for CBT in London, Newcastle and Oxford provided training in the therapy for depression and anxiety disorders, but limited instruction to those interested in working with schizophrenia. That has changed and these courses, and new ones developing since, now include modules on managing psychosis, although these still provide a limited focus on psychosis, albeit within a very valuable overall introduction to CBT.

SPECIALIST CBT COURSES

New specialist courses have also developed, for example, as multidisciplinary Masters Degrees in CBT for patients with severe mental illness in Manchester and Southampton Universities. These are two-year courses, with the first year focusing on CBT and the second year on research and development. Students first learn the general model of CBT in Module 1 before specialising in techniques in working with patients with severe mental illness in Module 2 and the families and severe mental illness in Module 3. The courses were first established in 1997 and 2000 respectively, but are limited in availability of places and appropriate local clinical supervisors, and also by travelling for many potential trainees. Funding can also be an obstacle, although many local funding organisations

A Case Study Guide to Cognitive Behaviour Therapy of Psychosis. Edited by
David Kingdon and Douglas Turkington. © 2002 John Wiley & Sons, Ltd.

(UK Workforce Confederations and their predecessors) have been supportive when approached with a good case.

PSYCHOSOCIAL INTERVENTION COURSES

'Thorn' courses and other courses in psychosocial interventions (e.g. in Sheffield) are more available around the UK, but these have generally recruited nurses and occupational therapists rather than other professions. These courses were originally set up in the early 1990s with a remit that was initially case management and family work, but the original courses at London and Manchester began to include CBT in the early-1990s and courses established since (e.g. in Nottingham, Hackney, Bournemouth and Gloucester) have followed this pattern (see further details in Chapter 14). CBT training on these courses has been structured in different ways but has usually included the elements shown in Table 13.1.

Understanding what it is like to have a psychotic illness

Introduction to this area is well described by O'Carroll (Chapter 14). Users of services have often been involved to convey their experiences of their mental health problems and the response from services. Exercises which can be particularly effective are those developed by people from the hearing voices networks, such as getting two trainees to talk to each other while another whispers or speaks loudly in one of their ears. This can help to get across the experience of distraction and the emotions evoked, especially where the speech is unpleasant in content. An exercise used in normalising psychosis can be to list the number of ways that one person could "drive someone else mad": e.g. stop them sleeping, give them amphetamines, deceive them in various ways (see Kingdon & Turkington, 1994, for further examples). This assists trainees in understanding the many ways that psychotic symptoms can be evoked and the many statements that people experiencing strange phenomena use to explain them. It also helps

Table 13.1 Sample topics for a basic course for CBT for psychosis

Topics covered
- Understanding what it is like to have a psychotic illness.
- Psychopathology of schizophrenia and other psychotic illnesses.
- Evidence base for CBT in severe mental illness.
- Training in CBT assessment.
- Working with hallucinations and delusions.
- Working with negative symptoms and thought disorder.
- Co-morbid conditions, e.g. depression, substance misuse, personality disorder, suicide, hostility.

them begin to think through what it must be like to have frightening things happening to you which you have difficulty explaining, and the powerful effect of finding an explanation—even if it is the wrong one.

Psychopathology of schizophrenia and other psychotic illnesses

Knowledge of the phenomena experienced with psychotic illnesses is often lacking, even in experienced mental health workers. They may be aware of voices, but not the range and types of delusions—and again, not just passivity, delusions of reference or thought interference: primary and secondary. Negative symptoms are also frequently misunderstood. The influences on them are many, e.g. medication, positive symptoms and depression, and the cognitive deficits that have been demonstrated are useful to understand in planning therapy.

Evidence base for CBT in severe mental illness

Critical evaluation of the evidence is important to understand what is, and is not, established in a rapidly evolving area (see Chapter 16 on Implementation).

Training in CBT assessment

CBT assessment, especially in this area, is based on an effective mental health assessment. Generic assessments identify needs, the presenting problem, history of that problem, personal history, medical and psychiatric history, social circumstances and relevant demographic details. A mental state examination determining the presentation of the person's psychological problems supplements this. There may be different ways of describing elements of the assessment but essentially the same core items will be noted. A cognitive assessment builds on this, identifying relevant cognitions, behaviours and emotions and the relationship between them.

Training in use of relevant rating instruments

The Thorn courses have used the KGV scale (Krawiecka, Goldberg & Vaughan, 1977) as a broad symptom measure for psychosis and supplemented this with the Social Behaviour Scale (Birchwood et al., 1990). More specific instruments for assessing hallucinations and delusions are available, of which PSYRATS (Haddock et al., 2001) is a good example. It assesses the dimensional nature of hallucinations and delusions—e.g. distress, preoccupations, disruption, attributions—which is valuable in focusing therapeutic strategies. There is also a case to be made for the use of the Health of the Nation Outcome Scales (Wing, Curtis & Beevor, 1996) which combine a range of important areas, e.g. social functioning, risk and symptomatology, in one brief scale and which is soon to become part of NHS mental health information requirements (minimum dataset) in the UK.

Working with hallucinations and delusions

Necessary skills in this area are described in the introduction. The ABC formulation can be a valuable way of enabling trainees to identify antecedents and link to relevant beliefs and consequences. Role-play, video interviews and, particularly, case discussion are useful training methods.

Working with negative symptoms and thought disorder

Negative symptoms are sometimes neglected but there is increasing evidence that they respond differentially to CBT compared to control groups. Taking the pressure off patients seems to be particularly important, combined with carer work, and again case discussion and supervision are important in getting this across in practice. Unfortunately the length of time available to work with negative symptoms on courses may mean that little progress is seen in the time available, even though the appropriate techniques are used. It took 18 months for such differential effects to emerge in our own study (Sensky et al., 2000).

Co-morbid conditions, e.g. depression, substance misuse, personality disorder, suicide, hostility

All these areas commonly present with patients and some discussion on the ways of proceeding are necessary. CBT for patients with depression and suicidality can proceed whether they have psychosis or not, and generally the same techniques can be used—working with faulty cognitions, assumptions and self-esteem. Similarly, some basic motivational interviewing techniques can be used for substance misuse, and even an introduction to Dialectical Behaviour Therapy may be relevant and possible, dependent on the teaching skills available. However, co-morbid areas inevitably involve greater levels of expertise, and it would be very ambitious to expect a Thorn trainee to pick these up solely within a relatively brief CBT module.

The Insight into Schizophrenia programme has been developed by a multi-professional group (Turkington et al., 2002) with funding from a pharmaceutical company (Pfizer) to make CBT and psycho-education available on a more widespread basis. A brief intervention using written materials has been developed with nurses trained in essentially the elements described for the Thorn courses above. Its format is described in Table 13.2.

Table 13.2   The Insight into Schizophrenia programme

Role of the Insight into Schizophrenia Nurse:
- co-ordinates the programme, enrols patients and carers and collects data
- counsels patients and carers and provides CBT
- introduces the Insight educational materials
- identifies training needs in conjunction with the unit
- delivers tailored training within the CMHT

Patients receive six sessions of CBT with the ISN:
- The ISN and patient together review a selection of the leaflets, which might be given to the patient to keep.

Carer counselling sessions with the ISN:
- The carer receives three sessions of CBT with the ISN.
- A selection of leaflets is reviewed by the ISN and carer together, and the carer might be offered the books to keep.

PATIENT SESSIONS
Session 1   Engaging/developing explanations
- *Aim*: To develop a range of explanations
- *Leaflet 1*: About your treatment

engagement
- collaboration
- understanding of diagnosis/symptoms/treatment
- unconditional positive regard
- jargon free/non patronising
- generating a problem list

stress vulnerability
- genetic/developmental/environmental
- individual threshold
- ambient stress
- life events/critical incidents
- raising the threshold

Session 2   Case formulation
- *Aim*: To develop a formulation linking critical incidents, schemas and psychotic symptoms
- *Leaflet 3*: Leisure time and relationships

Session 3   Symptom management
- *Aim*: To develop a clear focus on the management of one psychotic symptom
- *Leaflet 2*: Self-care and lifestyle
- *Leaflet 5*: Managing your symptoms

Session 4   Adherence
- *Aim*: The patient will develop an understanding of their attitude towards medication
- *Leaflet 1*: About your treatment
- *Leaflet 4*: Drug and alcohol advice

continues overleaf

Table 13.2   (*continued*)

Session 5   Core belief/attitude changes
- *Aim*: Patient will be clear about main core beliefs/attitudes and will have started to make one of them functional
- *Leaflet 3*: Leisure time and relationships

Session 6   Relapse prevention
- *Aim*: To collaboratively develop a relapse prevention plan
- *Leaflet 2*: Self-care and lifestyle

CARER SESSIONS

Session 1
- *Aim*: To engage with carer, start developing alternative explanations and problem list
- *Leaflet 1*: A positive outcome—working together
- *Leaflet 5*: About schizophrenia and similar illnesses

Session 2   Formulation, stress management and coping strategies
- *Aim*: To share a formulation and explore stress management and coping strategies
- *Leaflet 3*: Continuing medication—how you can help
- *Leaflet 4*: Coping with schizophrenia

Session 3   Goal-setting, problem-solving and relapse prevention
- *Aim*: To highlight a main problem and look at goal-setting and problem-solving. To produce a relapse blueprint/action plan
- *Leaflet 1*: A positive outcome—working together
- *Leaflet 2*: Hospital admission and difficult situations
- *Leaflet 3*: Continuing medication—how you can help

Programme materials
- A series of five leaflets for patients and five leaflets for carers
- Designed with advice from a panel of clinicians, users and help groups
- Offers advice/information to patients and carers on ways of coping
- Contains useful addresses/phone numbers for self help groups

PATIENT LEAFLETS

Leaflet 1
- Symptoms
- Drug treatments
- Non-drug treatments
- Side effects

Leaflet 2
- Reducing risk of relapse
- Healthy eating
- Relaxation
- Patient leaflets

Leaflet 3
- Establishing a daily routine
- Others' reactions to the illness

Table 13.2 *(continued)*

Leaflet 4
- Why take medication?
- Avoiding street drugs
- Patient leaflets

Leaflet 5
- Recognising symptoms
- Why attend therapy?
- Avoiding symptom triggers

Insight into schizophrenia is supported by an educational grant from Pfizer Ltd.

TRAINING IN COGNITIVE BEHAVIOUR APPROACHES FOR INPATIENTS

The developments that have occurred in CBT over the past decade have been predominantly with outpatients (although many studies have enlisted patients while they have been acute inpatients). Developing therapeutic skills in inpatient staff is very important as so many patients spend weeks or months of their time in such settings when they are at the height of their illness. There has been major concern at the state of wards and that users express that they do not feel listened to. In 1999, John Allen, at the time a nurse tutor, and I developed a staff training initiative to try to begin to address some of these issues (Allen & Kingdon, 1998). Staff from inpatient wards in Nottingham were offered the choice of one of three training days. They were given a basic introduction to CBT with specific discussion of its application to psychosis and their views on this. There then followed use of videos of patient interviews and participation in role-plays to use techniques for working with hallucinations and delusions. The aim of the workshop was to introduce CBT to staff such that they would be able to understand the potential for its use and consider it in the future. Supervision was then established on the three inpatient ward sites for ten sessions run by Thorn-trained nurses (supervised in turn by DK).

The training day was well attended by a total of 36 nursing and occupational therapy staff. The written, anonymous evaluation was positive with the workshop being described as relevant and practical. The supervision was more problematic: about half of the original group participated, but few came to more than three to five sessions. Evaluation suggested that there were problems getting time to attend (although funding for agency staffing to replace that time was available to nurses in charge of wards).

Although regular sessions with patients on the wards were not envisaged, discussion of how it might be valuable in their approach to patients was—but this was probably not conveyed well.

Lessons learned from the workshops were that many staff were very fearful of opening a "can of worms", and that stabilising rather than exploring and discussing difficulties was reinforced by senior staff. They anticipated increased patient aggression to others or harm to patients themselves. They also expressed the belief that their basic training had not given them skills to deal with emotional problems. With some justification, many also felt that they did not have time and were too easily pulled away from discussions with patients. There were some professional issues, including the question of who should perform CBT—psychologists or nurse therapists? There were also concerns about senior staff feeling underskilled and sometimes blocking access to supervision and support.

As general professional tuition begins to provide training in CBT, inpatient staff will begin to use this approach on wards. However, until the time pressures are addressed, it is clear that this will prove problematic although it may be possible to change attitudes to discussing important emotional issues as fears are found to be groundless. There is little evidence that such discussion inevitably opens "cans of worms" which cause increased distress and aggravation. More frequently patients say that they feel listened to, distress is alleviated and cooperation is developed. The one proviso is that CBT involves collaboration not confrontation, and when patients do become distressed, it must be realised that drawing back is more appropriate than driving onwards regardless.

CONCLUSION

Practical professional training, such as that offered by the Thorn programme (Gournay & Birley, 1998), enables mental health nurses and other keyworkers to become fully and actively involved in the management of schizophrenia and to improve outcome. In time, high-quality training in evidence-based techniques is overcoming a reluctance common among nursing staff to fully acknowledge the diagnosis of schizophrenia, and has the potential to prevent the use of inappropriate interventions. Moreover, training gives mental health professionals the confidence and enthusiasm to become fully involved in the management of patients with schizophrenia (Gamble, 1995).

Chapter 14

MODELLING THE MODEL: TRAINING PEOPLE TO USE PSYCHOSOCIAL INTERVENTIONS

Madeline O'Carroll

There is now a strong evidence base for the efficacy of psychosocial interventions for people with serious mental illness (see Chapter 15). Users of mental health services often ask for alternatives to medication, and policy initiatives such as the National Service Framework for Mental Health (Department of Health, 1999) also encourage their use. In addition, there is now a good range of manuals providing instruction on the use of these techniques (see Introduction). The challenge for those providing professional education and training is to translate and transform the clinical material in order to provide effective learning experiences.

Two key themes have emerged from my work as a lecturer and supervisor in psychosocial interventions. Firstly, it seems essential that the staff in effect "model the model" when teaching students. Secondly, there has been an evolving awareness that the course is perhaps less about exploring the beliefs of patients, service users and carers and more about uncovering the attitudes of the staff who are working with them. This fits with the view of the users movement which "has always said . . . mental health care is to do with issues of attitudes" (Rose, 2001).

In this chapter I will provide a brief introduction to the Thorn Initiative. I will then consider how aspects of a clinical model may be used to provide both content and a structure for training in psychosocial interventions, with particular emphasis on working with individuals.

A Case Study Guide to Cognitive Behaviour Therapy of Psychosis. **Edited by**
David Kingdon and Douglas Turkington. © 2002 John Wiley & Sons, Ltd.

THORN INITIATIVE

The Thorn Initiative began training mental health staff in 1992 at sites in London and Manchester with a grant from the Sir Jules Thorn Charitable Trust. Following the success of the first courses the intention was to develop training at other sites. Although there are variations in the academic level, structure and organisation of "Thorn" courses they nonetheless share certain key characteristics. The views of users and carers are central to both the clinical work and course development and delivery.

The courses are part time and students usually attend college for one study day per week. Students have to identify a minimum of four individual patients/service users and two families with whom they will work over a period of 12 months. All courses cover three broad areas:

- Case management: this includes policy and legislation and how services are organised and care is delivered
- Psychological interventions for psychosis: delivered on an individual basis
- Family work: offered to families and carers of people with schizophrenia.

Both the individual work and the work with families are derived from cognitive behaviour models. In addition, the work of Leff and colleagues (e.g. Leff & Vaughn, 1985) and the concept of expressed emotion is central to working with families.

USING A COGNITIVE BEHAVIOUR FRAMEWORK

Although the Thorn course does not aim to provide training in cognitive behaviour therapy, nonetheless it does draw extensively on this model. The principles of cognitive behaviour theory and therapy are taught on the course by practising therapists and follow the format described by Hawton and colleagues (1989). The course team was also aware that the study day provided a number of opportunities for modelling some of the skills. This enables a mirroring between the clinical and educational experience that can aid learning. There is also a repetition as the same material is presented in different ways. Clearly the relationship between the student and the lecturer/trainer is not the same as the relationship between the service user/patient and practitioner. However there are enough similarities to make the case for educators modelling characteristics or techniques that are deemed to be essential to good clinical practice.

The Cognitive Therapy Checklist has been used to assess the clinical skills of mental health nurses working with people with serious mental illness (Devane et al., 1998), and incorporates two sets of skills: general and specific. The five general skills are: agenda-setting, feedback, interpersonal effectiveness, understanding and collaboration. The second set is more specific to cognitive behaviour approaches and includes focusing on key cognitions and guided discovery.

Although some of the general skills may be used in a number of therapeutic models, collaboration and feedback are more common to cognitive behaviour approaches. At the centre of all work with patients and service users is the therapeutic alliance which in cognitive behaviour approaches is viewed as a collaboration. Devane and colleagues (1998) found that the community mental health nurses in their study were rated poorly on collaboration. For nurses, and probably doctors, it is likely that neither their initial training nor the roles in which they are currently employed include or encourage such an approach, and it will take some students time to develop the ability to work collaboratively.

Two of the skills—agenda-setting and feedback—can easily be incorporated into the study day. Although the timetable is generally set at the beginning of the course, it is nonetheless important to be flexible and respond to students' requests, for example, to review material that may have already been covered or to include additional related material. The lecturer's ability to respond to and manage these requests can be a useful learning experience for students.

Feedback can be sought and given in various ways. At the outset of the course the students identify the ground rules by which the group will operate. These are likely to shape how feedback is given. In addition, when students practise clinical skills or bring in audiotapes of their clinical work, it can be helpful if they identify the item(s) on which they would like feedback. Another example is asking students to evaluate the study day using a format such as "least and best". With this they are asked to make a statement reflecting what they liked least and best about the day. Thus the feedback can be quite broad and may relate to aspects of the environment, such as not liking the chairs, and can also provide useful information to the lecturers about the content or teaching strategies. Sometimes it is interesting for the group (and the lecturer) to hear that a particular approach will be commented on as being least liked by some students while others report it was the part they liked best. This helps to illustrate the idea that there are always multiple perspectives.

BELIEFS ABOUT PEOPLE WITH MENTAL ILLNESS

As noted above, the Cognitive Therapy Checklist is used to assess clinical skills. The general skills may also be used to structure some of the educational experience and provide some of the course content. However, the main model for individual work with patients and service users broadly follows the sequence outlined by Nelson (1997) and includes engagement, coping strategies, psycho-education and modification of beliefs. The teaching is timetabled and taught in the same order.

ENGAGEMENT

One of the difficulties for students already working in a professional capacity as they learn new skills can be the thought that much of their previous practice by implication must have been wrong. Not only is this incorrect as students come with a range of skills and have a wealth of experience to draw on, but perhaps more importantly it can be quite demoralising. It is helpful to ask students to produce an inventory of their skills and experience to clarify what they can access both individually and as a group.

Students are asked to develop collaborative relationships, and often this will be with people already on their caseload. It needs to be acknowledged that it is quite difficult to change approach within an existing relationship. One of the barriers to this may be the beliefs held by staff (often these are shared by the team as a whole) regarding working with a particular individual. The course team ask the students to adopt or adhere to two basic assumptions when working with people who are having distressing experiences or symptoms:

1. Patients and service users are honest.
2. They are trying to cope with their experiences (Fox & Conroy, 2000; Newell, 1994).

The discussion that follows students being asked what they think about these assumptions is usually very lively. The initial response tends to be a list of examples drawn from their own practice illustrating the opposite. Gamble (2000) raises the issue of staff attitudes towards people with mental illness and acknowledges that few of us are immune from adopting a judging or critical approach, at least at times.

A large part of the work of mental health practitioners involves observing patients but we should be mindful that Goffman's critique (1961) of the asylums may still be valid, and take care not to view all behaviour from within a pathological framework. Adopting a perspective that sees individuals as trying to cope is one way of trying to challenge this view. In this respect students are continually asked to think how particular behaviours that staff or carers view as problematic might actually be part of the person's way of coping. They also need to check this with the individual, but it is a useful framework for students to use.

PSYCHO-EDUCATION

There are a number of components to Nelson's work (1997) on promoting insight. The first involves eliciting the patient's views on mental illness and schizophrenia, and a similar approach is adopted in relation to students. Early in the course they are asked first to identify their personal beliefs regarding the causes of schizophrenia (they are not asked to share this with the group). Next the group as a whole are asked to brainstorm everything they have heard, or has been suggested, as a cause of schizophrenia. This generally covers a range of explanatory models, including biological, psychological, social and spiritual. The stress-vulnerability model is then offered as a framework for understanding how any of us can move from being well to unwell. This is followed by a discussion on how the factors identified by the students can be incorporated within a stress-vulnerability model.

Nelson (1997) says that, depending on the patient's response, it may be necessary to spend time destigmatising mental illness. An educational setting provides a useful space in which to reflect on how our experiences as mental health practitioners have shaped our beliefs about mental illness. Although training in mental health may help to assuage our personal fears about madness, the process of training is quite likely to result in stereotyped beliefs about "the mentally ill patient". The asylum system made patients and staff "creatures of each other" but the difference between the two groups was institutionalised (Hinshelwood, 1998). Psychiatry, too, and in particular the use of diagnostic classification systems, has been in part responsible for perpetuating the view that phenomena such as delusions are abnormal. More recently this dichotomous approach has been superseded by the view that experiences can be seen as being on a continuum (Craig, 2000). Nonetheless, although many recently qualified staff will not have trained within an asylum themselves, they are likely to have been either taught by staff or work alongside colleagues who were. There is a risk that the negative beliefs regarding patients may have been imported from the hospital to the community.

It is common in designing teaching and learning strategies to ask questions in order to allow students to explore issues (Ramsden, 1992). However, the way in which the questions are framed can inadvertently serve to reinforce rather than challenge existing stereotyped perceptions of people with mental health problems. For example, asking the students "How would you think, feel or behave in this situation?" often results in quite a different set of responses than asking "How would a person with a mental health problem think, feel or behave in this situation?". By approaching issues from a more personal perspective there is less of a tendency to make stereotyped responses. This approach can be used to address many questions from identifying the difficulties of accessing health services to considering why someone might not complete a course of prescribed medication.

Under the broad umbrella of psycho-education the next stage of the clinical work involves using a normalising rationale (Kingdon & Turkington, 1991). This follows on from the discussion earlier that phenomena such as hearing voices and having (what to some may appear to be) unusual beliefs are within the normal range of human experience. However, the practitioner can only put this view forward if it is one that is genuinely held. To this extent it is important that the students can recognise some of these experiences within themselves, again to challenge the notion that it is only "others" who have these experiences. Nelson (1997) and Gamble (2000) recommend asking practitioners and students to identify occasions when they might have had experiences such as hearing a voice or held beliefs that might be similar to the people with whom they are working. It is probably necessary to establish this view among practitioners initially before it can actually be seen as "normal".

CONCLUSION

While accrediting bodies will determine the content of academic courses, the method of delivery tends to be less prescribed. However it is important that there is consistency between clinical practice and teaching and learning, even though the nature of the relationships are not the same. To this extent lecturers should use the study day to model the techniques and skills.

In relation to attitudes Gamble (2000) acknowledges that staff working with people with serious mental health problems are as likely to respond as negatively as carers. Stereotyped beliefs about mental illness would seem to the norm, with mental health staff holding their own particular set of beliefs. As Nelson (1997) notes, socialisation and education can result in a new set of beliefs but they overlie the old beliefs, they do not erase them. Courses based in higher education are well placed to transform attitudes in a way that skills training are not (Harvey & Knight, 1996). The issue of the beliefs held by mental health practitioners about people with mental health problems requires further exploration.

Chapter 15

CLINICAL SUPERVISION

David Kingdon and Jeremy Pelton

Supervision is fundamental to developing skills in CBT, especially for patients with psychoses because of the need to adjust techniques learned in training to the realities of everyday clinical practice and to a very variable group of patients. Its goal has been described as modifying in-therapy behaviours by support and training. It can particularly enable the therapists to step back and review and reflect on their practice to learn and prepare for the next session. It is complementary and at least as important as workshops and lectures.

The natural consequence of the development of the courses for CBT and schizophrenia mentioned previously has been the need for good effective clinical supervision. Clinical supervision should be seen as the cornerstone of the therapist's practice and although generic supervision is often readily available in Trusts there is a distinct void for CBT with schizophrenia. Receiving the appropriate clinical supervision is imperative to the continuing development of the therapist and the safety of the therapy offered. Once the above courses were beginning to be established the problem for mental health professionals attending them was the limited access to clinical supervision on completion—clinical supervision is often provided during the course, but once complete there is an onus on the therapists to find their own supervisor.

Supervision can occur in group and individual settings by more experienced therapists or peers and is certainly a two-way process. Who should be your supervisor? Often little choice exists with few members of staff ready, available or sufficiently experienced to assist, but where options exist, choosing may well be more on personal grounds than for professional reasons. Supervision can feel a very personal process, exposing oneself and one's practice to the gaze of someone else may mean that a good personal relationship takes precedence over expertise and teaching ability. Issues such as gender, race/culture and power—a direct line manager may

A Case Study Guide to Cognitive Behaviour Therapy of Psychosis. Edited by
David Kingdon and Douglas Turkington. © 2002 John Wiley & Sons, Ltd.

not be the ideal supervisor—can influence this and certainly influence the supervisory relationship. Feeling comfortable in the relationship is important, but ensuring that the supervisor has the necessary experience and skills can save time being wasted for both. The needs of a student new to the area and of a more experienced clinician developing skills in this new area will lead to different arrangements, needs and interactions. Where experienced supervisors are not available, peer supervision is certainly not to be undervalued and, in a number of areas, we have seen therapists collaboratively develop their skills to a high standard through such mutual support and learning. It can also support supervision with experienced supervisors.

The raw material for supervision are process notes, tapes, and verbal reports and each is valuable. Notes help to prompt and, as a supervisor, notes of supervisory sessions are essential *aide-mémoires* for future sessions. Such notes can usefully include some verbatim commentary as this further illuminates the supervisory process.

Most supervision occurs in face-to-face interviews and this is certainly the ideal, but sometimes distance has meant that we have used telephones— one-to-one and using conference phones—and even correspondence. Supplemented with tapes of interviews this can be of some value, but the contribution of non-verbal communication, the writing down of formulations, or simple diagrams illustrating key points or looking at leaflets or research papers, becomes noticeably absent and can be difficult to compensate for—although fax, e-mail and post can help. The use of video technology may help as it becomes widely available, but unfortunately rarely seems to be sited in the areas where long-distance supervision is necessary, and neither is the availability of broad band transmission to webcams—but once it is more available, its potential will be well worth exploring.

Group supervision has advantages in providing multiple views, pooling knowledge, cost-effectiveness and emotional support, but lacks the individual attention of one-to-one supervision. Groups may serve more talkative members better than those who are less assertive.

What are the tasks of supervision? Carroll (1996) has described them generally as being:

- *Creating a learning relationship.*
- *Teaching.* This involves informal rather than formal teaching generally, using modelling of behaviours and techniques used in role-play. It may also be helpful to recommend relevant reading.

- *Counselling.* This is more controversial but involves helping supervisees to learn from their own reactions to and thoughts about patients. Where personal issues arise, as can be expected from work with patients, it may be possible to deal with relatively small matters in supervision but if not, giving advice to seek alternative interventions would usually be appropriate. If the supervisees are becoming too distressed or over-involved, it may even be appropriate to advise them to withdraw from such therapeutic endeavours until they are ready to return.
- *Consulting.* This involves helping the supervisees to develop a solid but flexible formulation based on a full assessment, and then work out strategies for change and relevant cognitive interventions.
- *Evaluating.* This refers to both supervisors and supervisees. This may be part of training and asking the trainees to evaluate themselves first makes a sometimes difficult job more collaborative. Monitoring of the supervision periodically and at completion is also an essential learning experience for supervisors.
- *Monitoring professional/ethical issues.* Circumstances, such as with a suicidal patient, can lead to professional and ethical issues about when to alert others, etc., and a supervisor's overview and support are invaluable. Unfortunately there are also times when personal or sexual issues arise between a therapist and a patient where the protection of a supervisor may be necessary for either, and a supervisor certainly needs to be aware of such possibilities and be ready to act if necessary.

General clinical supervision principles as so far described adapt well to a CBT context, but there is perhaps an advantage in basing supervision, itself, on a CBT model. So, setting agendas, monitoring automatic thoughts, and tackling assumptions are as relevant to supervision as to therapy and allow modelling of these techniques to occur in the supervision session. Clinical supervision often models the therapy session itself. The supervisor runs a time-focused session with an agenda that is collaboratively negotiated between the therapist and the supervisor. The session often starts with a review of the last clinical supervision and how the therapist has progressed since. Any actions from the last session should be revisited and evaluated and if necessary put onto the agenda. The agenda is then set with case studies, problem areas and session difficulties all being possible inclusions. The session then focuses on the agenda with the therapist and the supervisor working through specific examples and generating possible solutions/modifications. Developing a collaborative style where feedback is elicited, and which is regularly evaluated, is appropriate in these contexts. Presenting a full assessment from which a formulation can be drawn is an essential process. At the end of the session the supervisor should evaluate/review the supervision and appropriate negotiated action plans, together with a date and time, should be set for the next time they meet.

The supervisor can also take the analogy a step further by utilising the cognitive therapy scale as a checklist during supervision as all the points have a value. During the supervision session the supervisor should be collaborative, use Socratic questioning (to elicit the way forward from the therapist and not provide all the answers himself), ask for feedback and check for understanding.

Padesky (1996) discusses the format of clinical supervision in CBT and lists five questions that can form the backbone of the session.

1. *Is there a cognitive model for understanding and treating this patient's problem?*
   The therapist needs to be aware of the different models of CBT and how they help both him and the patient to understand the surrounding problem. The model can be drawn diagrammatically, allowing a powerful visual image to be shared with the patient.
2. *Is the cognitive model for formulation and treatment being followed?*
   The supervisor questions the therapist on the process of therapy and aligns it alongside the model for formulation and treatment. Does the formulation accurately portray the patient's circumstances and experiences and has the treatment been driven from the related hypothesis?
3. *Does the therapist have the knowledge and skill to implement the cognitive therapy treatment properly?*
   The therapist needs to be honest enough to highlight any deficits in their expertise and be able to approach the right person to help develop their approaches for the future.
4. *Is the therapeutic response following expected patterns?*
   Again the supervisor and therapist examine the process of therapy. Is it following the expected progress as predicted by the formulation? How does the original hypothesis match up to the current stage in therapy?
5. *What in the client formulation/therapy relationship/therapist response might be interfering with success?*
   If there are problems with the progress in Question 4, the supervisor and therapist can examine a number of avenues, as follows:
   - Does the therapist need to re-evaluate the original formulation and possibly look at another hypothesis?
   - Is there any thing in the therapist/patient relationship that may be interfering with the process of therapy—transference/counter-transference?
   - Does the process of therapy need examining—pacing of sessions, pitch of therapy, patient "buy-in" and understanding of the model?

CONCLUSION

Clinical supervision is underestimated in value, little training in this subject is offered, and it is often something picked up as you go along. It is too important for such a haphazard approach. There is an increasing body of knowledge about how to provide it most effectively. Clinical supervision should be a constructive and supportive process benefiting the patient, the therapist and the supervisor who can learn from each therapeutic contact, even by proxy, more about the application of CBT to psychosis.

Chapter 16

HOW DOES IMPLEMENTATION HAPPEN?

David Kingdon

So far, a variety of practitioners with a range of cases and training have described their experience of using CBT, but how can this training and experience be made more widely available? The widespread use of new evidence-based practices, like CBT of psychosis, develops through diffusion, dissemination and specific implementation initiatives (Koerner et al., 2001). Usually diffusion occurs through publication in scientific journals, conference presentations, etc., but this leads, at best, to very gradual incorporation into routine clinical practice. The exception is where the audience is open and seeking information, has minimal search costs for it, and staff are strongly motivated and highly reinforced by what they learn and their experiences. In the USA, this has been the case with the uptake of dialectical behaviour therapy (DBT) and to some extent this has also occurred with CBT for psychosis in the UK. Suicides, the repeated experience of treatment failure, and recurrent ineffective admissions has, according to Koerner et al. (2001), fuelled a groundswell of demand for training and implementation of DBT. Although it has a limited evidence base, the widespread perception of success in using these techniques has led to its spread. CBT for psychosis has had a major impact in the UK and Scandinavia but less so elsewhere despite its much stronger basis in evidence (see later). Some of this may be due to the need for time for the significance of the studies to penetrate, but there is also the need to develop "product champions" and development proposals to access resources. Koerner also cites the importance of having an RCT published in the journal *Archives of General Psychiatry* (e.g. Sensky et al., 2000), as being influential because it is where decision-makers look, not only in the USA but elsewhere. It may also be that the clinical impact has a less direct effect on patients' symptoms and quality of life, and possibly admission rates but not as dramatically as has occurred with DBT.

A Case Study Guide to Cognitive Behaviour Therapy of Psychosis. Edited by David Kingdon and Douglas Turkington. © 2002 John Wiley & Sons, Ltd.

Diffusion spreads interest but availability of high-quality training programmes with quantified outcomes are needed. UK developments in this area have been described (see Chapters 13 and 14). However developing opportunities to provide training for services as a whole, or teams within them, can be an appropriate route to disseminate good practice. Assistance in this is available from many of the groups who have published outcome studies and treatment manuals and from those running training courses (e.g. Thorn trainers).

With a team or service-based approach, pre-training consultation is important to inform and build consensus within the mental health service. This needs to be matched with needs assessment, costs, etc., and the initiator of the training request has to be able to sell the "product" with assistance from those offering the training. They also need to be persuasive—citing outcomes, relevance and personal meaning to individual patients, e.g. individual savings with specific patients or, more likely, improvement in quality of life. Usually the initiator has little time in which to do this. The individual training organiser will need to spend time on site to focus interest, sometimes even rein in enthusiasm until the organisation is committed and ready to move forward. With on-site training, effective methods need to incorporate follow-up—e.g. 5 days training, 6 months practice, then 2–5 days of further training and presentation by participants of the case(s) with which they have worked. There also needs to be careful attention to supervision arrangements during the training period and after. Who can provide it locally? What will it cost? in time and financial resources? How can that be put in place?

Obstacles to implementation of training schemes include the perception that "we can't" get involved because of lack of resources—financial and personnel—setting constraints on moving training forward. In contrast an approach that "you must", set by external managers or government, can lead to resistance, even rebellion, whereas an approach based on persuasion that high-fidelity training will be in everyone's best interests is more likely to be successful (and models the essence of a CBT approach). Assessing the contingencies that compete with people's time—initiators, participants and trainers (who usually have a "day job" as well)—can improve the successful implementation of a programme. Training as a team can lead to continuing development with support and understanding from the whole team. "Developing a learning environment" sounds good. In practice, it means changing attitudes, valuing training time, and providing training resources—books, manuals, videos, self-help materials, etc. Involving decision-makers early is also very important. Contingencies on performance, e.g. inclusion in appraisals, lead to actual use. Where private practice is relevant, different reimbursement rates for evidence-based practice may be paid or, alternatively, promotion and increased grades and subsequent remuneration may be individual advantages to participating in training. This can be viewed as a disadvantage to managers, but planning ahead to use skills effectively and retain staff can lead to the best of both worlds—highly motivated and appreciative staff who provide better service for clients within a budget that is less affected by the need to cover sickness and extra costs for exceptional but very expensive out-of-service placements. These latter may be more likely to be prevented by staff who are experienced and confident in their abilities with patients who appreciate the time and understanding that they are receiving.

So, how can cognitive behaviour therapy be made available to all those patients with psychosis that may be able to benefit from it? Inevitably resources are an issue, both for financial reasons and for trained personnel, but anyone who waits for resources to be made available will wait forever, or at least until someone with a more proactive approach comes along. In any service, enlisting the support of managers, training departments and clinical staff is critical (Tarrier et al., 1999). Assembling evidence is essential, and it is necessary to present it in a relevant way, taking national guidance into account.

WHO IMPLEMENTS?

Although the endpoint of any implementation strategy is for individual therapists to use CBT directly with patients, there are a number of groups who need to be involved to make this happen, and each group has different needs and issues.

Nationally

Evidence in support of CBT for severe mental illness from government in England goes back to the Clinical Standards Advisory Group report (1994) which advocated it as part of a service for patients with schizophrenia. The Review of Psychotherapy (NHS Executive, 1996) and accompanying supporting evidence on What Works? (Roth et al., 1988) similarly provided endorsement. In the National Service Framework (Department of Health, 1999), psychosocial interventions are given strong encouragement: "For schizophrenia there is growing evidence of effectiveness for psychological therapies including some cognitive approaches" (p. 46). Also, performance assessment of Standard 4, dealing with severe mental illness, will be "assessed by access to psychological therapies" (p. 66).

Professional groups

Professional organisations have also been supportive. The British Psychological Society has recently published a favourable review of the area (BPS, 2000). The development of techniques which fully utilise and build on the training of clinical psychologists, both CBT for psychosis and DBT, has led to a considerable increase in enthusiasm for working in the area of severe mental illness and the return of many to the practice. The late 1980s and early 1990s were a time when there had been a serious drift away, with the exception of a small number of stalwarts who remained working in rehabilitation services. Most have embraced the new developments and welcomed the increased interest, particularly among trainees, in the new developments.

Nurses have similarly been developing skills through Thorn (Gournay & Birley, 1998) and similar courses, and basic professional training in many areas is now incorporating CBT. The turmoil in which training has been over the past decade, and the severe shortages of qualified nurses, has seriously impaired development of practice, but support from training bodies has been forthcoming. There is a gradual movement away from generic community nurse courses to more specific postgraduate training which meets needs better.

The Royal College of Psychiatrists has also given invaluable support through, for example, providing a platform for presentation of results at workshops and scientific meetings, and inclusion of mandatory training in CBT for psychiatrists. This is despite CBT for psychosis apparently undermining some fundamental psychiatric assumptions, e.g. that delusions are not amenable to reason, and that an illness with demonstrable biological abnormalities can respond to psychological methods. In fact, what seemed to us to be fundamental and highly controversial has emerged not to hold in the UK, Australasia and Scandinavia. These do, however, remain issues in the USA and other parts of the world where CBT for psychosis has yet to make a substantial impact. However, the American Psychiatric Association published guidelines for the treatment of schizophrenia in 1998, and concluded:

> Several controlled and uncontrolled studies have extended Beck's cognitive therapy to schizophrenia, with encouraging clinical results, including reduction or removal of delusions and hallucinations. While cognitive therapy and remediation techniques appear promising, there have been no well-designed controlled studies demonstrating their efficacy. Furthermore, the techniques are still undergoing modification. At this stage of development, they are not recommended for routine clinical use. (APA, 1998)

Some positive consideration is occurring and interest is certainly growing with studies appearing as far away as Malaysia and China, although further developments (see evidence below) have yet to be incorporated in the US guidance.

Psychiatrists in the UK seem to have readily accepted that so-called delusions may have underlying meaning and are understandable. Consequently, working with them may assist in changing them. It may be that the impact of Laing (e.g. Laing & Esterson, 1970) paved the way. His work has had a wide general circulation among the general public and psychiatrists, and provided examples of patients where their symptoms seemed understandable in the context in which they lived. The social psychiatry school has also been strong such that links between social circumstances and schizophrenia were now accepted by psychiatrists. The shift to acceptance of the way such beliefs were perceived was relevant and has not been difficult for most. CBT has established a solid reputation as an effective and flexible method of working with patients who have a variety of mental health problems in conjunction with medication. The number of psychiatrists using CBT in a formal way is small, but many now refer or use some of the principles (see below in relation to cognitive behaviour approaches).

Acceptance has been easiest where stress-vulnerability models of mental illness (Zubin & Spring, 1977; Tyrer & Steinberg, 1998) are assumed. Where a biological model has been dominant, acceptance of psychosocial interventions has been more difficult. Our usual response has been to give the analogy of physiotherapy in stroke:

> The use of cognitive-behaviour therapy in schizophrenia may seem to be counterintuitive: How can a disorder for which evidence of brain dysfunction exists, respond to a treatment based on listening and talking? Perhaps, the most useful analogy is to the use of physiotherapy and other forms of rehabilitation after a cerebrovascular accident. Physiotherapy [probably] does not change the underlying brain dysfunction but can make a major contribution to overcoming the handicaps caused. Similarly cognitive-behaviour therapy may not change underlying functional abnormalities but may assist in coping and adjustment. The objection is sometimes raised that psychological treatments were clearly demonstrated to be ineffective in schizophrenia in the early 1980s in controlled trials... [However]... new evidence [now exists]... on recent adaptations of cognitive behaviour therapy to schizophrenia. (Kingdon, 2000)

Professional issues have nevertheless sometimes impinged on smooth implementation. Rivalry between psychiatrists, nurses and clinical psychologists may be an issue—the former defending a biological model against all comers—which can mean they fail to refer appropriate patients or fail to support and sometimes stymie the development of services. With psychologists, professional isolationism or elitism can interfere where work with teams and psychiatrists with complex patient problems is essential. Waiting for patients to attend an office and discharging them if they do not, means that many of the patients who could benefit fail to receive a service. Motivation and paranoia are key issues that can stop patients attending services. Safety issues do need to be considered carefully but should not block progress. Looking at integrating brief interventions may be necessary in the future. Certainly supervision and peer group support are essential to developing services. The integration of nurses with basic training (e.g. Thorn) has sometimes been too slow, and rather than being allies may be viewed as competitors.

Senior clinical staff in nursing, psychology or psychiatry may not wish to be involved personally or cannot free the time, but they can be invaluable allies. They will refer patients and can valuably support developments in the variety of forums, formal and informal, that exist from corridor conversations with managers to more explicit support from senior staff or within management committees. As clinical or medical directors, the more complete a case you can provide, the more help they can give.

Every service has staff with skills to understand the concepts behind CBT. Most of these staff, in our experience, have been only too delighted to become involved in training (see previous section), and many find the approach resonates with their current clinical practice but adds a dimension that substantially and very noticeably improves effectiveness and job satisfaction. Enlisting staff has not been found to be a problem, and competency levels were discussed in the section on training. However, finding the time to use the skills developed can be an issue, as different levels of CBT need to be considered:

- Specialised therapeutic input—advanced CBT
- Less specialised input—basic CBT
- A cognitive behaviour approach.

Each is valid and essential to consider for each service. A cognitive behaviour approach can:

- be therapeutic in its own right
- assist in patient management, e.g. of medication and social interventions ("compliance"/adherence)
- enable patients to accept more formal CBT and assist in them getting benefit from it.

Does such a piecemeal approach lead to inferior quality? We would argue it does not, as developing these levels of care is the most efficient way of using limited resources.

Levels of formal recognition of training and accreditation are available from workshop certificates to Thorn Diplomas, Diplomas and Masters courses in CBT, accreditation by national organisations such as the British Association of Behavioural Cognitive Psychotherapy (BABCP) or internationally, by the Academy of Cognitive Therapy (ACT). Details are available on the websites of the organisations. The ACT, for example, requires 40 hours' training to have been completed including, ideally, ten in supervised teaching, and a tape of a therapy session and a case study validated by them.

Users and carers

Nationally, the National Schizophrenia Fellowship, 'Rethink', MIND and other voluntary organisations have expressed support for the development of CBT in severe mental health problems. User and carer groups can be supportive, locally. The Hearing Voices Network in the UK and Holland (but not yet widespread elsewhere) has had a major impact on the way "voices" are perceived and, where necessary, managed by the patients with support from others. User groups generally favour non-pharmacological interventions (Rose, 2001) but there is little industrial support—either PR or marketing—and therefore prospects of making these forms of treatment available on a widespread basis are limited. One important example is of the Insight CBT programme as funded in several UK sites by Pfizer.

Funding or commissioning groups

Involving potential funders or commissioners of services at an early stage in proposals for any major developments is most likely to ensure their support for, and even commitment to, the implementation of CBT. Even with smaller projects, their influence on the use of the funding they provide can be critical to success. Commissioners and funders will often look to see a reconfiguration of existing services and as this continues to occur so opportunities for such developments emerge. Their concern is to see value-for-money and they need to demonstrate this to those who monitor them, e.g. the Regional Offices in the UK. Their priorities are to balance budgets, improve services and meet government objectives. The information given above about CBT in national priorities may be known to them, but if not it can be brought to their attention.

Provider managers

Provider organisations, e.g. NHS Trusts, will need to free up or increase resources for CBT implementation and cases need to be developed with them to do this. This may possibly be through drawing together consortia of organisations, if that is most economic way or if it relates geographically to areas covered by funding bodies, e.g. the Workforce Confederations or State/Health Authorities. Managers of services have responsibilities for the quality of services and financial viability. Their commitment to working in mental health services is often overlooked by clinical or research staff and yet they are usually strongly dedicated to the development of services and allies not enemies. Improvement in the quality of services is a requirement of clinical governance in the UK and accrediting bodies elsewhere. If the evidence supports such developments, managers are under an obligation to implement them.

Resources are limited, so development bids need to be realistic. If something can be obtained at no, or minimal extra cost, it will be favoured but will also be more likely to attract new resources. This usually means stopping doing something else or doing it less or more efficiently—an option that does not need to be permanent but can provide temporary funding as a pilot project. Such projects that are well evaluated can be invaluable. If word gets back to managers that patients are benefiting—especially if they can attest to this themselves—support and even workforce or financial resources often follow. Demonstrating that patients benefit and clinical staff approve is important to any service development proposal that could take the following form.

DEVELOPING A SERVICE DEVELOPMENT PROPOSAL

The formats for service development proposals differ between organisations, but the central structure tends to be the same although it is essential to adapt it to local circumstances. Components (see Table 16.1) could include the following.

Assessment of local need

Discuss with provider organisations' audit departments, local university departments and Department of Public Health (at health authority) or equivalent if any exercise to assess the number of patients with schizophrenia and related psychoses, e.g. schizoaffective/delusional disorder, has

Table 16.1 Service development proposal

Developing services

1. *Assess local need:*
   - Number of patients with schizophrenia or related psychoses
     For which of these will a service be relevant?
   - Number of available sessions of:
     Skilled therapist time
     - for therapy
     - for training
     - for support and supervision
     Trained therapist time
     - for therapy
     - for training
     - for support and supervision
     Basic cognitive behaviour approach
   - Number of patients seen already by therapists

2. *Assess the local support informally:*
   - psychology department
   - psychiatrists
   - local mental health teams
   - inpatient nurses
   - users and carers
   - general practitioners
   - commissioners of services
   - managers of services
   - local training/educational purchasing organisations (e.g. Workforce
     Confederation)

3. *If the local support is not strong, develop an educational strategy focused on individual groups*

4. *If the local support is strong, develop a case of need:*
   - assemble evidence
     research
     clinical—use local work to demonstrate effectiveness
   - develop an incremental plan for developing a service: training and practice
     e.g. places on CBT courses
   - negotiate costs with Trust/Provider management to develop a shared plan.

been done in the area and/or those in contact with services. If, as is usually the case, it has not, you can produce useful information by checking whether your Trust has any system of gathering such information, e.g. through a mental health computer information system or case register. Where this does not exist, you can proceed in some of the following ways:

- Gather a list of patients registered with depot injection and Clozapine clinics, where these exist.

- Obtain a list of patients with admissions with a diagnosis of above categories from patient administration systems that produce nationally required information returns.
- Contact a hospital and, possibly, other pharmacies who may hold lists of value, e.g. of patients on atypical antipsychotics such as Risperidone, Olanzapine, Quetiapine, Amisulpiride and Zotepine—or where Clozapine or depot clinics do not exist, hospital pharmacists may be able to assist with a list of such patients.
- Care Programme Approach (Kingdon, 1994) or similar registers may be useful in providing lists of patients with severe mental illness, many of whom will have psychosis.
- GP registers can also be useful but are not as readily available and rarely cover the geographical area that services do. Some GPs may have developed their own lists of long-term patients or can assist using medication data.
- Patients who have not been admitted or are solely in the care of GPs are most likely to be missed. Any service that you are able to set up is unlikely to target patients solely in the care of their GP first, but outpatients may be good candidates for referral. There are many with persisting symptoms who could benefit (Sensky et al., 2000).
- Lists of patients who are being seen regularly in outpatients should be obtainable from computerised outpatient management systems by consultant. If consultants are supporting your proposal, they may be prepared to indicate on such lists which patients have the above psychoses.

For whom is CBT relevant?

Studies demonstrating the successful use of CBT in the schizophrenia group of psychoses have included in and outpatients with positive and negative symptoms, early and later in their course, between 16 and 65. They have excluded patients who are too thought disordered to use rating scales with and who have a primary diagnosis of drug or alcohol misuse (although Barrowclough and colleagues have presented promising findings in this dual diagnosis group). Although some services have stressed that they are for patients with "persistent positive symptoms", the evidence is increasing that patients with negative symptoms, e.g. affective blunting, may benefit most.

On this basis, a case of need should distinguish which patients meet and do not meet these criteria as far as information allows—or should simply state these exclusions.

Forensic settings

There is currently very little evidence of effectiveness in forensic settings although these techniques are being used with patients with resistant symptoms in these settings (see Benn, above). The author has presented his experience (Kingdon, 1999) of being the responsible medical officer for a local long-stay forensic ward over a two-year period in Nottingham using a cognitive-behaviour approach with patients whose reasons for admission included sexual assault or exposure, arson, homicidal threats, serious aggressive/antisocial behaviour, danger to self: wandering, deliberate self-harm, neglect, threatening behaviour to children, incomplete/failure of response to Clozapine, and non-concordance with medication regimes. Over that period, patients were discharged who had symptoms such as that "...John Travolta...keeps interfering with me...", "...I am having a heart attack..." "...I'm dead...", "...the police are after me...", "...sexual interference from others...abusive voices" and "...I'm being poisoned through the taps..." to supported accommodation and their own flats. Of those remaining on the ward, CBT had some success with patients with abusive voices, grandiose compensation, beliefs that they were "...Bruce Lee..." and drug-induced hallucinations: "medication stops me breathing" but not with a persistent ruminator whose central concern was that he wanted "...no medication...no section". One patient worsened. He had delusional beliefs about "...heaven..." but initially presented as mute and severely neglected (having been in hospital for 5–6 years after a relationship break-up). He responded to gentle conversation about possible futures for him, started talking, shaved and eventually started going out. However, attempts to reform a relationship with his girlfriend, and mother of his child, failed. He was caught for theft, became hostile on the ward and was returned to the acute forensic ward. One patient who had made repeated serious suicide attempts unfortunately succeeded during the two-year period.

The experience of working with nursing staff and patients in this setting was instructive. Patience, persistence and dealing with issues of engagement were necessary. Attitudes changed slowly but when they changed, became very supportive and facilitated work with patients within an effective ward milieu. Joint interviews with nursing staff and patients were useful at modelling new approaches. Training was initiated and participated in by some. Risk assessment and management was facilitated as patients seemed more ready to disclose delusional beliefs and command hallucinations. Safety considerations took priority but a gentle, non-confrontational approach reduced hostility on many occasions. Use of medication reduced substantially as nurses successfully developed ways of analysing situations in terms of provoking factors and psychological measures to deal with them, instead of just having the availability of "as required" medication. Further exploration of the use of CBT in forensic settings—medium and high secure units—is being planned.

Therapist time

How many therapists are needed? Or, more specifically, what number of sessions of highly skilled therapist time is required for therapy, for training and for support and supervision? Similarly, how much trained therapist time is required for therapy, for training and for support and supervision? Finally, how can a basic cognitive behaviour approach to patients by all clinical staff be developed?

Most services develop incrementally, so that numbers of therapists needed becomes apparent as time progresses. Essential to a development case is an estimate of current numbers of patients being seen in each category and time being used. Most research studies using fully trained skilled therapists have provided 20 session courses, but for many patients continuing contact after the initial course often seems clinically indicated although, for some patients, 20 is more than enough. Indeed we have recently shown the effectiveness of six sessions in producing demonstrable (though not necessarily sufficient) improvement (Turkington et al., 2002). The number of patients that any therapist can work with at one time will vary, but 15–17 sessions per week is probably the maximum. Supervision and training for themselves and of others, with liaison, administration, travelling, etc., can readily account for the remainder of the working week.

However, for many patients, weekly sessions are too much and a session every two or four weeks is enough. Much of the work may also deal with issues of depression, anxiety, self-esteem or psycho-education rather than psychotic symptoms that can be exhausting work.

Groupwork

The value of groupwork is being established (see Chadwick et al., 2000). This may be more economic and can mobilise therapeutic factors that are not present in individual work. However, it is by its nature less individually focused and may not be as therapeutic. It is also acceptable to a limited number of patients, and selection is often an issue with the variety of patient needs that may be presented. Groups for patients hearing voices have been published (Wykes, Parr & Landall, 1999) and are also used for those with paranoia (Chadwick, personal communication). Their relationship to individual therapy needs further evaluation. Does the group obviate the need for individual work in some patients, or does it enhance such work, or shorten the time required? If so, can we predict the types of patients for which this form of therapy is most suitable?

Hearing voices groups that are run by the users themselves, or are facilitated by staff, have been developed in many areas. They meet the needs of many patients from their own testimony and support and encouragement for them seems self-evidently a good thing. Unfortunately, the amount of research evidence on their effects is still very limited and this may impede their further spread and development. Some groups vary in their level of membership and general level of activity, as can be expected from voluntary enterprises of this sort. Where users want support from mental health staff, it would seem beneficial to give it, as we are unaware of any evidence of harm (or adverse side effects).

Family work

The relevance of family work to the CBT of psychosis is commonly raised. In most cases, working with the family is part of a care programme approach and is strongly conducive to patient recovery (see "Jane" above). Work on expressed emotion is fully consistent with work on negative symptoms—managing expectations and reducing the pressure patients perceive. Rigidly working with patients to the exclusion of the family is guaranteed to lead to undermining of the therapeutic relationship and work being undertaken. It then seems logical to develop shared formulations with family and patient. The time involved is perhaps less than that described by proponents of family work (e.g. Barrowclough & Tarrier, 1992). Our brief intervention study (Turkington et al., 2002) offered three sessions to the families. Integrated family and individual work seems most economic in our experience, but skills for working with families need to be disseminated (as occurs in the Thorn courses).

Evidence for effectiveness of Thorn and CBT courses is referred to under training (Devane et al., 1998). An often unspoken fear of managers is that staff will be trained at their expense and leave for a better job elsewhere, or expect to be regraded. This certainly happens but can, of course, benefit services as well as disadvantage them. There is a very clear case for ensuring that such training is incorporated into career plans for the individual and service development plans for the organisation. There is too much evidence that Thorn-trained staff have completed courses and their skills have then been ignored, to the detriment of patients who have not benefited from their enhanced skills and the frustration of staff. Arranging for the allocation of cases to be more appropriate for their skills would seem reasonable to expect, but selecting caseloads is more difficult where pressure to allocate is intense. However, consideration of whether effectiveness of intervention might reduce demands on services could influence this, although such reduction in demands has not yet been directly demonstrated.

Assess and building local support

This can be done informally through local psychology departments, psychiatrists, local mental health teams, inpatient nurses, user and carers, general practitioners, and managers and commissioners of services. Training agencies, such as the local Workforce Confederation in the NHS, will also have a view.

If local support is not strong, it is more sensible to develop an educational strategy focused on individual groups by, for example, organising visits from speakers with expertise and experience in CBT of psychosis to local educational forums, or running workshops. Change may occur incrementally where there are examples of patients benefiting from contact with clinicians using CBT, although this may mean that just one or two people will develop such skills but demonstrate the value to others of gaining these skills in the future. Obtaining places on CBT courses (especially those focusing on SMI), Thorn (or equivalent) and in-service workshops/lectures can start the process moving with the development of individual CBT nurse/psychologist posts focused on psychosis. There is always a danger of isolation in such posts, but local centres (e.g. Newcastle and Southampton in the UK) can be a focus for peer support and supervision.

When local support is strong or growing, it is appropriate to develop a full case of need. This involves assembling evidence, developing training plans and negotiating costs with trainers and training funding bodies.

Evidence of effectiveness

The Cochrane Collaboration reviewed evidence in 1998 and their conclusion then was that:

> The results of well-conducted and reported ongoing trials are eagerly awaited. Currently for those with schizophrenia willing to receive CBT, access to this treatment approach is associated with a substantially reduced risk of relapse ... [it is a] scarce commodity ... how effective [is it] when ... applied by less experienced practitioners. (Jones et al., 1998)

Table 16.2 Randomised controlled trials of cognitive behavior therapy for psychosis

Authors	No.	Comparison groups	Outcome
Drury et al. (1996)	40	Individual and group CBT compared to structured activities and informal support.	Reduction in delusional conviction: 9 month CT. Fewer positive symptoms: 95% compared to 44% reported no or only minor positive symptoms on PAS. Recovery time reduced by 25–30%.
Lecompte, & Pelc (1996)	64	CBT & treatment as usual.	Length of admissions dropped in first year from 53.3 to 30.2 days CBT; 48.9 to 43.4 days in control.
Kuipers et al. (1997)	60	CBT vs. treatment as usual.	BPRS fell by 25% compared to no change in control at 9 and 18 months.
Kemp et al. (1996)	47	"Compliance therapy" vs. non-specific counselling: 4–6 sessions.	Significant improvements in attitudes to medication and insight. More effective and no more expensive: therefore, more cost-effective at 6, 12 and 18 months (Healey et al., 1998).
Tarrier et al. (1998)	87	Coping strategy/ problem solving/relapse prevention vs. control supportive therapy vs. treatment as usual.	Three months: significantly more CBT patients showed improvement of 50% or more in symptoms (18 of 33; 4 of 36; 3 of 28). Routine care—more exacerbations and time in hospital.
Sensky et al. (2000)	90	CBT vs. befriending (see text)	Significant differences in positive and negative symptoms at 18 months.

Table 16.1 summarises the studies that the Cochrane Collaboration reviewed, and two more recent ones awaited by them. One further article by authors involved in the original review has appeared to be of relevance, assessing the contribution of these studies positively (Adams, Wilson & Bagnall, 2000) and two further reviews appeared in the American literature (Dickerson, 2000; Rector & Beck, 2001).

The study by Sensky and colleagues (2000), in particular, provides evidence for effectiveness in patients whose symptoms have not fully responded to conventional neuroleptic medication. This controlled study compared a group of 90 patients, who received cognitive behaviour therapy, with a similar group, who received a "befriending" control intervention. This was intended to control for time and included the general therapeutic support that is available in any such intervention. Nurses trained in their delivery with patients who were randomly allocated to them for either treatment gave both interventions. Raters were independent and blind to treatment allocation. The interventions were given over nine months and averaged 45 minutes every two weeks. At the end of therapy, both groups had made impressive gains in positive and negative symptoms. The effects of CBT remained present nine months after the end of therapy but receded in the befriending group such that statistically significant differences emerged for both positive and negative symptoms. In the CBT group, 63% had made more than 50% improvement in symptomatology compared to 39% of the befriending group.

There have also been studies on cognitive remediation, which focuses on, for example, concentration, attention and social skills development, but these are reviewed elsewhere (Hodel & Brenner, 1998). Similarly an initial study by Hogarty and colleagues (1997) describing "personal therapy"—an individual psychotherapeutic intervention with some similarities to CBT—has shown it to be effective with patients with schizophrenia living with families, but not living alone. There is also published evidence of the effectiveness of a brief six-session intervention which may be relevant to a broader group of staff (Turkington et al., 2002).

The objection is sometimes raised that psychological treatments were clearly demonstrated to be ineffective in schizophrenia in the early 1980s in controlled trials such as that by Gunderson et al. (1984) but these were using very different models of therapy from those espoused today and described in this casebook.

Effectiveness of research in routine clinical practice

There are important effectiveness differences between research studies and practice, although the CBT studies have tried to allow for these as far as possible.

1. Selection of patients

Selection of patients for clinical trials is distorted by the essential need for patients to consent to participate in such a trial with the extra time and trouble for patients involved of meeting raters, the "risk" to them of receiving an ineffective control treatment, and an aversion, in principle, of involvement in research. It is probable that patients who are more severely ill are less likely to participate in studies, or to drop out of them, and so their results may have limited application. In practice, the studies cited below have been quite wide-ranging in their recruitment, and treatment and follow-up has been assertively offered in patients' homes where necessary. Exclusion criteria can also have effects, e.g. patients with dual diagnosis, especially of substance misuse, have been excluded from the studies cited below although many of the patients were abusing cannabis or amphetamines to some degree. Pilot studies in this group using motivational interviewing followed by CBT have, however, been successfully completed (Barrowclough et al., 2001).

2. Therapist quality

Training and supervision in research studies can be expected to be of higher quality and the therapists themselves are likely to have prior experience and skills above those expected in usual practice. This inevitably also affects how studies can be interpreted where staff with less skill, time and commitment are involved. The Insight into Schizophrenia study (Turkington et al., 2002) has attempted to address this concern by developing a brief intervention delivered by a range of nurses recruited directly from inpatient and community services with a basic, two-week training.

3. Relevance of outcome measures

Finally the outcome measures used may not be as relevant, e.g. symptom scores may not be as meaningful as social change or reductions in admission rates, and evidence on these is still quite limited.

Developing a training plan

Having assembled information on need, therapist time and supporting evidence, an estimate can be made of the number of therapists required from the information given above—i.e. How many sessions are required immediately to meet demand?; How many on a continuing basis for newly presenting patients? In practice, however, developments take time, are incremental, usually commence with a workshop or two, and some staff are given the time and resources for training. However, it is useful to try to plot, for planning purposes, the number of staff that require training to advanced levels or need to be recruited with this level of training; the number that require it at a more basic level; and the number that would benefit from a broad cognitive-behaviour training.

When such a plan is developed, there may be an obvious route for funding, again usually incrementally, but often there still needs to be consultation with professional groups, management teams, service planning committees and funding bodies with a gradual process of refinement (and usually reduction) of the proposals. A long-term strategy—over 3 to 5 years—can allow for flexibility but enduring, collaborative persistence, as in CBT itself, has a good chance of producing good outcomes in the end.

CONCLUSIONS

Implementation of CBT in psychosis can mean pushing against open doors, but even where this is the case, enlisting support and planning carefully is least likely to waste resources—financial, personnel or time. Where the door seems closed, even locked, it may take time to find the key, but gradual enlisting of support through information and examples of clinical success can make progress even where resistance seems strongest. We have certainly found it to be worth the trouble, and hope you do too.

REFERENCES

Adams, C., Wilson, P. & Bagnall, A.-M. (2000). Psychosocial interventions for schizophrenia. *Quality of Health Care*, **9**, 251–256.

Allen, J. & Kingdon, D.G. (1998). Using cognitive behavioural interventions for people with acute psychosis. *Mental Health Practice*, **1**, 14–21.

APA (1993). *Diagnostic and Statistical Manual* (4th edition). Washington, DC: American Psychiatric Association.

APA (1998). *Guidelines on Schizophrenia*. Washington, DC: American Psychiatric Association.

Asberg, M., Montgomery, S.A. & Perris, C. (1978). The Comprehensive Psycho-pathological Rating Scale. *Acta Psychiatrica Scandinavica*, Suppl. **271**, 5–27.

Ballard, C.G., Chithiramohan, R.N., Bannister, C. & Handy, S. (1991). Paranoid features in the elderly with dementia. *International Journal of Geriatric Psychiatry*, **6**, 155–157.

Barham, P. (1995). Manfred Bleuler and the understanding of psychosis. In J. Ellwood (Ed.) *Psychosis; Understanding and Treatment*. London: Jessica Kingsley.

Barker, P. (1999). Therapeutic nursing and the person in depression. In M. Clinton & S. Nelson (Eds.) *Advanced Practice in Mental Health Nursing*, Oxford: Blackwell Science.

Barnard, P.J. (in press). Asynchrony, implicational meaning and the experience of self in schizophrenia. In A. David & T. Kirchner (Eds.) *The Self in Schizophrenia: A Neuropsychological Perspective*. Cambridge: Cambridge University Press.

Barrowclough, C. & Tarrier, N. (1992). *Families of Schizophrenic Patients. Cognitive Behavioural Intervention*. London: Chapman & Hall.

Barrowclough, C. & Tarrier, N. (1997). *Families of Schizophrenic Patients. Cognitive Behavioural Intervention*. Cheltenham: Stanley Thornes.

Barrowclough, C., Haddock, G., Tarrier, N., Lewis, S.W., Moring, J., O'Brien, R., Schofield, N. & McGovern, J. (2001). Randomized controlled trial of motivational interviewing, cognitive behavior therapy, and family intervention for patients with comorbid schizophrenia and substance use disorders. *American Journal of Psychiatry*, **158**, 17.

Bartram, D., Lindley, P. & Foster, J. (1991). *Culture-Free Self-Esteem Inventory: Some British Normative Data Based on Research carried out for the Employment Service*. Windsor, NFER-Nelson.

Battle, J. (1980). *Culture-Free SEI: Self-Esteem Inventories for Children and Adults*. Manual. Seattle, Special Child Publications.

Beck, A. & Greer, R. (1987). *Beck Depression Inventory Scoring Manual*. New York: Psychological Corporation.

Beck, A.T. (1967). *Depression: Clinical, Experimental and Theoretical Aspects*. New York: Hoeber.

Beck, A.T. (1976). *Cognitive Therapy of the Emotional Disorders*. New York: International Universities Press.

Beck, A.T., Rush, A.J., Shaw, B.F. & Emery, G. (1979). *Cognitive Therapy of Depression.* New York: Guilford Press.

Bentall, R. & Haddock, G. (2000). Cognitive-behaviour therapy for auditory hallucinations. In D. Mercer, T. Mason, M. McKeown & G. McCann (Eds.) *Forensic Mental Health Care: A Case Study Approach* (pp. 67–75). London: Churchill Livingstone.

Bentall, R. & Kinderman, P. (1998). Psychological processes and delusional beliefs: Implications for the treatment of paranoid states. In T. Wykes, N. Tarrier & S. Lewis (Eds.) *Outcome and Innovation in Psychological Treatment of Schizophrenia* (pp. 81–100). Chichester: John Wiley & Sons.

Bentall, R.P. (1990). The syndromes and symptoms of psychoses: or why you can't play 'twenty questions' with the concept of schizophrenia and hope to win. In R.P. Bentall (Ed.) *Reconstructing Schizophrenia.* London: Routledge.

Berne, E. (1968). *Games People Play.* Harmondsworth: Penguin.

Birchwood, M., Todd, P. & Jackson, C. (1998). Early intervention in psychosis. The critical period hypothesis. *British Journal of Psychiatry*, Suppl. **172**, 53–9.

Birchwood, M. & Iqbal, Z. (1998). Depression and suicidal thinking in psychosis: A cognitive approach. In T. Wykes, N. Tarrier and S. Lewis (Eds.) *Outcome and Innovation in Psychological Treatment of Schizophrenia* (pp. 81–100). Chichester, UK: Wiley.

Birchwood, M., Smith, J., Cochrane, R., Wetton, S. & Copestake, S. (1990). The Development and Validation of a New Scale of Social Adjustment for use in Family Intervention Programmes with Schizophrenic Patients. *British Journal of Psychiatry*, **157**, 853–859.

Blackburn, I.M. & Davidson, K. (1990). *Cognitive therapy for depression and anxiety.* Oxford: Blackwell.

Bleuler, E. (1950). *Dementia Praecox or the Group of Schizophrenias.* New York: International Universities Press (translated from the German edition, 1911).

Bloom, J.D., Mueser, K.T. & Muller-Isberner, R. (2000). Treatment implications of the antecedents of criminality and violence in schizophrenia and major affective disorder. In S. Hodgins (Ed.) *Violence Among the Mentally Ill: Effective Treatment and Management Strategies* (pp. 145–169). Dordrecht: Kluwer Academic.

Brabban, A. & Turkington, D. (2001). The search for meaning between life events, underlying schema and psychotic symptoms—formulation driven and schema focused cognitive behavioural therapy for a neuroleptic resistant patient with a delusional memory. In A.P. Morrison (Ed.) *A Case Book of Cognitive Therapy for Psychosis.* Brighton: Psychology Press.

British Psychological Society (2000). *Recent Advances in Understanding Mental Illness and Psychotic Experiences.* Leicester: Division of Clinical Psychology, BPS.

Burns, D.D. (1980). *Feeling Good—The New Mood Therapy.* New York: Morrow.

Burns, T., Creed, F., Fahy, T., Thompson, S., Tyrer, P. & White, I. (1999). Intensive versus standard case management for severe psychotic illness: A randomised trial. UK 700 Group. *Lancet*, **353**, 2185–2189.

Carroll, M. (1996). *Counselling supervision. Theory, skills and practice.* London: Continuum.

Carroll, R.T. (1994). *The Skeptics Dictionary: A Guide for the New Millennium.*

Carton, G. (1999). *Multi-disciplinary Training in a Shared Model of Care. Programme Development Outline.* Rampton, UK: Rampton Hospital Authority.

Chadwick, P. & Birchwood, M. (1994). The omnipotence of voices: A cognitive approach to auditory hallucinations. *British Journal of Psychiatry*, **164**, 190–201.

Chadwick, P. (1997). *Schizophrenia: The Positive Perspective. In Search of Dignity for Schizophrenic People*. London: Routledge.

Chadwick, P., Birchwood, M., & Trower, P. (1996). *Cognitive Therapy of Voices, Delusions and Paranoia*. Chichester, UK: Wiley.

Chadwick, P., Sambrooke, S., Rasch, S. & Davies, E. (2000). Challenging the omnipotence of voices: Group cognitive behavior therapy for voices. *Behaviour Research and Therapy*, **38**, 993–1003.

Chadwick, P.D.J. & Trower, P. (1996). Cognitive therapy for punishment paranoia: A single case experiment. *Behavioural Research and Therapy*, **34**, 351–356.

Chadwick, P.K. (1997). *Schizophrenia: The Positive Perspective—In Search of Dignity for Schizophrenic People*. London: Routledge.

Claridge, G. (1997). *Schizotypy: Implications for Illness and Health*. Oxford: Oxford University Press.

Clarke, I. (1999). Cognitive therapy and serious mental illness. An interacting cognitive subsystems approach. Clinical Psychology and Psychotherapy, **6**, 375–383.

Clarke, I. (2001). Psychosis and spirituality: The discontinuity model. In Clarke, I. (Ed.) *Psychosis and Spirituality: Exploring the New Frontier*. London: Whurr.

Clarke, I. (2002). Introducing further developments towards an ICS formulation of psychosis: A comment on Gumley et al. (1999). An Interacting Cognitive Subsystems Model of Relapse and the course of psychosis. *Clinical Psychology and Psychotherapy*, **9**, 47–50.

Clinical Standards Advisory Group. (1994). *Schizophrenia. Report of a CSAG Committee*. London: HMSO.

Craig, T. (2000). Severe mental illness: Symptoms, signs and diagnosis. In C. Gamble & G. Brennan (Eds.) *Working with Serious Mental Illness. A Manual for Clinical Practice*. London: Harcourt Publishers Limited.

Dalal, B., Larkin, E., Leese, M. & Taylor, P.J. (1999). Clozapine treatment of long-standing schizophrenia and serious violence: A two-year follow-up study of the first 50 patients treated with clozapine in Rampton high security hospital. *Criminal Behaviour and Mental Health*, **9**, 169–178.

Day, J.C., Wood, G., Dewey, M. & Bentall, R.P. (1995). A self-rating scale for measuring neuroleptic side-effects: Validation in a group of schizophrenic patients. *British Journal of Psychiatry*, **166**, 650–653.

Department of Health (1999). *A National Service Framework for Mental Health*. London: Department of Health.

Devane, S.M., Haddock, G., Lancashire, S., Baguley, I., Butterworth, T., Tarrier, N., James, A. & Molyneux, P. (1998). The clinical skills of community psychiatric nurses working with patients who have severe and enduring mental health problems: An empirical analysis. *Journal of Advanced Nursing*, **27**, 253–260.

Dickerson, F.B. (2000). Cognitive behavioral psychotherapy for schizophrenia: A review of recent empirical studies. *Schizophrenia Research*, **43**, 71–90.

Drury, V., Birchwood, M., Cochrane, R. & Macmillan, F. (1996). Cognitive therapy and recovery from acute psychosis: A controlled trial. I. Impact on psychotic symptoms. *British Journal of Psychiatry*, **169**, 593–601.

Ehlers, A. & Clark, D. (2000). A model of persistent post traumatic stress disorder. *Behaviour Research and Therapy*, **38**, 319–345.

Ellis, A. (1962). *Reason and Emotion in Psychotherapy*. New York: Lyle Stuart.

Ewers, P., Leadley, K. & Kinderman, P. (2000). Cognitive-behaviour therapy for delusions. In D. Mercer, T. Mason, M. McKeown & G. McCann (Eds.) *Forensic

Mental Health Care: A Case Study Approach (pp. 77–89). London: Churchill Livingstone.

Falloon, I.R.H., Laporta, M., Fadden, G. & Graham-Hole, V. (1993). *Managing Stress in Families; Cognitive and Behavioural Strategies for Enhancing Coping Skills.* London: Routledge.

Fenigstein, A. (1996). Paranoia. In C.G. Costello (Ed.) *Personality Characteristics of the Personality Disordered.* New York: Wiley.

Fenigstein, A. (1997). Paranoid thought and schematic processing. *Journal of Social and Clinical Psychology*, **16**, 77– 94.

Fenton, W.S. & McGlashan, T.H. (1997). We can talk: Individual psychotherapy for schizophrenia (Editorial). *American Journal of Psychiatry*, **154**, 1493–1495.

Foudraine, J. (1971). *Not Made of Wood.* London: Quartet.

Fowler, D., Garety, P. & Kuipers, L. (1995). *Cognitive Therapy of Psychoses.* Chichester, UK: Wiley.

Fox, J. & Conroy, P. (2000). Assessing client's needs: The semistructured interview. In C. Gamble & G. Brennan (Eds.) *Working with Serious Mental Illness. A Manual for Clinical Practice.* London: Harcourt Publishers Limited.

Frank, A.F. & Gunderson, J.G. (1990). The role of the therapeutic alliance in the treatment of schizophrenia. *Archives of General Psychiatry*, **47**, 228–236.

Gamble, C. (1995). The Thorn nurse training initiative. *Nursing Standard*, **9** (15), 31–34.

Gamble, C. (2000). Using a low Expressed Emotion approach to develop positive therapeutic alliances. In C. Gamble & G. Brennan (Eds.) *Working with Serious Mental Illness. A Manual for Clinical Practice.* London: Harcourt Publishers Limited.

Garety, P.A., Fowler, D. & Kuipers, E. (2000). Cognitive-behavioral therapy for medication-resistant symptoms. *Schizophrenia Bulletin*, **26**, 73–86.

Gehrs, M. & Goering, P. (1994). The relationship between the working alliance and rehabilitation outcomes of schizophrenia. *Psychosocial Rehabilitation Journal*, **18**, 43–54.

Gilbert, P. (1998). The evolved basis and adaptive functions of cognitive distortions. *British Journal of Medical Psychology*, **71**, 447–463.

Goffman, E. (1961). *Asylums.* Harmondsworth: Penguin.

Goldberg, D. & Williams, P. (1988). *A Users Guide to the General Health Questionnaire.* NFER-Nelson.

Gournay, K. & Birley, J. (1998). Thorn: A new approach to mental health training. *Nursing Times*, **94**, 54–55.

Gournay, K. (1996). Setting clinical standards for care in schizophrenia. *Nursing Times*, **92** (7), 36–37.

Grassian, G. (1983). Psychopathology of solitary confinement. *American Journal of Psychiatry*, **140**, 1450–1454.

Gresswell, D.M. & Kruppa, I. (1994). Special demands of assessment in a secure setting: Setting the scene. In M. McMurran & J. Hodge (Eds.) *The Assessment of Criminal Behaviours of Clients in Secure Settings* (pp. 35–52). London: Jessica Kingsley.

Gumley, A., White, C.A. & Power, K. (1999). An interacting cognitive subsystems model of relapse and the course of psychosis. *Clinical Psychology and Psychotherapy*, **6**, 261–279.

Gunderson, J.G., Frank, A.F., Katz, H.M., Vannicelli, M.L., Frosch, J.P. & Knapp, P.H. (1984). Effects of psychotherapy in schizophrenia: II Comparative outcome of two forms of treatment. *Schizophrenia Bulletin*, **10**, 564–598.

Gunn, J. & Maden, A. (1999). *Should the English Special Hospitals be Closed? Maudsley Discussion Paper No. 6.* London: Institute of Psychiatry.

Haddock, G. & Slade, P.D. (Eds.) (1996). *Cognitive-Behavioural Interventions with Psychotic Disorders.* London: Routledge.

Haddock, G., Devane, S., Bradshaw, T., McGovern, J., Tarrier, N., Kinderman, P., Baguley, I., Lancashire, S. & Harris, N. (2001). An investigation into the psychometric properties of the Cognitive Therapy Scale for Psychosis (CTS-Psy). *Behavioural and Cognitive Psychotherapy,* **29,** 221–233.

Haddock, G., McCarron, J., Tarrier, N. & Faragher, E.B. (1999). Scales to measure dimensions of hallucinations and delusions: The psychotic symptom rating scales (PSYRATS). *Psychological Medicine,* **29,** 879–889.

Haddock, G., Bentall, R.P. & Slade, P.D. (1996). Psychological treatment for auditory hallucinations: Focusing or distraction. In G. Haddock & P. Slade (Eds.) *Cognitive-behavioural Interventions with Psychotic Disorders.* London: Routledge.

Harrow, M., Rattenbury, F. & Stoll, F. (1988). Schizophrenic delusions: An analysis of their persistence, of related premorbid ideas, and of three major dimensions. In F. Oltmanns & B.A. Maher (Eds.) *Delusional Beliefs* (pp. 185–211). New York: John Wiley.

Harvey, L. & Knight, P.T. (1996). *Transforming Higher Education.* Buckingham: SRHE.

Hawton, K., Salkovskis, P., Kirk, J. & Clark, D.M. (1989). *Cognitive Behavioural Therapy for Psychiatric Problems. A Practical Guide.* Oxford: Oxford Medical Problems.

Healey, A., Knapp, M., Astin, J., Kemp, R., Kirov, G. & David A. (1998). Cost-effectiveness of compliance therapy for people with psychosis. *British Journal of Psychiatry,* **172,** 420–424.

Hemsley, D.R. & Garety, P.A. (1986). The formation and maintenance of delusions: A Bayesian hypothesis. *British Journal of Psychiatry,* **149,** 51–56.

Hinshelwood, R.D. (1998). Creatures of each other. Some historical considerations of responsibility and care, and some present undercurrents. In A. Foster & V. Zagier Roberts (Eds.) *Managing Mental Health in the Community. Chaos and Containment* (pp. 15–26). London: Routledge.

Hodel, B. & Brenner, H.D. (1998). State-of-the-art approaches in the treatment if information-processing disorders in schizophrenia. In Perris, C. & McGorry, P.D. (Eds.) *Cognitive Psychotherapy of Psychotic and Personality Disorders: Handbook of Theory and Practice.* Chichester, UK: Wiley.

Hodgins, S. (Ed.) (2000). *Violence Among the Mentally Ill: Effective Treatment and Management Strategies.* Dordrecht: Kluwer Academic.

Hogarty, G.E. (1993). Prevention of relapse in schizophrenia. *Journal of Clinical Psychiatry,* **54,** 18–23.

Hogarty, G.E., Kornblith, S.J., Greenwald, D., DiBarry, A.L., Cooley, S., Ulrich, R.F., Carter, M. & Flesher, S. (1997). Three-year trials of personal therapy among schizophrenic patients living with or independent of family. I: Description of study and effects on relapse rates *American Journal of Psychiatry,* **154,** 1504–1513.

Honig, A., Romme, M.A, Ensink, B.J., Escher, S.D., Pennings, M.H. & Vries, M.W. (1998). Auditory hallucinations: A comparison between patients and non-patients. *Journal of Nervous and Mental Disease,* **186,** 646–651.

Horowitz, M., Wilner, N. & Alvarez, W. (1979). Impact of events scale: A measure of subjective distress. *Psychosomatic Medicine,* **41,** 209–218.

Jones, C., Cormac, I., Mota, J. & Campbell, C. (1998). *Cognitive Behaviour Therapy for Schizophrenia (Cochrane Review), Issue 4.* Oxford: Update Software.

Juniger, J. (2001). The paradox of command hallucinations. *Psychiatric Services,* **52,** 385–386.

Kane, J., Honigfeld, G., Singer, J. & Meltzer, H. (1988). Clozapine for the treatment-resistant schizophrenic. A double-blind comparison with chlorpromazine. *Archives of General Psychiatry*, **45**, 789–796.

Kaye, C. (2001). A state of siege: The English high security hospitals. *Criminal Behaviour and Mental Health*, **11**, 1–5.

Kemp, R., Hayward, P., Applewhaite, G., Everitt, B. & David, A. (1996). Compliance therapy in psychotic patients: A randomised controlled study. *British Medical Journal*, **312**, 345–349.

Kingdon, D. (1999). *Cognitive behaviour therapy in forensic settings*. Presentation to Special Hospitals Research Conference, Nottingham.

Kingdon, D. (1998). Cognitive behavioural therapy of psychosis: Complexities in engagement and therapy. In N. Tarrier, A. Wells & G. Haddock (Eds.) *Treating Complex Cases: The Cognitive Behavioural Therapy Approach* (pp. 176–194). Chichester, UK: Wiley.

Kingdon, D.G. & Turkington, D. (1994). *Cognitive-behavior Therapy of Schizophrenia*. New York: Guilford.

Kingdon, D.G. & Turkington, D. (1998). Cognitive behaviour therapy: Styles, groups and outcomes. In T. Wykes, N. Tarrier & S. Lewis (Eds.) *Outcome and Innovation in the Psychological Treatment of Schizophrenia*. Chichester, UK: Wiley.

Kingdon, D.G. (1994). The care programme approach. *Psychiatric Bulletin*, **18**, 68–70.

Kingdon, D.G. (1997). *Understanding Voices* (Leaflet). www.e-mentalhealth.co.uk.

Kingdon, D.G. (2000). Cognitive therapy for schizophrenia. *New Directions in Psychiatry*, **20**, 265–273.

Kingdon, D.G. & Turkington, D. (1991). Preliminary report: The use of cognitive behaviour therapy and a normalizing rationale in schizophrenia. *Journal of Nervous and Mental Disease*, **179**, 207–211.

Kinsley, J. (1998). Security and therapy. In C. Kaye & A. Franey (Eds.) *Managing High Security Psychiatric Care* (pp. 75–84). London: Jessica Kingsley.

Koerner, K., Swenson, C.R., Dimeff, L. & Sanderson, C.J. (2001). *Linking enthusiasm to evidence-based practice: disseminating dialectical behaviour therapy*. Presentation at Association for the Advancement of Behavior Therapy 35th Annual Convention.

Krawiecka, M., Goldberg, D. & Vaughan, M. (1977). A standardised psychiatric assessment scale for rating chronic psychotic patients. *Acta Psychiatrica Scandinavica*, **55**, 299–308.

Kuipers, E., Garety, P., Fowler, D., Dunn, G., Bebbington, P., Freeman, D. & Hadley, C. (1997). London–East Anglia randomised controlled trial of cognitive-behavioural therapy for psychosis. I: Effects of the treatment phase. *British Journal of Psychiatry*, **171**, 319–332.

Laing, R.D. & Esterson, A. (1970). *Sanity, Madness and the Family*. Harmondsworth: Penguin.

Lecompte, D. & Pelc, I. (1996). A cognitive behavioral program to improve compliance with medication in patients with schizophrenia. *International Journal of Mental Health*, **25**, 51–56.

Leff, J. & Vaughn, C. (1985). *Expressed Emotion in Families*. New York: Guilford Press.

Lewis, S.W., Tarrier, N., Haddock, G., Bentall, R., Kinderman, P., Kingdon, D., Siddle, R., Everitt, J., Benn, A., Leadley, K., Grazebrook, K., Drake, R., Haley, C., Akhtar, S., Davies, L., Palmer, S. & Faragher, B. (in press). A randomised controlled trial of cognitive-behaviour therapy in early schizophrenia: Acute phase outcomes in the SoCRATES trial. *British Journal of Psychiatry*.

Liddle, P., Carpenter, W.T. & Crow, T. (1994). Syndromes of schizophrenia. *British Journal of Psychiatry*, **165**, 21–27.

Linehan, M.M. (1993). *Cognitive Behaviour Therapy for Borderline Personality Disorder and Skills Training Manual for Treating Borderline Personality Disorder*. NewYork: Guildford.

Lyon, H.M., Kaney, S. & Bentall, R.P. (1994).The defensive function of persecutory delusions. Evidence from attribution tasks. *British Journal of Psychiatry*, **164**, 637–646 .

Maden, A., Curle, C., Meux, C., Burrow, S. & Gunn, J. (1995). *The Treatment and Security Needs of Special Hospital Patients*. London:Whurr.

Maher, B.A. (1988). Anomalous experience and delusional thinking: The logic of explanations. In T.F. Oltmanns & B.A. Maher (Eds.) *Delusional Beliefs* (pp. 15–33). New York: Wiley.

Malan D. (1979). *Individual Psychotherapy and the Science of Psychodynamics*. London: Butterworths.

Manchanda, R., Saupe, R. & Hirsch, S. (1986). Comparison between the brief psychiatric rating scale and the Manchester scale for the rating of schizophrenia symptomatology. *Acta Psychiatrica Scandinavia*, **74**, 563–568.

McFadyen, J. & Vincent, M. (1998). A reappraisal of community mental health nursing. *Mental Health Nursing*, **18** (4), 19–23.

McPhillips, M. & Sensky, T. (1998). Coercion, adherence or collaboration? Influences on compliance with medication. In T. Wykes, N. Tarrier & S. Lewis (Eds.) *Outcome and Innovation in Psychological Treatment of Schizophrenia* (pp. 161–177). Chichester, UK: Wiley.

Milne, D., Claydon, T., Blackburn, I.-M., James, I. & Sheikh, A. (2001). Rationale for a new measure of competence in therapy. *Behavioural and Cognitive Psychotherapy*, **29**, 21–33.

Moorhead, S. & Turkington, D. (2000). The cognitive behaviour therapy of delusional disorder: The relationship between schema vulnerability and psychotic content. (in prep.)

Morrison, A.P. (2001). The interpretation of intrusions in psychosis: An integrative cognitive approach to hallucinations and delusions. *Behavioural and Cognitive Psychotherapy*, **29**, 257–276.

Mueser K.T., Trumbetta, S.L., Rosenberg, S.D., Goodman, L.B., Osher, F.C., Auciello P. & Foy, D. (1998). Trauma and post traumatic stress disorder in severe mental illness. *Journal of Consulting and Clinical Psychology*, **6**, 493–499.

Muijen, M. (1996). Scare in the community; Britain in moral panic. In T. Heller et al. (Eds.) *Mental Health Matters: A Reader*. London: Macmillan.

Nelson, H. (1997). *Cognitive Behavioural Therapy with Schizophrenia. A Practice Manual*. London: Stanley Thornes.

Newell, R. (1994). *Interviewing Skills for Nurses and other Health Care Professionals. A Structured Approach*. London: Routledge.

NHS Executive (1996). *NHS Psychotherapy Services in England. Review of Strategic Policy*. London: NHS Executive.

Nuechterlien, K.H. & Dawson, M.E. (1984). A heuristic vulnerability-stress model of schizophrenic episodes. *Schizophrenia Bulletin*, **10**, 300–312.

Orr, M. (1998). Describing the patients. In C. Kaye & A. Franey (Eds.) *Managing High Security Psychiatric Care* (pp. 111–122). London: Jessica Kingsley.

Oswald, I. (1974). *Sleep* (3rd Edition). Harmondsworth: Penguin.

Padesky, C.A. (1996). Developing cognitive therapist competency: Teaching and supervision models. In P.M. Salkovskis (Ed.) *Frontiers of Cognitive Therapy* (pp. 266–292). New York: Guilford.

Peralta, V. & Cuesta, M.J. (1998). Factor structure and clinical validity of competing models of positive symptoms in schizophrenia. *Biological Psychiatry*, **44**, 107–114.

Peters, E.R., Joseph, S.A. & Garety, P.A. (1999). Measurement of delusional ideation in the normal population: Introducing the PDI (Peters et al. Delusions Inventory). *Schizophrenia Bulletin*, **25**, 553–576.

Pinto, A., La Pia, S., Mennella, R., Giorgio, D. & DeSimone, L. (1999). Cognitive-behavioral therapy for clozapine clients with treatment-refractory schizophrenia. *Psychiatric Services*, **50**, 901–904.

Ramsden, P. (1992). *Learning to Teach in Higher Education*. London: Routledge.

Raune, D., Kuipers, E. & Bebbington, P. (1999). *Psychosocial stress and delusional and verbal auditory and hallucinatory themes in first episode psychosis: Implications for early intervention*. Paper presented at the Cognitive Behaviour Therapy for Psychosis Conference, Oxford, England.

Rector, N.A. & Beck, A.T. (2001). Cognitive behavioral therapy for schizophrenia: An empirical review. *Journal of Nervous and Mental Disease*, **189**, 278–287.

Reeves, A. (2000). Creative journeys of recovery: A survivor's perspective. In M. Birchwood, D. Fowler & C. Jackson (Eds.) *Early Intervention in Psychosis*. Chichester: Wiley.

Richards, D. & Lovell, K. (1999). Behavioural and cognitive behavioural interventions in the treatment of PTSD. In W. Yule (Ed.) *Post-traumatic Stress Disorders: Concepts and Therapy* (pp. 239–246). Chichester: Wiley.

Rogers, C. (1959). A theory of therapy, personality and interpersonal relationships as developed in the client-centered framework. In S. Kock (Ed.) *Psychology: A Study of a Science: Vol. 3. Formulations of the Person and the Social Context*. New York: McGraw-Hill.

Rogers, C.R. (1977). *On Becoming a Person*. London: Constable.

Romme, M. & Escher, S. (1993). *Accepting Voices*. London: MIND.

Romme, M. & Escher, S. (2000). *Making Sense of Voices*. London: MIND.

Romme, M.A.J. & Escher, A.D.M.A.C. (1989). Hearing voices. *Schizophrenia Bulletin*, **15**, 209–216.

Rose, D. (2001). *Users' Voices. The Perspectives of Mental Health Service Users on Community and Hospital Care* (p. 93). London: The Sainsbury Centre for Mental Health.

Roth, A., Fonagy, P., Kazdin, A.E. & Shapiro, A.D. (1988). *What Works for Whom?* New York: Guilford Press.

Roth, M., Tym, E., Mountjoy, C.Q. & Huppert, F.A. (1986). CAMDEX: A standardised instrument for the diagnosis of mental disorder in the elderly with special reference to the early detection of dementia. *British Journal of Psychiatry*, **149**, 698–709.

Salzberger-Wittenberg, I., Henry, G. & Osborne, E. (1990). *The Emotional Experience of Learning and Teaching*. London: Routledge.

Sensky, T., Turkington, D., Kingdon, D., Scott, J., Scott, J.L., Siddle, R., O'Carroll, M. & Barnes, T.R.E. (2000). A randomized controlled trial of cognitive-behavioural therapy for persistent symptoms in schizophrenia resistant to medication. *Archives of General Psychiatry*, **57**, 165–172.

Slade, P.D. (1984). Sensory deprivation and psychiatry. *British Journal of Hospital Medicine*, **32**, 256–260.

Smith, A.D. & Taylor, P. (1999). Serious sex offending against women by men with schizophrenia: Relationship of illness and psychotic symptoms to offending. *British Journal of Psychiatry*, **174**, 233–237.

Smith, A.D. & Taylor, P.J. (1999). Serious sex offending against women by men with schizophrenia. *British Journal of Psychiatry*, **174**, 233–237.

Smucker, M. & Dancu, C. (1999). *Cognitive-behavioral Treatment for Adult Survivors of Childhood Trauma: Imagery Rescripting and Reprocessing*. London: Jason Oronson.

Stanton, A.H., Gunderson, J.G., Knapp, P.H., et al. (1984). Effects of psychotherapy in schizophrenia: I. Design and implementation of a controlled study. *Schizophrenia Bulletin*, **10**, 520–562.

Steels, M., Roney, G., Larkin, E., Jones, P., Croudace, T. & Duggan, C. (1998). Discharged from special hospital under restrictions: A comparison of the fates of psychopaths and the mentally ill. *Criminal Behaviour and Mental Health*, **8**, 39–55.

Swinton, M. & Haddock, A. (2001). Clozapine in special hospital: A retrospective case-control study. *Journal of Forensic Psychiatry*, **11**, 587–596.

Swinton, M. & Ahmed, A.G. (1999). Reasons for non-prescription of clozapine in treatment-resistant schizophrenia. *Criminal Behaviour and Mental Health*, **9**, 207–214.

Tarrier, N. (1992). Management and modification of residual positive psychotic symptoms. In M. Birchwood & N. Tarrier (Eds.) *Innovations in the Psychological Management of Schizophrenia*. Chichester, UK: Wiley.

Tarrier, N., Beckett, R., Harwood, S. et al. (1993) A trial of two cognitive behaviourl methods of treating drug resistant residual symptoms in schizophrenic patients: I. Outcome. *British Journal of Psychiatry*, **162**, 524–532.

Tarrier, N., Barrowclough, C., Haddock, G. & McGovern, J. (1999). The dissemination of innovative cognitive-behavioural psychosocial treatments for schizophrenia. *Journal of Mental Health*, **8**, 569–582.

Tarrier, N., Haddock, G. & Barrowclough, C. (1998). Training and dissemination: Research to practice in innovative psychosocial treatments for schizophrenia. In T. Wykes, N. Tarrier & S. Lewis (Eds.) *Outcome and Innovation in Psychological Treatment of Schizophrenia* (pp. 215–236). Chichester, UK: Wiley.

Tarrier, N., Yusupoff, L., Kinney, C., McCarthy, E., Gledhill, A., Haddock, G. & Morris, J. (1998). Randomised controlled trial of intensive cognitive behaviour therapy for patients with chronic schizophrenia. *British Medical Journal*, **317**, 303–307.

Taylor, P., Garety, P., Buchanan, A. et al. (1993). Measuring risk through delusions. In J. Monahan & H. Steadman (Eds.) *Violence and Mental Disorder: Developments in Risk Assessment*. Chicago: Chicago University Press.

Taylor, P.J., Garety, P. & Buchanan, A. (1994). Delusions and violence. In J. Monahan & H. Steadman (Eds.) *Violence and Mental Disorder: Developments in Risk Assessment*. Chicago: Chicago University Press.

Taylor, P.J., Lees, M. & Williams, D. (1998). Mental disorder and violence. *British Journal of Psychiatry*, **172**, 218–226.

Teasdale, J.D. & Barnard, P.J. (1993). *Affect, Cognition and Change: Remodelling Depressive Thought*. Hove: Lawrence Erlbaum Associates.

Teasdale, J.D., Segal, Z.V., Williams, J.M.G., Ridgeway, V.A., Soulsby, J.M. & Lau, M.A. (2000). Prevention of relapse/recurrence in major depression by mindfulness-based cognitive therapy. *Journal of Consulting and Clinical Psychology*, **68**, 615–623.

Thornicroft, G. & Susser, E. (2001). Evidence-based psychotherapeutic interventions in the community care of schizophrenia. *British Journal of Psychiatry*, **178**, 2–4.

Truax, C.B. & Carkhoff, R.R. (1967). *Towards Effective Counselling and Psychotherapy*. Chicago: Aldine.

Turkington, D. & Kingdon, D.G. (1991). Ordering thoughts in thought disorder. *British Journal Psychiatry*, **159**, 160–161.

Turkington, D., John, C.H., Siddle, R., Ward, D. & Birmingham, L. (1996). Cognitive therapy in the treatment of drug resistant delusional disorder. *Clinical Psychology and Psychotherapy*, **3**, 118–128.

Turkington, D. & Kingdon, D.G. (2000). Cognitive-behavioural techniques for general psychiatrists in the management of patients with psychoses. *British Journal of Psychiatry*, **177**, 101–106.

Turkington, D., Kingdon, D.G., Turner, T. & Insight into Schizophrenia Research Group (2002). Effectiveness of a brief cognitive-behavioural intervention in the treatment of schizophrenia. *British Journal of Psychiatry*, **180**, 523–527.

Tyrer, P. & Steinberg, D. (1998). *Models for Mental Disorder* (3rd edition). Chichester: Wiley.

Tyrer, P., Sievewright, N., Kingdon, D. et al. (1988) The Nottingham study of neurotic disorder: comparison of drug and psychological treatments. *Lancet*, **2**, 235–240.

Verdoux, H., Maurice-Tison, B., Van Os, B.G., Salamon, R. & Bourgeois, M.L. (1998). A survey of delusional ideation in primary-care patients. *Psychological Medicine*, **28**, 127–134.

Warner, R. (1985). *Recovery from Schizophrenia; Psychiatry and Political Economy*. London: Routledge & Kegan Paul.

Weissman, A.N. & Beck, A.T. (1978). *Development and validation of the dysfunctional attitude scale*. Paper presented at the Annual Meeting of the Association for Advancement of Behavior Therapy, Chicago, Illinois.

Wilkin, P. (2001). The other side. *Mental Health Nursing*, **21**, 5.

Wing, J.K., Curtis, R. & Beevor, A. (1996). *The Health of the Nation Outcome Scales*. London: Royal College of Psychiatrists.

World Health Organisation (1990). *International Classification of Diseases. Tenth Revision*. Geneva: Author.

Wykes, T., Parr, A. & Landau, S. (1999). Group treatment of auditory hallucinations: Exploratory study of effectiveness. *British Journal of Psychiatry*, **175**, 180–185.

Yalom, I. (1970). *The Theory and Practice of Group Psychotherapy*. New York: Basic Books.

Young, J., Beck, A.T. (1980). *The Cognitive Therapy Scale*. Unpublished Manuscript.

Zigmond, A.S. & Snaith, R.P. (1983). The Hospital Anxiety and Depression Scale. *Acta Psychiatrica Scandinavica*, **67**, 361–370.

Zubin, J. & Spring, B. (1977). Vulnerability: A new view on schizophrenia. *Journal of Abnormal Psychology*, **86**, 103–126.

AUTHOR INDEX

SUBJECT INDEX

The Wiley Series in

CLINICAL PSYCHOLOGY

Carlo Perris, *Willem A. Arrindell and* *Martin Eisemann (Editors)*	Parenting and Psychopathology
Chris Barker, *Nancy Pistrang* *and Robert Elliott*	Research Methods in Clinical and Counselling Psychology
Graham C.L. Davey and *Frank Tallis (Editors)*	Worrying: Perspectives on Theory, Assessment and Treatment
Paul Dickens	Quality and Excellence in Human Services
Edgar Miller and *Robin Morris*	The Psychology of Dementia
Ronald Blackburn	The Psychology of Criminal Conduct: Theory, Research and Practice
Ian H. Gotlib and *Constance L. Hammen*	Psychological Aspects of Depression: Toward a Cognitive-Interpersonal Integration
Max Birchwood and *Nicholas Tarrier (Editors)*	Innovations in the Psychological Management of Schizophrenia: Assessment, Treatment and Services
Robert J. Edelmann	Anxiety: Theory, Research and Intervention in Clinical and Health Psychology
Alastair Agar (Editor)	Microcomputers and Clinical Psychology: Issues, Applications and Future Developments
Bob Remington (Editor)	The Challenge of Severe Mental Handicap: A Behaviour Analytic Approach
Colin A. Espie	The Psychological Treatment of Insomnia
David Peck and *C.M. Shapiro (Editors)*	Measuring Human Problems: A Practical Guide
Roger Baker (Editor)	Panic Disorder: Theory, Research and Therapy
Friedrich Fösterling	Attribution Theory in Clinical Psychology
Anthony Lavender and *Frank Holloway (Editors)*	Community Care in Practice: Service for the Continuing Care Client
John Clements	Severe Learning Disability and Psychological Handicap